Praise for *When Time Stopped*

'A beautifully told story of personal discovery, of almost unimaginable
human bravery and sacrifice, and a harrowing portrait of living,
dying and surviving under the yoke of Nazism.'
John le Carré

'*When Time Stopped* is Ariana Neumann's journey of discovery,
lyrically set down in this truly exceptional book. She shines an intimate
light upon a time unique in its horror, and tells a story of bravery
and rare survival . . . This is a work of very great talent.'
Jon Snow, journalist and Channel 4 presenter

'Ariana Neumann's story may strike a chord, and rightly so . . . What makes this
account so effective is that it's personal and, because of the dogged extensiveness of
her research, Neumann reminds us of the small details that make the Nazi persecution
of the Jews all the more chilling . . . It's not always a grim story. Alongside anger and
despair, there is love and hope. But the message is stark. This is the way bullies work.
When Time Stopped is more than just history. It's a warning.'
Michael Palin

'Through her painstaking work, Neumann takes lifeless fragments that ensured her
family's obscurity, and magically brings them back to life in this carefully woven and
beautifully written tapestry. She not only has done justice to those closest to her, but
to understanding our shared humanity. If you are in any doubt about the power and
importance of knowing family history before you read this, you will be in no
doubt after. This is a work of resistance against oblivion, a reminder
against forgetting, an investigation driven by true love.'
Stephen D. Smith, UNESCO chair on Genocide Education

'Ariana Neumann's beautiful, meticulously researched memoir is an
extraordinarily moving story of a family's lost history, a father's well-kept secret
and a daughter who pieces it all together with courage, tenacity and love.'
Dani Shapiro, author of *Inheritance*

'This book is utterly riveting . . . reads like a detective novel, as she unravels her
late father's complex, agonising yet inspiring trajectory. Conjuring the lives of her
relatives murdered in the Holocaust, she brings their lost world to vivid life.'
Claire Messud, author of *The Emperor's Children*

'This is non-fiction that reads like a detective thriller.'
Tilar J. Mazzeo, author of *Irena's Children*

'*When Time Stopped* is a remarkable and beautifully written book. Hans Neumann's story is astonishing, confirming that, when it comes to the Holocaust, we should expect only the unexpected. This is one of the most powerful and profoundly moving family stories of the Holocaust to have been published in many years and a must-read.'
Dan Stone, professor of modern history and director of the Holocaust Research Institute, Royal Holloway, University of London

'A fascinating and beautifully constructed memoir . . . a testimonial to the power of meticulous research and family love.'
Caroline Moorehead, historian, journalist and author

'*When Time Stopped* is an astonishing family memoir that will imprint itself on your psyche as only the best books can, forever changing the way you look at your own family. With a mastery of the dogged art of research rarely seen, and with an exquisite narrative sensibility to match, Ariana Neumann has breached the hidden surface of her family's tumultuous past and brought not only their tragedies and sorrows, but also their joys and loves, to indelible light. I will carry the experience of this book with me for a very long time.'
John Burnham Schwartz, author of *Reservation Road* and *The Commoner*

'Never in my reading life have I ever come across anything akin to this magical, brilliant and gripping work of art. To call this moving is an understatement. It is a journey of untold grace, sorrow and love.'
Deborah Copaken, author of *Shutterbabe* and *The Red Book*

'Remarkable . . . Through painstaking, meticulous research Neumann tells the true story – part memoir, part history – of her heart-wrenching and ultimately life-affirming journey in uncovering her family's long hidden past.'
Georgia Hunter, author of *We Were the Lucky Ones*

'Part literary memoir, part mystery tale, Ariana Neumann's tribute to her father is a classic story of redemption and love.'
Janine di Giovanni, journalist and author of *The Morning They Came for Us*

'My wife Helena and I both survived the Holocaust. Part of our childhoods were spent in hiding and in the concentration camp of Terezín. We lived through the events and knew some of the people so perfectly and creatively depicted in these pages, so this book is important to us. It is a story that has crossed the world, but it vitally confirms our experience as survivors and carries our same message of hope: Nothing will be forgotten. All will be passed down and remembered. Thank you Ariana Neumann for writing this book.'
Helena Klímová and Ivan Klíma, winner of the Franz Kafka Prize and author of *My Crazy Century* and *Love and Garbage*

OSLAV T[...]VII 1910 JIŘINA 5.III 1915 ~ 20.11 1943 FREUND
HERMÍNA 25.II 1887 ~ 20.11 1943 *HELLER EVŽEN 1.IV 188[...]
[...]43 *KAUFMANN OTA 23.XI 1889 MARIE 20.V 1888 VĚ[...]
1943 IDA 30.XI 1880 ~ 28.III 1943 HELENA 16.XII 1888 HAN[...]
PICK OTAKAR 9.VI 1883 VALESKA 5.X 1883 VÍTĚZSLAV.[...]
AGEROVÁ RŮŽENA 1.X 1864 ~ 22.11 1943 * SILBERST[...]
F 9.IV 1856 ~ 26.II 1943 *LIBČANY: *BERAN EVŽEN 20.[...]
U: NEUMANN OTA 17.X 1890 ~ 29.IX 1944 ELA 2.IV 189[...]
[...]IX 1943 *JOSEF 18.X 1912 OLGA 3.XII 1911 JIŘÍ 14.XI 1937 [...]
[...]A 1.III 1852 ~ 27.VII 1942 *ČERVENKA LEOPOLD 4.IV[...]
[...] 1943 HEDVIKA 16.II 1905 ~ 23.IV 1942 *LIBEŘ: *SC[...]
N 24.IV 1879 ~ 18.X 1942 *LÍBEZNICE: *HERMANN[...]
75 ~ 15.X 1942 *KÖNIG JOSEF 23.VII 1913 ~ 6.IX 1943 R[...]
A 14.III 1910 ~ 27.IV 1942 *LÖWIDT OSKAR 16.V 1894 E[...]
NK JINDŘICH 26.VI 1919 ANNA 22.IV 1923 ~ 26.X 1942 P[...]
ZDENĚK 25.XII 1911 ~ 8.X 1942 BOHUMIL 8.V 1920 ~ 22.[...]
1888 ~ 17.V 1942 *REITLER ANTONÍN 6.VII 1891 AL[...]
[...]7.11 1885 REGINA 4.11 1889 EMIL 25.XII 1912 ARNOŠT[...]
[...]0.11 1943 *LIBICE NAD CIDLINOU: *FREUND KAR[...]
EMIL 10.X 1910 BERTA 23.IX 1882 ~ 12.VI 1942 *MEIS[...]
[...]OVÁ EDITA 1.IV 1890 ~ 12.VI 1942 *ROGEL ABRAHAM 2[...]
MAGDALENA 20.VII 1876 ~ 27.IV 1942 *LIBIŠ: *PRIE[...]
[...]ŠKA 3.11 1893 ~ 20.11 1943 *LIBÍV: *ŠULC JOSEF 31.V[...]
KOVÁ KAMILA 12.VI 1884 ~ 22.11 1943 *LIBLÍN: *BLU[...]
1944 *GROSSMANNOVÁ AMÁLIE 17.X 1914 ~ 1.1[...]
ANKA 27.VI 1896 KAREL 4.11 1923 HEŘMAN 23.IX 1924[...]
4.VIII 1885 MARIE 30.III 1912 ~ 13.VI 1942 *FLORA 28.[...]
27.IV 1942 *EISERTOVÁ EMILIE 3.IX 1863 ~ 15.[...]
BERT 11.IX 1898 ~ 6.IX 1943 ADOLF 1.XII 1861 ~ 15.X[...]
1942 *GLÄSNER JOSEF 1.XI 1890 OLGA 28.X 189[...]
R 25.X 1885 ~ 27.IV 1942 *HAHN LEO 6.XI 1876 ~ 27.1[...]
[...]LÍMOVÁ LUDMILA 15.VIII 1892 ~ 17.III 1942 *KATZ[...]
[...]5.X 1895 ~ 17.III 1942 *KOCH ALOIS 14.V 1909 ~ 17.III 1942 J[...]
[...]2 *LANGEROVÁ KAROLÍNA 4.XI 1855 ~ 29.IX 1942 *LAUE[...]
~ 17.III 1942 *NOVÁK OTAKAR 4.XII 1887 ~ 11.III 1942 *PER[...]
[...]VÁ HEDVIKA 10.X 1896 ~ 17.III 1942 *POPPEROVÁ IDA[...]
[...]4.11 1942 ~ 18.V[...]

[...]IX 1854 ~ 9.11[...]
[...]ROUBÍČEK [...] OŠTKA 9.V 189[...]
[...]X 1942 *STE[...] [...]A 28.III 1901 HE[...]

WHEN
TIME STOPPED

A Memoir of My Father's War
and What Remains

ARIANA NEUMANN

SCRIBNER

LONDON NEW YORK SYDNEY TORONTO NEW DELHI

First published in the United States by Scribner, an imprint of Simon & Schuster, Inc., 2020
First published in Great Britain by Scribner, an imprint of Simon & Schuster UK Ltd, 2020
A CBS COMPANY

Copyright © Ariana Neumann, 2020

SCRIBNER and design are registered trademarks of The Gale Group, Inc.,
used under licence by Simon & Schuster Inc.

The right of Ariana Neumann to be identified as the author of this work has been
asserted in accordance with the Copyright, Designs and Patents Act, 1988.

3 5 7 9 10 8 6 4 2

Simon & Schuster UK Ltd
1st Floor
222 Gray's Inn Road
London WC1X 8HB

www.simonandschuster.co.uk
www.simonandschuster.com.au
www.simonandschuster.co.in

Simon & Schuster Australia, Sydney
Simon & Schuster India, New Delhi

Extract on p.vi © Pablo Neruda, 1973 and Fundación Pablo Neruda. Pablo Neruda, 'If each
day falls…,' translated by William O'Daly, from *The Sea and The Bells*. Copyright © 1973
by Pablo Neruda and the Heirs of Pablo Neruda. Translation copyright © 1988, 2002 by
William O'Daly. Reprinted with the permission of The Permissions Company, LLC on
behalf of Copper Canyon Press, www.coppercanyonpress.org.

Dylan Thomas, 'Do Not Go Gentle Into That Good Night' from the Poems of Dylan
Thomas, copyright ©1952 by Dylan Thomas. Reprinted by permission of New Directions
Publishing Corp.

The author and publishers have made all reasonable efforts to contact copyright-holders
for permission, and apologise for any omissions or errors in the form of credits given.
Corrections may be made to future printings.

A CIP catalogue record for this book is available from the British Library

Hardback ISBN: 978-1-4711-7940-2
Trade Paperback ISBN: 978-1-4711-7941-9
eBook ISBN: 978-1-4711-7942-6

Typeset in Perpetua by M Rules
Printed and bound by CPI Group (UK) Ltd, Croydon, CR0 4YY

MIX
Paper from
responsible sources
FSC® C020471

For Sebastian
For Eloise
For Maria-Teresa

This book is dedicated to the memory
of those who could not tell their stories.

Si cada día
cae dentro de cada noche,
hay un pozo donde la claridad
está encerrada.

Hay que sentarse a la orilla
del pozo de la sombra
y pescar luz caída,
con paciencia.

If each day falls
inside each night,
there exists a well
where clarity is imprisoned.

We need to sit on the rim
of the well of darkness
and fish for fallen light
with patience.

— PABLO NERUDA,
'Si cada día cae', *El Mar y las Campanas*

Things are not as easy to understand or express as we are mostly led to believe; most of what happens cannot be put into words and takes place in a realm which no word has ever entered.

— RAINER MARIA RILKE,
Letters to a Young Poet, 1903

CONTENTS

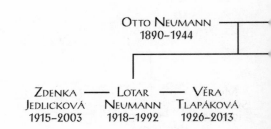

OTTO NEUMANN
1890–1944

ZDENKA — LOTAR — VĚRA
JEDLICKOVÁ NEUMANN TLAPÁKOVÁ
1915–2003 1918–1992 1926–2013

OTTO'S FAMILY

JOHANNA ROUBIČEK
1853–1910

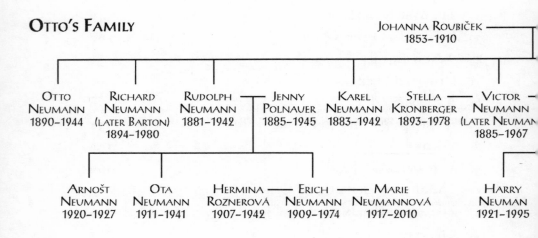

OTTO
NEUMANN
1890–1944

RICHARD
NEUMANN
(LATER BARTON)
1894–1980

RUDOLPH
NEUMANN
1881–1942

JENNY
POLNAUER
1885–1945

KAREL
NEUMANN
1883–1942

STELLA
KRONBERGER
1893–1978

VICTOR
NEUMANN
(LATER NEUMAN
1885–1967

ARNOŠT
NEUMANN
1920–1927

OTA
NEUMANN
1911–1941

HERMINA — ERICH — MARIE
ROZNEROVÁ NEUMANN NEUMANNOVÁ
1907–1942 1909–1974 1917–2010

HARRY
NEUMAN
1921–1995

ELLA'S FAMILY

SALOMON HAAS
1855–1938

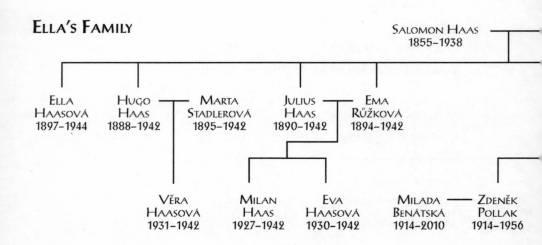

ELLA
HAASOVÁ
1897–1944

HUGO — MARTA
HAAS STADLEROVÁ
1888–1942 1895–1942

JULIUS — EMA
HAAS RŮŽKOVÁ
1890–1942 1894–1942

VĚRA
HAASOVÁ
1931–1942

MILAN
HAAS
1927–1942

EVA
HAASOVÁ
1930–1942

MILADA — ZDENĚK
BENÁTSKÁ POLLAK
1914–2010 1914–1956

-HAAS FAMILY

Ella Haasová
1897–1944

Milada — Hans — Maria Cristina
Svatoňová Neumann   Anzola
1922–1990 1921–2001   1941–

Ignatz Neumann
1850–1902

Elsie   Josef — Hilda   Oskar — Jolana   Hermine — Moritz
Einhorn   Neumann Weissová Neumann Hoffmanová   Neumannová Weil
1893–1932 1887–1945 1902–1944 1892–1942 1906–1942   1880–1919   1874–1938

Milton   Arno   Hana   Richard
Neuman   Neumann Neumannová   Neumann
1925–2011 1925–1944 1928–1944   1933–1942

Klara Dörflerová
1858–1937

Martha — Rudolf   Josefa
Haasová   Pollak   Katzová
1894–1923 1884–1943   1894–1943

Hanuš — Hana — Jindrich   Arnošt — Zita — Jaroslav   Jiříi
Mandelík Polláková Schick   Freudenheim Polláková Chuchvalec Pollak
1911–1945 1916–1985 1923–1985 1912–1945   1917–1985 1917–1970   1927–1943

EUROPE AT THE OUTSET OF WAR - 1938

PROLOGUE

There is a question mark, almost lost in a sea of names on the walls of an old synagogue in Prague. Visitors hush children as they pass through each chamber of the Pinkas memorial. It is hard not to be overwhelmed by the dizzying display of black and red letters. They memorialise 77,297 individuals. Each was a resident of the Czech districts of Bohemia and Moravia during the war. All were victims of the Nazis.

Next to every name is stencilled the date of birth, and next to each date of birth neatly sits the date of death.

One entry bears the name of my father, Hanus Stanislav Neumann, born on 9 February 1921. It is different. Unlike the others on that wall, it has no date of death.

Instead, carefully calligraphed, there is an incongruous and bold black question mark.

My father's name with the question mark, tenth line from the top,
in the Pinkas Synagogue, Prague.

I visited the memorial in 1997 as a tourist, unaware of any link
with the synagogue. Scanning across the top wall to my right
as I descended the steps into the first chamber, I was astounded
to see my father's name. He was then very much alive, settled
and working in Caracas. And yet the bold question mark was
there, both jarring and oddly apposite.

This was the first time I had seen the query inked on the
wall, but questions about my father had emerged long before.
My quest for answers started when I was just a little girl, living
across an ocean and a sea in a very different world.

The questions began with a photograph. They started with a
picture that was kept hidden but was then found. A memento
left behind by accident or on purpose, perhaps subconsciously,
that engendered doubt. An image that was out of sorts with

reality, as I saw it, forcing the present into an unfamiliar focus. It prompted questions. It demanded answers of the past.

My childhood memories hum with the songs of troupials, crickets and frogs. My recollections are cradled by tranquil breezes; they sway to the rhythm of tall palm trees and are lit by the reds and oranges of birds of paradise. Yet in all their warmth, colour and chaos, they are punctuated by the crisp metal rotors, wheels, pivots and mainsprings of mechanical watches, of beautifully intricate movements with complications. Among enormous sculptures, my mother recites verses from Rubén Darío and Andrés Eloy Blanco, and my father dances as he sings 'Yellow Submarine'. In most of my early memories, there are people moving around the open rooms, terraces and gardens – politicians, diplomats, industrialists, writers, filmmakers, ballet dancers – gesticulating, chatting, laughing, sitting or standing, invariably surrounding my parents. There is the noise of success, the prattle of happiness, but in some of the memories, the hubbub fades and there is just enough silence to hear the watches tick, click, whirr and chime.

Embedded in my memory is the image of a particular watch. It is a round silver pocket watch, perfectly polished, lying face down, with its cover off and the gold insides visible.

It is an odd piece – different from the others in my father's collection. The watch has four cases. It is rendered in an easily tarnished silver. Most of the others are gold and ornately decorated with precious stones. It is large and heavy, and the first case is indelicate, with a braided burgundy cord attaching a key. It has a thick relief motif that would perhaps be more familiar if it were carved in wood.

Press a button on the side, and the first case pops open to

3

reveal a much finer silver face, surrounded by tortoiseshell and silver screws. You can then see the dial, the curved gold hands and the face of light and darkened silver ringed with symbols for numbers; the letters in the centre spell the maker's name.

Inside this second cover is an aged piece of paper trimmed to fit roundly inside the back of the case. In beautiful black script, it reads: '*Thomas Stivers, London, England. Made in 1732 at the Old Watch Street Shop for Export Trade India*'.

Inside this is a smaller plain polished silver case.

Within this third unremarkable metal shell sits another polished silver case that houses the device itself. Eyes are drawn to the beauty of the hands and face, and without the outer cases the watch now seems rather small and delicate, fragile, even. As you lift the glass and inspect the piece closely, additional hinges are revealed within, and if you examine the face, at the six o'clock mark there is a tiny, almost invisible lever. If you move the lever lightly – being careful not to damage the enamel – towards the centre, the back of this case clicks open, disclosing a magnificent movement with ornate wheels of interwoven filigree that resemble flowers and feathers of silver and gold.

Most people never look at the movement. They rarely open the mechanism to understand what is behind the meticulous time-keeping. For the majority, observing the dial and knowing that the watch functions within a beautiful case is marvel enough. Yet when you examine this beguiling mechanism, you find it is not functioning – the thin silver thread that forms the spring is torn, and the watch cannot keep time.

When my memories pan back from the watch, my father is hunched over, his back cocooned by a white chair. He is wearing a black plastic visor with two rectangular magnifying lenses in front of his eyes. His thick white hair is tousled around the adjustable band. He is unaware of the world outside, oblivious to me as I tilt my head through the crack of the door and stare at him. He sits at a purpose-built wooden table, his slim fingers grasping pointed tweezers. He is trying to tease out a thin silver thread from a part of the watch that looks to me like a spool made of gold. He is moving very gently, with absolute precision and fathomless patience. If his fingers were not playing over the watch, just a millimetre here and there, his stillness would suggest that time had stopped.

He is trying to repair the mechanism. He needs his watches to be accurate to the second. It seems a necessity rather than a want. He keeps most of them in his bedroom: some on stands in a Louis XV vitrine, some carefully laid in the drawers of a nineteenth-century tulipwood chest that have been specially lined with thick burgundy velvet. He opens and checks a few at least once a week, the winding mechanisms, the springs, the levers, the chimes. If they need to be regulated, he will take them to his workshop, the long windowless room in my memory, the one off a long corridor by the kitchen. The room that is narrow and resembles the carriage of a train. The room that unfailingly remains locked, its key kept in my father's pocket, attached to a gold chain clipped to a belt loop in his trousers. There, he will sit at the table upon which his minuscule tools are arrayed. He will don one of the black magnifying visors that hang on hooks aligned on the wall. Depending on the watch, he will push the lever or prise the case open and examine the movement. The first thing he will do is ascertain that the escapement and the train are functioning. The train should be in constant motion; that is crucial to provide energy for the mechanism to run for many hours. Usually, trains are made up of four wheels, one each for hours, minutes and seconds, and a fourth connected to the escapement. The latter consists of tiny pallets, a lever and two further wheels, one for escape and another for balance. It allows just the right amount of power from the train to escape at precise intervals, sufficient to allow the correct movement of the hands. It makes the ticking sound and ensures exactness. Both train and escapement are critical components. They must work together faultlessly, or time will not be kept. The workshop drawers are filled with lights, magnifying glasses and tools. He owns 297 pocket watches. Sometimes, if he spots me nearby, he calls me to his side and winds the one I love. Not the one he tries to fix but the one with complications, the one that works perfectly, which plays a song in chimes and has two cherubs with moving arms knocking little golden hammers against a bell.

My father wakes every morning by six-thirty. Every morning, regardless of how much he has slept, he dons a navy cotton robe and walks to his study, where a tray is neatly laid out on a small table. Every weekday by six-thirty-five a.m., with the dark thorny green leaves from the bromeliads coming through the cast-iron bars of the window, he is sitting on the edge of the daybed to eat half a grapefruit and read a newspaper. He pours a third of a sachet of sweetener into a small cup of black coffee and drinks it in one gulp. He showers, opens his mirrored cupboard, picks one from his dozens of suits, straightens his tie, grabs a perfectly pressed handkerchief, chooses his wristwatch and is headed to the office by seven a.m. sharp.

At the end of the day, the drive home from the office takes him between nine and thirteen minutes, depending on the day of the week. He times his departure accordingly and arrives at the house promptly at six-thirty every night. If he is not going out, he leaves his briefcase in his study, mixes himself a Campari and soda stirred with a long, curled silver spoon, and sits in an armchair on the terrace. Every night that my father is home, the curled spoon leaves a pink mark on the crisp white linen napkin on the drinks cabinet. Dinner is at exactly seven-thirty p.m.

If the Campari spoon is untouched when I walk past the library after my piano practice, I know that my parents are dressing to go out. Then I rush to my mother's room and watch her put on her make-up in front of the illuminated swivel mirror. I sit on the floor and chat about my day as she carefully applies make-up, puts on a gown and chooses her jewellery. My father usually walks in wearing an immaculate black tie or a crisp dark suit and says impatiently that they are going to be late. They kiss me goodnight and head down the long corridor, my father straight and tall in his suit, my mother mesmerising in her flowing gown, with her fiery-speckled brown hair dancing as they disappear from view.

2

Unlike most houses in our neighbourhood, ours did not have a name. There was, however, a sign on the green metal gates with two words printed in copperplate: *Perros Furibundos*. There is no precise English word for *furibundo*. Roughly translated, the sign meant *frenziedly furious dogs*. To our visitors, the house was known as the House of the Frenziedly Furious Dogs. The dogs spent more time lazing in the sunshine than they did in frenzied fury, but the name stuck. *Perros Furibundos* was an oasis protected from the bustle and chaos of 1970s Caracas by tall mango trees, high white walls and two guards who, though placid, were methodical in their alternating patrol of the perimeter.

The garden of my childhood had an imposing ceiba tree, dozens of different palms, mango, guava, acacia and eucalyptus trees, and bushes covered in orchids, flores de mayo, frangipanis, all surrounding a sky-blue pool. My mother had played in the house as a small girl, when it had belonged to family friends. When my parents started their life together, my father bought it for them to live in.

A bright and sprawling single-storey house, it was full of high-ceilinged rooms and airy terraces. It had been designed in 1944 by Clifford Wendehack, an American architect who built grand houses and designed the colonial villa that forms the main building of the Caracas Country Club. Our single-storey home stood amid the seemingly boundless sea of gardens in the neighbourhood of Los Chorros in the eastern part of Caracas. It was close to El Avila, the regal mountain that towers above the city and separates the capital from the coast.

The country that I grew up in was filled with promise.

There were serious problems – social disparity, corruption and poverty – but there was also a sense that such issues were being addressed. Social and educational programmes were being implemented; government housing, schools and hospitals were being built. The Venezuela of the 1970s and '80s was seen as a model for Latin America. It had a stable democracy, a rising literacy rate, a flourishing art scene and, thanks to oil, a well-funded government intent on developing further industries, infrastructure and education. It was alive with potential. Businesses, both local and international, were keen to invest. Migrants were attracted by the quality of life, relative safety, climate and opportunities. Most of the country benefited from clement weather and fertile land, and the nature that surrounded the cities, the beaches, the jungles, the biodiversity, was without equal in variety and beauty. As I was growing up, new buildings, museums and theatres were being constructed all around the capital. It was a hustling, modern metropolis. There were daily flights from Caracas to New York, Miami, London, Frankfurt, Rome and Madrid. Even Concorde made regular flights from Paris to the Maiquetía airport.

The tremendous energy of the place was the harvest of a crop sown several decades before. In 1946 Venezuela decided to welcome and support displaced Europeans who could not return to their homes after the war. Tens of thousands of refugees, mostly from Southern and Central Europe, arrived in Venezuela, to be followed in later decades by many more escaping the political turmoil of countries on the Continent.

As a child, I was aware that my father, together with his older brother Lotar, had migrated to Venezuela because their country had been broken by war. I am not sure how I knew this, as it was certainly not something my father discussed. His focus was always on life now, not that which had gone before. By the time I came along over two decades later, any vestige of refugee hardship had entirely vanished. On the surface, all that was incongruous about him was his pale skin, his heavy Eastern European accent and his obsession with timekeeping and punctuality.

On arrival in Venezuela, he had started a paint factory with Lotar. My father had prospered in Venezuela. His drive, knowledge of chemicals and wide-spanning interests had led him to seize the opportunities that the country offered. By the time I was born, he was a leading industrialist and intellectual. Billboards around the city advertised his businesses: paints, building supplies, juices, yogurts. People read his newspapers. Every hardware shop bore the logo of his paint factory, Montana. He also headed charitable institutions, spearheaded educational programmes and was a patron of the arts. My mother came from a European family who had migrated to Venezuela in 1611, and their marriage firmly ensconced my father in Venezuelan society. In 1965 a writer named Bernard Taper wrote a lengthy article entitled 'Dispatches from Caracas' in the *New Yorker*:

> The Neumanns are considered prime examples of a breed of industrialist new to the Venezuelan scene for they simultaneously exhibit technical competence, entrepreneurial drive and a sense of social responsibility – an almost unknown combination here.

He then described my father:

A vigorous, well-built man of forty-three, Hans has close cropped gray hair, alert green eyes, a bent nose (it was broken in a youthful boxing match), and a mouth rather more sensitive and expressive than one might expect to accompany a broken nose and a decisive personality. He is a lover of art and has a splendid collection of modern paintings and sculpture. In addition, he is the president of the Museo de Bellas Artes, and has done much to foster the development of Art in this country . . .

Hans Neumann and Maria Cristina Anzola in Caracas, c. 1980.

My father had filled every part of our house with art. Every wall in every room opened up his collection to visitors; even the large garden was dotted with sculptures. There were beautiful artworks by well-known European masters alongside some lesser-known young Latin American artists. Peppered among the gentler pieces was disturbing surrealist and expressionist art, pictures of fragmented bodies, deconstructed landscapes, and even one of warring body parts. There were sculptures, small and huge, of naked women. I remember the shocked silence of a particularly pious mother of a friend from my Catholic school who had come to my birthday party. She shielded her daughter's eyes with a blue balloon as she led her towards the door, past an immense bronze of a nude woman with legs apart that leaned against a hammock in the entrance hall. I do not remember that girl ever coming to play at my house again.

3

When I was very young, I wanted to be a detective or, even better, a spy. I often said I wanted to be a doctor, but I think I was just trying to sound clever, as the sight of blood has always made me feel faint. The reality is that I wanted to solve mysteries. To further this ambition, at age eight I started a spy club with my maternal cousins and a few friends. We had read and been inspired by Enid Blyton's 'Famous Five' and 'Secret Seven'. We were unfazed by the fact that we lived in the tropics and not in rainy England. We called it the Mysterious Boot Club. My friend Carolina and I had chosen the name carefully. Carolina, a year older than I, was one of the best students in her class at the British School. We had known each other and got along not because our families were friends but because she understood, like I did, the gravity of our investigative endeavours. We had initially thought of naming it the Mysterious Footprint, but that seemed too bookish and obvious for a club of young detectives. We did not want our enterprise to be dismissed as childish – we needed to be taken seriously by the other children and, more important, by the adults. Too many pages in books with mystery stories were filled with enigmatic footprints in the mud. So we decided to call it after the boot that had made the puzzling footprints – it seemed better somehow, less silly: both more cryptic and more worldly.

Nestled along the garden's northernmost wall, surrounded by trees cackling with parrots and the odd wild monkey or sloth, sat a large disused kennel: the official clubhouse of the Mysterious Boot Club. I had asked my father to give us a tin of white paint and some thick brushes so we could make it look the part. He had obliged and we duly decorated the kennel. Carolina had the best handwriting, and she fastidiously inked the letters *CBM* (*Club Bota Misteriosa*) in bold black permanent marker on a part of the outside wall that was protected from the rain. Every Saturday before the meetings, we would crawl through the low doorway next to the letters. Equipped with a small broom and a box of tissues that we had borrowed from the supply cupboard, we swept the cement floor, cleared the cobwebs and attempted to shoo away the caterpillars, ants and bugs that had sought shelter in its tin walls. Wooden crates served as bookshelves, stools and a table. The place was stuffed with mystery books and notepads half-filled with our attempts at finding enigmas to spice our mundane and protected lives.

In the absence of substantive mysteries with which to wrestle, I had occupied myself in composing by-laws that set out the hierarchy and objectives of the club. Given that role, I was unsurprisingly appointed president. The two most sensible and organised members of our group, Carolina and my cousin Rodrigo, were the vice presidents. We had decided that all prospective members should undertake IQ and physical agility tests. The intelligence test I had torn from a *Reader's Digest* left lying around the kitchen, and the agility test consisted mostly of running ahead of the not very furious dogs with pockets full of kibble before climbing a tree. We had to bend the rules a little sometimes to ensure that anyone invited could belong. A disappointed aunt heard about our by-laws and coerced us into accepting my youngest cousin, Patricia, who tended to bite when angry and was too young to read, let alone pass, any written test. My parents were adamant that I behave in a kind and inclusive manner, so the entrance requirements were malleable and existed principally to give the members a certain aura of prestige.

On those Saturday mornings, we would swap books and collect pocket money in a washed-out mayonnaise jar with a slit in the lid, for club supplies and to help an old people's home down the road. We would all bring notebooks and spy on the people who lived, visited or worked in my house. We would set one another tasks in half-hour slots and then gather at the clubhouse to drink mango or watermelon juice and read out our reports in serious tones.

The bulletins were mostly tedious. We all, of course,

pretended that they were riveting. Often, we had to spy while taking turns guarding the tiny biting cousin. Carolina observed that the gardener repeatedly picked up leaves from the same patch in the garden, over and over, week after week. It was clear to her, she solemnly reported, toying with a dark curl of her long hair, that he was simply killing time. My older cousin Eloy, who had big blue eyes and a musical voice, read in great detail his notes about a cleaner whom he had watched dusting and who had suspiciously moved books from one library shelf to another. He had also seen her as she switched around LPs in my father's colour-coded collection. Rock and roll (alphabetically arranged by band with red tape on the spine) had been exchanged with opera (alphabetically arranged by composer with yellow tape). Eloy could not detect whether this had been an act of playfulness, defiance or absentmindedness. He said what we all knew: when my father spotted the displacement, he would be irate. My father's constant desire for organisation was mystifying and slightly unnerving to all the members of the Mysterious Boot Club.

We would ask everyone who visited or worked in the house if they had seen anything out of the ordinary. Months would pass and our gatherings continued, in the main, identical. We diligently monitored the activity in the house and patiently recorded every mundane detail. We would encounter small puzzles, gather and whisper excitedly only to realise with abject disappointment that, after a few queries, all was too easily explained.

I remember once feeling exhilarated, during school holidays, when we found a red waxy rind in the rubbish after the worried cook had complained that an entire ball of Edam

cheese was missing. We ineffectively dusted the rind for fin-
gerprints and patrolled with an ink pad that I had borrowed
from my father's desk, demanding that everyone at the house
cooperate and be fingerprinted. It turned out that Maria, the
Galician lady who was missing two fingers and came to do the
daily ironing, had skipped breakfast and lunch that day, was
famished, and had a passion for the imported yellow cheese.
She wearily confessed just as Carolina and I asked to press her
remaining fingers against the ink pad. There always seemed
to be a straightforward explanation for such puzzles. All of
us children yearned desperately for a real conundrum against
which to test our skills.

Then one day my cousin, after what seemed like hundreds
of unmemorable reports, the gentle and pragmatic Rodrigo,
relayed that my father had moved a strange grey box from
a locked drawer in the watch workshop to a cupboard in
the library.

Quite why that particular bulletin caught my attention, I
cannot say. Perhaps it was because Rodrigo told us that my
father had been acting awkwardly and seemed to move more
slowly than he should, considering he was just carrying a cardboard box. He reported that it seemed to contain something
heavy or precious. After my father left the library, Rodrigo had
opened the cupboard but had not dared touch the box.

I did not disclose the slightest interest in the incident to
my fellow spies. I am not sure why. Perhaps it was because it
involved my father.

That afternoon, as soon as the spies left after their lunch
and swim, I went to look for the box. I found it easily enough.
It was dark grey and made of board and cloth. It sat below

the shelf where the draughts board and the wooden chess set were kept. It was not concealed, it just lay there inside a cupboard in which it did not belong. I remember thinking at the time that it may be filled with broken watches. I moved it and, contrary to Rodrigo's intelligence, was struck by how very light it was.

I sat on the carpet in front of the bookcase and lifted the lid with the tips of trembling fingers. I sensed that this was the mystery we had been waiting for. The box contained only five or six papers and cards. On the top was a long-expired Venezuelan passport, much smaller than the ones I had seen. It was dated 1956 and bore a picture of my father as I knew him, smiling and already wrinkled, with glasses balanced on a boxer's nose. Underneath the passport lay other documents, thin and fading.

They were printed in a foreign language. The paper seemed delicate and old. I lifted each sheet with my two hands and placed it on the lid of the open box. Then, at the bottom of the box, I saw it. A picture of my father's face on a pink card. He was much younger than I had ever seen him, with no broken nose, no wrinkles or white hair. Still, I had no doubt that it was him – I recognised the eyes. His lips seemed to be about to smile, but his eyes stared out at me with an acute and questioning intensity.

At the bottom of his picture, below his chin, almost covering his tie, was a stamp. I was too young to know much history, but I recognised the man on the stamp. I had no doubt he represented evil, and the sight of my father's face above it made no sense. I tried to find more clues.

The identity card I found as a girl in Caracas.

I could see that it was some form of identification. I looked for my father's name, but it was not there. Instead, the card seemed to belong to someone called Jan Šebesta. It was dated October 1943 and was valid until October 1946. On the reverse, the bearer's date of birth was recorded as 11 March 1921. I knew my father's birthday was 9 February 1921.

I do not remember much else from that moment other than being terrified. I had to find my mother. My father was not called Hans. He was lying about his name and about his date of birth. The evidence was undeniable, printed on an official-looking document. I ran down the long chequered granite terrace, past the sofas and armchairs and the enormous bronze and limestone sculptures. I flew through the white hallway, thinking then that the eyes of the Botero portrait of my father watched me as I ran. I prayed I would not see my father before I found my mother. I could

19

hear music in my parents' bedroom. My mother was sitting on the daybed in their room, holding the libretto from a cassette box and mouthing the words to a loud *Rigoletto*. I threw myself at her. I sobbed and shook. I remember that she held me and then carried me to the stereo to lower the volume. Her hair brushed my cheek as she asked if I had hurt myself again, playing with the dogs.

'No. No. Mami, no. He is not who he says he is. It is not him.'

'Who?'

'Papi,' I said. 'He is pretending, I have proof. He is not Hans, his real name is Jan, Mami. He wasn't born on February the ninth, he is lying. He is an impostor.'

I don't remember anything else from that day.

The identity card, with the stamp of Hitler and its photograph of my father, jolted me to a sharp and unexpected focus. It brought to the fore every other tiny fissure in my understanding, all the minuscule silences and unanswered questions that had been invisible before. It was then that I first sensed that, hidden beneath my father's strength and triumphs, were shadows cast by nameless horrors so terrible they had to remain unuttered.

The averted eyes, the pauses a second too long, the eschewing of reminiscence had until then passed mostly unnoticed. Finding that photograph in the box was the pivot. It marked the exact moment when the unfilled spaces, the cracks in the narrative, emerged.

And slowly, very, very slowly, I realised that in those gaps, buried and interwoven within the silences and minute instances of discomposure, lay the real story.

The next time I looked, the box had been moved from the library. I never discovered where it was kept. Much later, my mother told me that she never, in her many years of living with my father, saw that box. Decades would pass before I found it again.

4

There were hints before. Peppered across my memories were moments that jarred, instances of disquiet. The cracks had been there all along. I remember when I was about seven, after a nightmare, going down the corridor to find refuge in my parents' bed. It was something I rarely did, not because I did not have nightmares, but because my father slept naked and seemed irritated to have to put pyjamas on under his dressing gown when I showed up. So I remember quite distinctly the few times when I did sneak in.

That night, after some comforting, I dozed off wedged between him and my mother. I woke to hear my father screaming, desperate, in a language that I did not understand. My mother reached out to him over me and hugged us both. She stroked his arm, his white hair, and murmured: 'Handa, it's okay, you are home in Caracas. You are here with us. It's a nightmare.'

My father sat up, nervous and sweaty, and left the room, almost at a run. He had seemed in so much pain. My mother whispered, 'Don't worry, little mouse. He too has nightmares.'

'What about?' I asked.

'He had a hard time during the war in Europe. But that was a long time ago.' And then she left to go after him.

I curled up on my father's side of the bed, put my head on my hands and stared at the velvet fabric that covered the walls. I recall thinking at the time that if he was having nightmares, whatever was causing them could not have taken place so long ago. And why did my mother have to remind him that he was in Caracas? Where else could he be? My eyes rested on the picture in the faded leather frame that sat alone on my father's mirrored bedside table. The picture was dark and faded; it was hard to tell exactly what was there. It was the only picture of them in a house filled with photographs: my father's parents seated at a table, not really looking at the camera or at each other. The table was covered with a white cloth, and on it was a newspaper, some glasses and a bottle of wine. My grandmother was looking down at something in her hands, almost smiling at it. Perhaps she was knitting. My grandfather was also looking down, a cigarette held in between the long fingers of his right hand. On his left he was holding something that looked like a pencil. I remember thinking that despite my grandmother's expression, they both looked sad. Sad and old. Distant from each other and from the photographer. In the greying picture, they seemed far removed from my life too, certainly from our life that was filled with sunlight and bright colours. I remember that night I felt scared. Scared by them, scared by what I did not know about them, and scared for my father.

The only photograph of my grandparents kept in our home in Caracas.

5

My father and me in his study, *c.* 1978.

When I was a child, my father seemed ancient and inaccessible. He was busy, always in meetings, unfailingly doing something important. I was desperate to be close to him, to find ways of connecting. We solved word and logic puzzles together. He talked to me about politics and the social inequalities of the society we lived in. He enjoyed debate and intellectual discussion. I remember when I was nine, he had been watching the BBC dramatisation of *I, Claudius*. Keen to discuss it with him, I read the first in the series of Robert Graves' books, which I found on a shelf in our library. It was, I can now see, an unusual choice for a young girl who liked Enid Blyton. I felt so proud as my father tugged at one of my plaits and looked down approvingly when I told him I had finished the book. I recall the moment he announced to my mother at dinner that night that I was clearly very clever and that I had just been discussing *I, Claudius* with him. I am not sure that I made head or tail of the book and can certainly not recall any part of the story now, but I had read it furiously from cover to cover. I just remember the joy of having impressed him.

When I had first told him I was setting up the spy club, he was enthralled. He suggested I prepare a diagram of how we would divide responsibilities. He particularly liked it when I said that we would give everyone a voice but have a structure that would assure clear leadership in case of an impasse. I had heard him discuss the management structure of one of his companies when we had been spying. I repeated what I had heard to give the impression that I had a precocious aptitude for business and management.

'Your father is so brilliant'; 'A true Renaissance man'; 'You are so lucky', people would say without exception. I often wished he were a little less brilliant and spent a bit more time watching football matches on television like other fathers. When you are a child, you do not want to be different. You do not want to have a family who stands out or parents whom your friends talk about. I already had an impossibly beautiful mother, the kind of beautiful that people would stop in the street and stare at. People spoke about her beauty, and that was bad enough.

Then there was my father.

People consistently spoke about my father in hushed tones. Twenty years older than my mother, he was almost fifty when I was born and utterly unlike the fathers of my friends. He seemed so much busier, so much more complicated. As I grew older, I had to call his secretary to ask for a meeting if I wanted to have a proper chat during the week. He was so much more serious than my friends' parents. So much more wrinkled, with that pale skin and those circles under his eyes. And then there was that day when he picked me up from school and all the other girls in my fourth-grade class sniggered when one announced, 'Ariana – your grandfather is here.'

I remember my disappointment when people said I looked like him. I desperately wanted to be petite with a turned-up nose, to be delicately exquisite, like my mother. I did not want the pallor, the under-eye circles or the round, enormous green eyes.

My father in 1993 with his portrait by Colombian artist Fernando Botero.

It was clear that there were things that my father could not talk about. This was evident from the nightmares, the reticence. These boundaries made him even less accessible. His Spanish was thickly accented. Whenever he addressed his brother Lotar, his first wife Míla or my half-brother Miguel, who was 23 years my senior, my father would inevitably speak in effortless Czech. Languages came easily to me and I wanted to learn it. I coveted both the challenge and the bond it might forge between us. 'No, no. It would be a waste of time. Czech is a useless language,' he said the only time I asked, in a tone so firm and hostile that it was obvious that I should not ask again.

Yet there were moments when, speaking Spanish, he was endearing and vulnerable. He repeatedly used the wrong word. Sometimes he would say a phrase that would make sense but sound odd. I remember him apologising once when he had a cold: 'My nose is jogging,' he said, his expression stern as he produced his handkerchief.

6

The last time I saw my father, then very frail and infirm, he had a runny nose. 'It's that jogging nose of yours again,' I mumbled through tears, his and mine. I had locked my green eyes on his, and with the hand he could still use, he squeezed mine because he could not speak clearly. Despite everything, we both laughed. I was living in London and was five months pregnant with my first child. I had answered a late-night call from his doctor in Caracas saying that I must come at once. My husband and I boarded a plane that same day.

In 1996, Corimon, the international conglomerate that had

grown from my father and his brother's paint factory Montana, almost completely disintegrated. My father had retired from the business five years earlier but had kept all his shares as a vote of confidence in the management. After the collapse, caused by economic headwinds and strategic errors, only a shell was left, which had been taken over by banks. My father had worked for four decades to build an empire that encompassed many industries across the Americas. He felt immensely proud of the publicly traded company and personally responsible to its hundreds of employees and shareholders. The distress at watching his life's work disappear was enormous but it had not stopped him. His spirit remained undaunted though the blow on his body was severe; the stress probably brought on his first massive stroke a few months after the debacle. My father had then defied all odds by living for a further five years. Although wheelchair bound, he stayed active enough to continue to work, write, marry for a third time, divorce again and establish a new daily newspaper in opposition to the Chávez regime. Regardless of the initial dire prognosis and for the years that followed, every morning at six-forty-five my father ground through vocal exercises, swam laps aided with a float and then traipsed up and down the chequered corridor with a walking frame three times a day.

In 2001, my father suffered a series of further strokes that weakened him and paralysed his legs completely. Despite the setback, after we arrived in Caracas following the late-night summons, he rallied once more. We spent a week together in June that year at *Perros Furibundos* mostly chatting about politics and technology. We watched spy films as well as *Cabaret* on DVDs. I remember his nurse, a stern and spindly woman, poking her head through the door, bewildered as the three of us sang along to '*Willkommen*'. It was not until my husband and I were back in London a few months later, on the morning of Sunday, 9 September, three weeks before I was due to give birth to my first child, that I received another call. Through the crackly static I heard the voice of Alba, my father's trusted assistant of over twenty years. 'He had more strokes last night. We brought him to the hospital, he is alive, but there is nothing to be done. The doctor wants to speak to you.'

I remember being struck by the doctor's firm and unfussy tone. As next of kin, I had to decide when to disconnect the machines. He explained that the strokes had been so damaging that the doctors were keeping my father's heart beating artificially. The scans showed that there was no brain stem function left. Total brain death, he called it. The doctor knew I could not travel. He explained that he wanted me to take some time to think and to let him know when I had reached my decision. He used the medical terminology, unvarnished and brutal, that flows easily from those for whom the cessation of life is commonplace. Aware that I was absorbing few of his words, I agreed to call him back.

I dialled my mother in New York, who had remained close to my father even though they had divorced decades before. She reminded me that my father had never wanted to be dependent on machines. Losing the use of his arm and legs six years earlier had been arduous enough. Yet, with his capacity to think intact, he had battled on. If he could not use his brain, he would not want to go on. I had just needed to hear my mother say it. I made the call to the doctor in Caracas. 'It might not be immediate,' he warned. 'His instinct throughout has been to survive.'

Half an hour later came a sobbing phone call from Alba to say that he was gone.

My father was cremated on 11 September 2001. As I watched the tragedy of the attacks that day unfold, I grieved more privately too. I could not attend my father's funeral. My pregnancy meant that I had to wait until my son was born before flying. It was some months later that I travelled to our house in Caracas.

We held a memorial service late one January morning under the shade of the ceiba tree. My husband addressed the gathered group and read Dylan Thomas's famous poem that ends with the stanza:

> *And you, my father, there on the sad height,*
> *Curse, bless, me now with your fierce tears, I pray*
> *Do not go gentle into that good night*
> *Rage, rage against the dying of the light.*

That afternoon, when friends, family and colleagues had left, I walked into my father's study. Everything looked immaculate, exactly as it had months before. My father's computer was on his desk, and to its left, still on its stand, was his pipe.

The last moments I had spent with him in this room were on the day I had flown back to London. He had been in a wheelchair, smoking that pipe, held with his only mobile hand, a glass of Coca-Cola and ice with a blue and pink paper straw before him on the desk. His desk had been covered in books, papers and letters, and every drawer had been bursting with files. My father had compulsively collected things. He was a collector of watches and clocks, books, medieval objects, paintings, sculptures. He catalogued everything. Every single thing he had ever bought was listed in files by category, with the pertinent receipts and history arranged chronologically. Every paper that anyone had sent him, every note or memo, personal or professional, no matter how trivial, was filed either under the person's name or by subject, within a range of dates. There were entire rooms in his office dedicated to his files. A long wall in his study was also packed with filing cupboards. I expected to spend days going through all his papers, sorting out what to keep and what to throw away.

Now, in the silence of this study, I pulled open the top drawer of his desk to start the task of sorting his papers. There was nothing in it. I opened drawer after drawer in the room only to find them entirely empty. I walked to the terrace to ask Alba where she had placed his files and I found her talking to Eric, our sage family lawyer.

'Your father made me throw them all away after you visited in June,' she said, her eyes full of tears. 'He asked me to clear everything but a few of the files. He didn't want you to be overwhelmed with his things.'

As we entered the study, she pointed to a cupboard in the corner behind his leather chair. It housed the only drawer in the room that was still full. On the top lay a yellowing folder holding every note that I had ever written to him. It contained an embarrassingly bad poem I had composed for him as a teenager that began with 'I have your eyes'. There were various notes and cards, most of them from my years at boarding school. Beneath this was another thick folder with dozens of letters and notes from my mother. Everything she had ever written to him, during their romance, their marriage, and even after their divorce, was there. He had asked that all other personal files and romantic notes be shredded, Alba explained. She then hugged me and she left me to look through the papers.

There would have been many folders filled with notes and letters, as my father had through the years been involved with many women. He knew that I would be the one to sort through his papers once he was gone. Erasing entire aspects of his past made his departure more real, but I was grateful for this gesture of kindness.

Underneath the pale yellow file of love letters, my father had left the box with his identity card from the war. It was the same box that I had found as a child detective, with that photograph of my father as a young man with intense and hopeful eyes and that enigmatic name, Jan Šebesta.

Only this time, the box was crammed with papers.

I

BOXES

On the middle shelf of the vitrine that held my father's collection, nestled between the intricate pocket watch embellished with chiming golden angels and a red enamel, gilt and diamond fob watch in the shape of a beetle, sat a very simple round smooth gold piece which always struck me as dull. It did not *do* anything. It played no music. It sounded no alarms. It lacked complications to intrigue or delight. It was not beautiful, delicate or ornate. It simply told the time.

I asked my father why he liked it. He replied that it was accurate, and he mentioned his own father. 'Was it my grandfather's?' I must have asked. 'No,' he replied, 'I bought it because it reminded me of a watch he owned.'

Now I own the watch from my father's vitrine. It was

manufactured in England in the eighteenth century by John Arnold. Apparently, in the world of watch collectors, Arnold and the Swiss manufacturer Abraham Breguet are generally considered the inventors of the modern mechanical watch. One of Arnold's skills was manufacturing watches so precise that they could even be used for navigation. He was the first to design a watch that was both accurate and practical. This type of watch is called a chronometer; its main purpose is to be exact in the keeping of time. In Switzerland, the country with the most watchmakers in the world, there are very stringent rules as to what type of watch may be called a chronometer. Chronometers must be independently certified as such. To my untrained eye, this pocket watch still seems rather plain, with its flat white face and generic Roman numerals. And yet it is a very collectible piece because, above all, it keeps time accurately.

The connection with my grandfather had intrigued me. As a child, I never felt that I had any grandparents on my father's side. Questions on the topic were answered curtly, without apparent emotion, met with only the most basic of details and in a tone that made it clear that this was not a subject for exploration. Perhaps talking about them to me would have made their absence more real. It was easier for everyone if they faded into the background, unmentioned and barely visible in a haze of greys, like the only photograph of them in our family home. Against a background of silence, that washed-out black-and-white image by my father's bedside was all I had of the two of them.

My mother did not seem to know much about my grandparents either. As a teenager, even as I explored limits and tested rules with stereotypical determination, I knew that to raise the subject of my father's past was to stray beyond what was allowed. We could freely discuss politics, religion, sex, drugs or my parents' marriage, any topic except that. I was never told this, but somehow I knew. It was the one taboo. At the height of my angsty rebellion, I flaunted a punk hairdo and would storm off from the dinner table, but asking about my father's own childhood or his parents was something that I never dared to do. As I became an adult, I learned to calibrate questions with care. Despite the unspoken prohibition, whenever an opportunity arose, I tried to sneak in a furtive question. I was grateful for whatever titbit my father was willing to share. It was clear that speaking about my grandparents was painful for him. He seemed unable even to talk about Czechoslovakia. He never volunteered any details about this period of his life. Later, after he became very ill, he let slip a little more. I allowed him to set the pace, and I learned to desist when the narrative faltered. For a long time, all I knew of my grandparents was that they were Czech, that they never made it to Venezuela and that my grandfather had owned a dull gold watch.

Much later, during my research into my father's family, I encountered a strong and wise woman whose parents had escaped the Holocaust and prospered in the UK. I asked her what she knew about the family they had left behind. 'Very little,' she replied. I asked her why she had not researched it. She answered simply, 'Because my parents never gave me permission. Your father did.' I had not thought of it like that until that moment, but I realised that she was right. My father had left me the box. Traumatised people often construct defence mechanisms strong enough to deter those closest to them. When an area is deemed out of bounds for so many years by an authority figure, the need for permission to enter persists even after they are gone.

Feeling that my father had given his consent made all the difference. When he intentionally left me the papers from the war years, he surrendered evidence of his other life. Even more important, he gave me his implicit blessing to explore his past and find out who his, and my, family were. Often, I have felt that it was more than just permission. At times it seemed almost an exhortation.

I opened the box my father had left in his vacant study, the one with the identity card I had glimpsed as a child, and realised that I must solve the mystery of what had happened if I was ever going to be able to understand him. My enquiries led me to other boxes, from different sources, inevitably holding clues but which also prompted more questions. My father left the world of which he seldom spoke as a riddle for me to unlock, the answer perhaps being the key to his complex and hermetic personality. The boxes held a jigsaw puzzle for me to reconstruct, with pieces just large enough to allow a sense of the theme. But there were also missing parts, fragments that I had to find to complete the picture.

As soon as I saw his papers in the box, it was clear that this was his way of showing me who he had been. It was his means of illuminating himself and also of remaining with me, of surviving as he had always done. He left it as a puzzle because he could not tell the story in its completeness. The truth of his past, for him, was a horror that could be barely even glimpsed and then only through the cracks between his fingers.

I have now spent years researching my father's life before he arrived in Venezuela. When I started enquiring, locating people and attempting to assemble a family tree, another box that my uncle Lotar's second wife, Věra, had kept untouched in Switzerland emerged. Věra was moving to a smaller, more manageable place and had rediscovered this box as she packed. Věra and Lotar's youngest daughter, my cousin Madla, who is a painter and lives in London, shared this box of relics with me.

This second box also contained documents from the war. A handful were faded or torn, some were wrinkled, their edges softened, but most were intact, crisply preserved as if time had not passed. The box held Lotar's papers and permits. There was also an identification document in a different name. And then there was a trove of letters from the 1930s and early '40s sent by my grandparents to family in the US and to their sons. There were dozens. Most of the ones to Lotar and my father were written from Terezín, also known as Theresienstadt, which I knew to be a concentration camp in Czechoslovakia. The letters were all handwritten, every inch of the paper covered in tiny characters. The words seemed uncensored, and my grandparents' state of mind was further signalled by the care or the speed with which they wrote. Despite my lack of Czech, I recognised some names. Many others presented a challenge. Eventually I sought help, and it took a Czech Holocaust expert almost a year of patient deciphering to unlock the correspondence. It took me several more years to be able to read more than a few lines without finding myself almost stupefied by a sadness that would render me incapable of absorbing any detail whatsoever. Initially, the letters, and what I assumed would be the desolation and hopelessness described within them, terrified me. I wanted to understand my father, unlock the mystery, but the idea of journeying through the letters was daunting. I was raising my young children at the time and dared not read the letters for fear of the darkness that would confront me. I had just embarked on the most optimistic adventure of my life, building my own family. I had to be forward-thinking, positive and strong. The letters gave real voices to the people who, until then, had remained silent and stilled in grey photographs. Their words summoned my lost grandparents and people who had endured misery and injustice. I just could not face them and then turn easily back to a cheerful narration of *The Very Hungry Caterpillar*.

But I remained intrigued as the years passed. Little by little, generally for just a few minutes at a time, I chipped away at the pages and pages of text that the translator had sent me by email. My children grew and, as they did, I became more comfortable, allowing myself to feel and show them a wider range of emotions. As they became more independent, I no longer felt the need to shield them or myself from life's darker moments. I felt the letters embodied this darkness. I allowed myself to read a few pages here and there. Each time I spent a little longer with them, especially as I realised that when you looked carefully, interspersed amid the horror were wisps of beauty and love. Their darkness was laced with vivid glimmers of light. It was this realisation that first rendered me capable of tackling the correspondence at all.

Also I was intrigued by the idea that there were traits in my children's personalities that I could not recognise in my husband, their grandparents or myself. And as we reared our family, other, more intrinsic questions arose about identity, to do with heritage and traditions, about what it is that one, as a parent, needs to pass on. Gradually, I realised that uncovering what had remained concealed concerned me and my children as much as it did my father. Finding out about those who came before us had as much to do with the present and with the future as it did with the past. The desire to understand my father was there all along. And despite my original hesitation, my burgeoning little family provided further motivation. Yet I was still afraid.

Finally, my maternal aunt, who had just retired from working at the department of peacekeeping at the United Nations in New York, in an act of boundless generosity, offered to spend the many hours necessary to read the letters alongside me. She loved history and had known and been close to my father in Venezuela, so she too was curious. Having a fellow reader, a companion with whom to share the emotional burden that came with a detailed knowledge of the letters, made the deciphering easier and the journey bearable. It was her offer of support that emboldened me to finally delve into the words and the world of my lost family, to attempt to retrieve their unspoken story.

So, four years after first receiving the translations of the family correspondence, I plunged fully into the past. The majority of the letters were from the 1940s and gave an account of daily life in Terezín, the concentration camp a few miles northwest of Prague. The Nazis had established it in 1941 to hold Jews as prisoners before sending them on to extermination camps. Over 140,000 residents of Central Europe went through it. There were no gas chambers there, yet tens of thousands died within its confines.

I read and reread the letters until the names, the dates and the places interconnected seamlessly. I familiarised myself with the authors' writing habits. My grandparents modified first names slightly, reflecting affection or humour or frustration and sometimes from melancholy or fear of reprisal. My grandfather Otto was at times *Ota* and even *Grumpy*. My grandmother Ella could be *Elka*, *Mother*, or *Dulinka*. Their boys were *darlings* or *dearests* or *golden ones*. Lotar could be *Lotík*. Hans was often *Handa*, and later, from mid-1943 on, he was seldom mentioned and became an oblique reference, *H*.

Once I was able to navigate the distress and gained a fluency in the way the letters were written, familial lines were revealed that had hitherto been invisible, lost in time. I noted each name in the letters and tried to ascertain who they were. Often there were clues that helped me to deduce the approximate age of these new acquaintances, details that hinted at their previous professions or where they hailed from. Armed with this, Magda — a tenacious and resourceful researcher from Prague — and I scoured lists from the camps, trying to find the correct record for each person mentioned and, wherever possible, identify his or her fate and find the family. Thus I traced unheard-of relatives and their friends of over half a century before. In many cases, I actually found the children of those friends of my grandparents, now older themselves. The openness of all those I contacted amazed me then, and it does so still. They warmly welcomed me into their own histories, recalling anecdotes and experiences of their childhood and adult lives. Their stories connected with my own family — the one I had never met. My questions sometimes led to answers and often also to further puzzles, to more documents, photographs and objects stored in boxes, stowed away in cupboards and attics.

A letter from my grandfather Otto dated December 1942.

And so it was that additional boxes filled with clues from the past began to appear – usually unannounced and unexpected, and always as if by magic.

With the help of Magda who scoured public records, I found out that my great-uncle Victor had left Prague for America in 1919. For reasons unknown, there he had changed his last name slightly by dropping the last n. I traced his grandchildren to California. After scrolling through phone books online and leaving messages on a dozen answering machines, I located his grandson, also Victor, the first of many long-lost cousins, in San Diego.

Victor Neuman is an American engineer who was wholly unaware of his Jewish heritage. After our initial Skype call, what struck me was that we had spoken for over an hour, and somehow the conversation had flowed easily. This was in spite of many apparent differences between us. Victor is few decades older than I am and grew up in California. He received a master's degree in engineering from Cambridge and is a practising Methodist, while I was raised in Venezuela, studied humanities and have no formal religious leanings at all. We had never spoken before, and yet we laughed at the same things with an unexpected familiarity. During our call, Victor mentioned that he had lost touch with another California cousin, Greg, who was involved in real estate and might have more information on the family. But Victor did not have any further details and could not help me find Greg. I played with the spelling, googled every real estate agent named Greg Neumann on the West Coast of the US, and even stalked a real estate agent called Gregg Neuman on Facebook. That Gregg finally answered numerous messages and calls with a very polite, if slightly alarmed, email. He clarified that he had initially thought I might be part of a scam, and while he would love to help, his family had been in America for generations, and his background was not Czech but Hungarian. Eventually, the California White Pages yielded some possible phone numbers. I left a few messages on answering machines, and the correct Greg replied with a joyous email. I had found another cousin. On Skype once more, I tried to explain our very large family tree, told him how to get in touch with his cousin Victor – who, it transpired, lived close to him – and explained about my father's box of papers.

To my astonishment, Greg told me that his own father had also left a box behind. He believed it was still in his attic and contained some old postcards written in German and Czech. As a boy in California, his father, Harry Neuman, had been a keen philatelist who kept the letters simply for the collectible stamps on the envelopes. A few days later, Greg graciously posted this box of his father's stamps to me. Carefully packaged with layered cardboard and secured all around with strong-bonding brown tape, it was filled with postcards, envelopes containing letters, and photographs sent in the 1920s, '30s and '40s from my grandparents and the family in Europe to their relatives in the US.

I opened the box and, for a moment, understood what people mean when they say things are fated. Greg had not known whom these cards were from. He had never seen our family tree. I turned around the first postcard at the very top of the pile that he had sent, one with a French stamp dated 1936. I immediately recognised my grandfather in a bathing suit, nonchalantly sitting on a beach, smiling. It was an instant of inexplicable concordance, one of many that drove me on with the research, echoing the luminosity and magical realism of Latin America more than the darkness of Europe during the Second World War.

Items from Greg's box included a postcard photograph
of Otto on the beach in Cannes in 1936.

In a similar manner, I traced and spoke to a dozen other
people. I located cousins in California, Paris, Leeds in
England, Bern in Switzerland, Prague and the Czech town of
Teplice. I discovered connected friends in Florida, New York,
Australia, Indonesia and the Czech village of Staré Město. I
have collected memories and evidence from every reliable
source I could find. Each unhesitatingly opened and shared

troves of family documents, photographs, written memoirs, saved notebooks and childhood tales to help me piece together the puzzle of my father's family and what happened to them during the war.

I have now listened to and read so many stories from people who knew my family in the 1930s and '40s, and read enough of their written words, to be able to sense the personalities of those who have gone, to hear their voices, to glimpse the people they were. I have gone to the paint factory that the family owned, to the houses and apartments that were once theirs. I have paced the same rooms and hallways, climbed the same stairs, held on to the same railings, crossed the same streets, tripped on the same chipped cobblestones of Prague sidewalks, walked on the paths of the Vltava that smell of the same magnolias and geraniums, knocked on the same doors, turned the same handles and entered the same rooms. From their windows, I have looked out at their world. I have imagined them so many times that it is almost as if I have my own memory of my grandparents and of who and how they were.

Perhaps all remembrance is a process of compilation and creation. Every day we absorb what is around us and assemble observations of a specific time: sounds, smells, textures, words, images and feelings. Of course, we prioritise and edit as we go, subjective witnesses to our own lives, providing recollections that are often biased and incomplete. It is, I suppose, why even honest and reliable witnesses in a courtroom can describe the same event differently. And yet I am told that they tend to agree on the essentials even while the details can vary wildly. As a number of witnesses provide their diverse accounts, a distinctive picture frequently emerges – even if it is a mosaic of impressions rather than a series of identical overlapping images.

I realise now that I too have created a mosaic of assembled reminiscences. It is a remembrance because the words, the feelings, the impact left on others mean that those who shaped them are still present, retained as a mental perception. I have collated these recollections that capture my grandparents' essence and consolidated them with the photographs and the hundreds of documents. Now my family are no longer a passed-over palette of faded shadows. I can conjure them.

I can see them vividly.

Hans with his uncle Richard, Otto and Ella Neumann in Prague, *c.* 1934.

2

THE WATCH ON THE PLATE

The first time I saw a photograph of my father as a child, he had been dead for over fifteen years. Halfway into my research, my uncle Lotar's daughter, my cousin Madla, brought me an album from her father's house. She had forgotten about its existence, though, as a small girl, she had been shown the contents. It is covered in black vinyl and, despite its obvious age, is in perfect condition. An adhesive black label reads *Famille Lotar* in lettering of white relief. Its cardboard pages are laden with black-and-white photographs, some with corners curling as they have become unglued. As I turned the pages carefully, trying to recognise my family, the tiny image of a boy jumped out at me. It startled me because the face was so familiar. It does not immediately remind of my father, it just looks like my son. The way my eldest holds his hands is the same. Their noses are different, the shade of the hair is dissimilar, but the eyes are uncannily identical. I have seen that expression, that half grin, the eyes gazing up, a million times. In the photograph, the family is in the woods near their holiday house in Libčice just outside of Prague. My grandparents Ella and Otto, and Otto's youngest brother Richard, pose for the camera while two smiling boys sit on picnic blankets in the foreground. They are my uncle Lotar and my father, Hans. It must have been taken in

1928 or 1929. Lotar appears to be about ten, and Hans could not be more than seven or eight. The boys are dressed in pin-striped jackets and shorts, and their hair is styled in matching pudding-bowl cuts. When I look closely, despite the blur of time passed, I recognise my father's smile. There is a distinct impishness in his eyes.

Lotar and Hans with their parents and uncle Richard, *c.* 1928.

I have read, researched, asked and asked again so many questions of so many people who knew of them that I can almost hear their breaths, their laughs, their sobs.

I can picture the family in 1936, moving about their lives. When it is quiet enough, I can hear their voices.

They are in a large airy living room with a beamed high ceiling and a chimney at one end. From the windows, you can see the wind create waves of needles on the pines in the garden. It is a weekend in late September, and the chill of the winter's evening has already impregnated the air. Otto leans against the back of an armchair next to the crackling fire, absorbed in a book about Mahatma Gandhi. He is forty-six, but his white hair and down-turned lips make him seem older. Ella is almost forty, looks closer to thirty as she floats about the rooms humming a melody. They have two teenage boys, Lotar, who is eighteen, and Hans, who is fifteen. That evening Lotar is at home with his parents. He has just brought more firewood from the supply outside. Again, they are in their country house in Libčice, about 25 kilometres north of Prague, on the banks of the Vltava river.

Ella had received a gift of money from her parents and bought the farmhouse in Libčice, ignoring Otto's protests about the extravagance of owning a second home. In the city, they had a comfortable apartment in a nineteenth-century building chosen specifically for its location: a two-minute walk from the main building of the family's paint factory. 'It is most practical to live nearby,' Otto would say over and over, as Ella complained that being so close just meant that home and work fused into one. 'It is so much better to have to travel a little,' she protested, 'to have a journey that allows you to separate and disconnect.' She would say to Otto, who was no longer listening: 'You have to have a different place to rest, a place that is just for family and that allows you the space to think of other things. In Prague, the factory just there means that someone is always knocking on the door whenever there is a problem at work.' Even though he never admitted it, Ella knew that her husband also came to treasure their weekends away.

Ella had spent her childhood in a rambling house in Chlumec nad Cidlinou, a small medieval town in northeastern Bohemia. She had met Otto there, when he had been employed as an accountant at the local sugar refinery. He had conducted a determined court-ship of Ella which had been as respectful as it was resolute. Ella's father, a successful stockbroker, had immediately approved of his serious prospective son-in-law. Ella had found Otto's gravitas and candour endearing. She and her three siblings had grown up with the easy nonchalance that comes from a childhood unclouded by financial worries. Her family baffled Otto. He considered them too preoccupied with trivia. They certainly did not spend their time studying politics and philosophy, as he did. They seemed to devote most of their attention to parties and music.

Everyone in her family played either the piano or the violin, and as a young girl, Ella had loved to sing. She had wanted Hans and Lotar to learn an instrument, but Otto had not allowed it. It was not that Otto did not enjoy music, it was just that he considered playing an instrument inconsequential. He did relish listening to the Bohemian composers from the last century, Smetana and Dvořák, though Otto maintained this was mostly from a sense of national pride. Ella, on the other hand, liked the more modern composer Martinů, and shared her boys' love of jazz, swing and political cabaret. She missed the constant music and the happy chaos of her childhood. Her older sister, Martha, who had married Rudolf Pollak and had three children, had died of pneumonia in 1923. The remaining family and Martha's brood regularly gathered in Roudnice, where one of her brothers and her parents still lived. Every moment there was a hubbub of dis-cussion, music and laughter.

When she first moved to Prague with Otto, Ella had been exhilarated by the bustle of the capital. Yet, with the years, she would come to take pleasure in it only sporadically. She longed to live outside of it, where time passed more slowly. This was why she loved the house in the sleepy town of Libčice. They spent most weekends and school holidays there. Otto would join them only when circumstances at the factory allowed. Hans and Lotar had grown up cycling on the paths and rowing their boat on the Vltava. They had caught butterflies, built huts in the woods, swum in a calm part of the river – in Libčice, they had found the space and freedom to be boys. Ella especially enjoyed the people and the natural life that bustled and thrummed around the river. She would walk its banks every morning after breakfast and watch the colours and shadows thrown by the rising light change with the seasons.

A portrait of Ella from the early 1930s.

Otto was the seventh of eight siblings. He had grown up in the area of České Budějovice in southern Bohemia. His parents had struggled to keep some order in a household with seven boys by imposing strict rules. His father had died when Otto was twelve, and he had found comfort in discipline and order. He had embraced the role of the sensible and cautious one in the family, and took pride in having all rely on him for advice. All the Neumann children were earnest and hardworking. They had, by turns, taken care of their mother until her death in 1910. When one of the brothers faced difficulty, the others rallied around to help. Otto had studied business because he enjoyed the predictability of numbers. He remained close to all his brothers, and especially to the youngest, Richard, with whom he had started the Montana paint factory in 1921. Letters show that he also often spent time with his elder brother Rudolf and with Oskar, who was only two years younger and who ran one of the factory branches. His older brother, Victor, an engineer who had helped the Austro-Hungarian army build bridges, had migrated to America after the First World War to try his luck there. Despite the distance, they were in constant contact.

A portrait of Otto from the 1920s.

Otto and Ella had worked on the house for years, modernising it, decorating it, planting the garden. It had been three years since they had begun using it regularly, and it was just coming into its own, shaped to the contours of the family. The rooms were by now cosy and familiar, the walls filled with prints, every nook explored and cherished. The trees and shrubs in the garden surrounding the house had rooted deeply, filled out and blossomed. The path to the riverbank had been re-paved and weeded, and in spring and summer was traced with wild-flowers. In autumn and winter, the damp fallen leaves plastered the stones.

Early that evening, as his father worked at his desk, Lotar sat in an armchair and gazed out of the window, warmed by a fire that danced in the hearth. He sat upright, supported by a needlepoint pillow, with a half-read book face down on his knee. Ella bustled about him, going in and out of the kitchen as she checked on the stew. She chattered and pestered Lotar for more information about his sweetheart. Lotar tried to concentrate enough to tune out his mother's nonsense and focus on his book.

That August, the rest of the family had vacationed in Cannes while Hans was away at a YMCA summer camp near the town of Sázava, southeast of Prague. Otto and Ella had gone to collect Lotar, who had spent his second summer learning French at a language school in Cannes. There, the previous summer, he had met a fellow Czech from Prague, Zdenka Jedličková. The beautiful Zdenka with the confident cascading laughter and the dreamy blue eyes had transformed his life. Lotar had fallen in love before they had even spoken. She had been in the middle of a group of young men, and as one lit her cigarette and she shielded it from the breeze, she had glanced across the street at Lotar and smiled. It took a full day for him to muster the courage to speak to her. After their first early evening walk along the promenade, they spent together every second that remained of the summer. She was almost fluent, while this was only Lotar's first summer in France, so she had helped him with his French. Seeing each other had been harder in Prague. In France, everything had been easy, both this summer and the first. It had been perfect. They had even performed together onstage. An article appeared in a local paper, *L'eclaireur*, on 24 August 1935, mentioning them both by name in a review of the artistic evening of the International School. Lotar kept it as his bookmark and, many years later, stored it in his box.

Lotar (standing) and Zdenka (second from left) in Cannes, 1936.

Zdenka was fiercely independent. Her grandfather worked in property and had constructed many buildings in the New Town area of Prague. Her grandparents did not trust their son-in-law, Zdenka's father, and had placed the properties they owned in their granddaughter's name. They had given Zdenka ownership of a residential building on Trojanova Street, and the income and the responsibility had helped her grow in confidence and maturity. She was in her first year of studying law at Charles University and, rather outrageously, raced around the city in her own car. She was three years older than Lotar, a fact he had not yet shared with Otto and Ella. Zdenka's own parents knew about the age difference and were less than thrilled. However, they were unhappier still when they learned that he came from a Jewish family. 'But we are not a religious family,' Lotar had explained to her mother one evening when the topic had arisen soon after they returned from France. 'My father is more moved by Gandhi's philosophies than anything. We were all forced to be vegetarians for a year!'

'They celebrate our holidays, even Christmas,' Zdenka had insisted. 'They are also fluent in Czech and German, like us. Really, they are as Czech as you and me.'

Ella adored Zdenka. She could tell that Lotar was happily distracted. He was completely absorbed by the girl. His customarily grave mood had lifted so noticeably that he seemed physically lighter on his feet since his return. He laughed more easily, and often he appeared to do so for no reason at all. Otto, however, was unimpressed and preoccupied. Lotar had to focus on his studies; these were not times to dawdle. He had finished the last two years at the Grammar School, taken his maturita final exams and enrolled at the Czech Technical College in

Prague to study chemical engineering. Lotar had toyed with the idea of becoming an actor but, under some pressure from Otto, he had soon realised that drama was not a 'proper' career.

Hans had not been expelled from school despite his truancy and had attained the grades to start a four-year course at the Chemical Industrial School. But Otto knew that this was just luck. His younger son oscillated between obsessions: one day it was poetry, another sculpture, another collecting stones. Hans was mercurial; it was obvious to everyone that he took after Ella and her side of the family. Uncle Richard was talking of migrating to America, and if he did, Otto would be left alone at the helm of the business. Otto beseeched Lotar to focus on school and work. Otto needed his elder son to study, work and keep the company running. Hans could not be relied upon.

When Lotar had first introduced his parents to Zdenka at the café on the promenade of La Croisette, Ella had been chatty and warm. Otto, on the other hand, had been so cold that it bordered on the impolite. He had barely looked at Zdenka. Later that evening, as Lotar walked her to her building on a quiet side street, he felt the need to apologise. 'I am sorry about my father – he is very serious and doesn't know how to charm. But deep down he is kind, and he adores you, I know,' he whispered.

Otto had been irate at the end of that summer when he found out that Lotar had seen Zdenka every night in Cannes. He was furious that his son had auditioned for the stage again. 'He must remember his priorities, he is there to study French. He cannot be derailed by a relationship that will never amount to anything.' After the fight, Otto had not spoken to Lotar for days. Ella, on the other hand, had been relieved that he was having fun. 'Let the boy live a little,' she said, laughing. As she was keen to point out, any whimsical behaviour was entirely unusual for Lotar; he took nothing lightly. He actually took life so seriously that he had to be treated for ulcers and exhaustion during the final exams at the Prague Grammar School in June.

On this autumn evening in Libčice, as Jerry the elderly fox terrier nuzzled up to him by the fire, Lotar's stomach pains now seemed a distant memory. Hans, his lanky and disorganised younger brother, who lived in a fantasy world of ideas and poems, was predictably late.

Despite every chastisement and incentive, Hans was never on time. He had spent the day with Zdeněk Tůma, his new friend from school. The two had met on the first day. A teacher had asked a question about a chemical reaction, and Hans and Zdeněk had been the only ones to know the answer. Zdeněk — who, Hans soon realised, was always joking — had come up to Hans as they had left the classroom and said, 'I think it is extremely important that we idiots join forces.'

Hans liked him immediately. Zdeněk was no idiot. He was the only pupil in the year to have gained a scholarship to attend the school.

Unlike Hans', Zdeněk's childhood had been marred with difficulty. His mother, Marie, hailed from Benátky, a farming town close to the Slovak border, where her family had worked in the fields. She had raised him alone for the first few years, as his father, a wealthy married farmer, had denied any responsibility. Life for a single mother in the strict Catholic farming community had been untenable. Marie needed to find a job so, in the hope of making a better life for them both, had moved them to Prague. In the capital, she had found work as a cleaner at the famous

U Fleků restaurant and brewery and had enrolled her boy in a school. When Zdeněk was eight, Marie married Antonín Tůma, a caretaker of a nearby building. Antonín adored little Zdeněk and had adopted him in 1929. The three of them lived a simple but happy life in the city. Zdeněk, ever chatty and precocious, had flourished in Prague and soon started arriving home with report cards filled with accolades. The staff from the Chemical Industrial School of Prague regularly ate and drank at U Fleků, which was only a few yards away. Marie, who was proud and ambitious, had made sure that they met her cheerful and bright young son. The teachers were so taken with the boy that they had reviewed his reports and arranged for him to take the chemistry degree course at the school for free.

But you would not have known that Zdeněk and Hans were high-achieving students. In the first days of the term, they had decided to join a society of practical jokers in Prague called the *Klub Recesistů*, or Prankster Club. In June 1936, the club had published the first *Almanach Recesse*, stating the aims of its prankster members: 'Everything is a joke. We must have fun because nothing can be done seriously. Egomaniacs and know-it-alls rule the world, so we must use the only weapon against them that has stood the test of time – humour.' Hans and Zdeněk had passed the club's entry examination by lying down in the middle of the main street in Nove Mesto amid the midday traffic. When concerned passers-by asked if they were unwell, they had replied, 'Oh no, just a little tired,' and run away. This jape had elicited the requisite number of laughs from the fellow members, and they were now full members of Recesistů.

That Saturday in September 1936, Zdeněk had come up from

Prague to spend the day in Libčice with Hans. Ella had wrapped some sandwiches in a basket for them, and they had headed for the promenade by the riverbank. They had whiled away their afternoon sitting on the grass, coming up with possible pranks to discuss at their next Recesistů club meeting. And they had chatted about novels and poetry – both Hans and Zdeněk loved poems and wrote verse. As they threw stones into the Vltava and tried to make them skip, they took turns reciting stanzas from a lyrical poem by Rilke.

As usual, they had lost track of time. Hans had taken his friend on the back of his bicycle to catch the train from a neighbouring stop. Zdeněk had just managed to clamber onto the train, but the detour meant that Hans was late.

Dinner at home in Libčice, or in Prague, was always at seven-thirty p.m. As Hans raced back up the path to the house on his bicycle, he missed a stone in the shadows cast by the waning sunlight. He lost control. He fell off. He picked himself up, blew the dust off his glasses and rearranged the chain. He had scraped his arms and legs, and reddened dirt had lodged in his cuts. Tomorrow, undoubtedly, the contusions would be obvious, but this was of no consequence. Hans seemed to be perpetually covered in bruises. He struggled with coordination and constantly walked into things, mis-stepping, losing his hat or scarf, or leaving his school books behind. He frequently fell off his bicycle. Organising his body, his things or his time was not a strength or, as he liked to clarify, a priority. As a result of the mishaps to which he was prone, his parents, with a mixture of pity and affection, had nicknamed him the 'unfortunate boy'.

At seven-thirty-four that evening, scratched and grimy, that unfortunate boy dumped the bicycle by the side door and rushed in through the kitchen. Ella, Otto and Lotar were already sitting in the dining room. The stew and dumplings on the sideboard had been served. Jerry wagged his tail as he waited for crumbs beneath the table. Hans quickly sat down and stared at his father with defiant green eyes that seemed more olive as his face reddened with embarrassment. 'Handa . . .' Ella sighed with resignation as he apologised for being late. Hans looked down and rubbed his muddied hands under the table. Before him he could see the elaborate pattern of cobalt-blue vines and flowers meandering across the white plate. This was visible everywhere except in the centre.

There, in rebuke, instead of dinner, his father had placed his plain gold pocket watch.

3

IT THUNDERS EVERYWHERE

In the late 1970s, when I was a young child in Caracas, my parents would wake at different times. My mother liked to sleep longer and then linger in bed. My father used to say that he needed to 'stretch the hours' and, weekday or weekend, would rise no later than six-thirty a.m. and disappear into the study that connected with their bedroom. From there, he enjoyed watching the sky lighten.

I was not to disturb them in the mornings. I was allowed into my parents' rooms only once either was awake and reading the newspapers. There were very few rules in our house, but my parents were strict about this one. Eager to please as the only child at home, I scrupulously obeyed. My parents would call for their breakfast through an internal intercom. My own bedroom was on the other side of the house, so I had no way of hearing the phone ring or the bustle of preparations in the kitchen. I only knew that my parents were awake because of the newspapers.

So I would wait patiently for my cue. The routine hardly altered. The night guard received the papers in a bundle in the small hours and handed them to the housekeeper in the kitchen when he collected his breakfast. She would cut the string that bound them and place them on the cream-carpeted floor just outside the closed white door that led to my parents' room. She carefully arranged them in a half-opened fan so that the name and headline of each was visible at a glance. When the papers disappeared from the end of the hall, I knew that I was allowed in.

First, my father would take the papers from the floor and withdraw to his study for breakfast. It was then that I joined him. Often I brought my own breakfast tray so we could eat together. There was only room for one at the table by the daybed, so he would help me place my tray on an armchair as I positioned myself cross-legged on the floor. He would hand me the comic strip, the puzzle pages and a pencil. He gently enquired how I was, but aside from discussing the crossword clues, the sporadic conversation would habitually revolve around the news that he read.

When he finished with the papers, he would carefully arrange them again on the hallway carpet for my mother. He would then go away for meetings, make calls at his desk or vanish into the room where he repaired watches, leaving me to finish the puzzles on my own.

I would return to my room and wait for the papers to disappear once more, signalling that my mother was up. She ordinarily woke around nine or ten a.m. and had her breakfast in bed, elegant in a nightgown even then. My mother was not interested in puzzles, so I left those behind. I was allowed to usher in the three enormous dogs, and we all nestled in the bed around her while we listened to music or talked about her friends or mine. She worked in the arts and told marvellous stories about the quirks of conductors, musicians and ballet dancers. Sometimes as she dressed, we would pretend that we were on a stage and dance around the room. On occasion, we sang at the top of our voices, my mother melodically and I, unfailingly, off-key.

One morning in 1979, when I was eight years old and before I had found the false identity card in the box, my father woke much earlier than usual.

It was not yet dawn. The hallway lamp that was kept on, because I was afraid of the pitch-dark, had not yet been switched off. I had heard a rustling and looked down the hall to find the papers gone. The garden leaves rippled in shades of black through the bars of the windows. Yet the lights were turned on in my father's study. It was too early for breakfast, and I did not have my tray to bring in. I crept down the long hall, pushed gently at the half-open door and peered through. My father sat, dressed in his navy cotton kimono decorated with white seagulls, lost as he gazed out of the window. Outside, the garden was feebly patched with the promise of light. The newspapers lay in a pile unopened on the daybed. I installed myself in my usual spot on the floor. His hair seemed especially white in the shadows. The characteristic poise was absent, and he seemed somehow disjointed, unsettled. He did not hand me the comics or the page with the puzzles. Instead, he turned to me, profoundly serious, and announced that something odd had happened the night before during his dinner at the restaurant. As he had chatted with his friends, he had felt a sharp pain in his left leg.

'When we got home, I looked under my trousers, and I saw these.'

He lifted the edge of his gown slightly, uncovering part of his shin. He pointed at two small red wounds, one exactly above the other, that were clearly visible on his pale skin. 'Do you see these holes in my leg?'

I did.

'What do you think they are?' he asked slowly. He seemed exhausted, as if he had not slept.

'Mosquito bites, Papi?'

'I hope you are right. I am not sure at all. They are very round, and their position is unusual. I think they're something else.'

I was reminded of a news story that he had recounted a few weeks earlier of a Bulgarian dissident in London. The man had been poisoned by spies with a tiny bullet fired from an umbrella as he waited for a bus. The bullet had been shot into his leg and left a minute wound. My father's meaning struck me. 'Like the one in the man's leg in London?' I ventured.

He nodded. 'Exactly. They can just shoot you when you are no longer useful. If they don't like you, if they think you are a traitor, just like that, without process or trial, they just kill you. And the worst thing is, nobody would ever know.'

His words threw me. I inspected his leg again. The perfect dots, with fine red scratch lines around them, definitely looked like insect bites to me.

'But Papi, no one wants to kill you. Don't they itch? Are you sure they aren't mosquito bites?'

His evident fear unnerved me. I wanted it to go away, I longed to dispel it. I bent my elbow towards him and pointed at a scab of my own, which I had just scratched.

'Look, Papi! See, yours are the same.'

'You are right,' he said, his gaze still adrift.

Then, after a pause, he looked at me again and murmured

63

affectionately a term that he had derived from the French word for mischievous and that he used for both my mother and me.

'Coquinita. That's what they probably are.'

He looked away, but his laugh, intended to reassure me, sounded wrong. He was nervous still, I could tell. It was obvious to me then that he did not think he had been the victim of a biting insect. It was as if he had forgotten that I was his young daughter and just wanted me to be a witness to these strange wounds on his leg. He passed me the comics, opened a paper and hid behind it.

It did not make sense. My father was not fearful, he was resolute and strong. He personified security, success. Yet he seemed frightened. Why would he think that anyone wanted to kill him? But I did not say anything more, and neither did he.

When I went into my mother's room that morning, I told her about my father's bites. My mother repeatedly maintained that children must never be lied to. I knew this and found it reassuring. It did mean that she was uncommonly candid with her explanations and opinions.

'It's probably that he's concerned about malaria . . . there used to be lots of cases here. But no longer.'

I countered that was not it at all, that he was not afraid of mosquitoes or malaria. He thought someone was trying to kill him, as they had the Bulgarian.

'Don't pay attention, he is like that at times,' she replied casually. 'It doesn't happen usually, but sometimes he is a little afraid.'

Then she told me about a similar incident during their last

skiing trip. On those journeys, my parents usually flew direct from Caracas to Zurich while I stayed at home and went to school. They travelled regularly, and I particularly liked their trips to Switzerland because they returned home laden with giant boxes of chocolates for me.

My mother explained that when it was nearly time to land, the pilot announced that, due to bad weather, the plane might have to be diverted to Vienna or Stuttgart. My father's reaction had been striking. He clutched the metal hand rests and started to shake and sweat, she said, so much that just patting his forehead had soaked his handkerchief completely.

'Was it the turbulence? Were there thunderstorms?'

'Oh no, he wasn't scared of the weather,' she said. Hoping to reassure me, she continued: 'It just happens sometimes, he is afraid. He has not been back to Central Europe since he left all those years ago. I just told him to stay calm, reminded him that as a Venezuelan, he had nothing to worry about. And in the end the storm cleared, and we landed in Zurich after all. There was no reason to be anxious.'

'So things to do with some countries in Europe make him nervous?'

'Not often, but they sometimes do,' she said. 'He is very far away from Europe now. And you, my little mouse, certainly should not spend any time worrying about it.' I did not understand at all but left the issue there.

Why had the murder of a man at a bus stop in Europe made my father uneasy at home in Caracas? How was Switzerland different from Austria or Germany? Why would being Venezuelan have made a difference? Why would my father be scared for no reason? Who were *they*, those people who could just kill you? And what did all of that have to do with red dots on your shins? I had no clue how mosquitoes, nationality, poison, spies and turbulence could be connected. I did not understand why any of these things made my formidable father afraid.

There were no immediate answers, but if my mother thought it was fine that my father was nervous at times, then that meant I must do the same. She evidently was not remotely worried about anyone trying to poison him. Like her, I would try not to give the matter further thought.

Anyone observing us then wouldn't have noticed that anything was out of kilter at all. Our lives carried on as normal, the usual routines unaltered. My father's bites healed and no one mentioned poison again. For a while, I forgot about it too. My father's days continued to pass in Venezuela, replete with work, philanthropy, hobbies, friends and family. Seemingly, he had no real worries at all.

Could my family in the Czechoslovakia of the late 1930s possibly have imagined what was coming? If you look at the letters and photographs of the time, everything suggests that life for them during the mid-1930s retained a sense of normality. And yet, behind the smiles in the pictures, concealed within the words that filled their letters and emphasised the positive and the mundane, doubtless there must have been intimations of fear.

As Otto read the papers and oversaw production at the Montana factory, as Hans and Lotar continued with their studies, pranks, poems and boyish romances, it must have been there. Silent, ever present, but just out of sight.

Perhaps Hans was a bit too immature, but Lotar was more thoughtful. Otto was anything but a fantasist; he must have been apprehensive, even perhaps foreseen it. He must have discussed it with his brothers. By the middle of the decade, Victor, one of his brothers, had already asked the family to join him in America, and the youngest, Richard, had been arranging to emigrate. Surely, Ella's every instinct, even with her perpetually optimistic disposition, would have been to protect her brood. Perhaps during her walks along the Vltava, when the noise of everyday life quietened and she allowed her thoughts to wander, she had some presentiment, felt some anxiety at the impending threat.

Czechoslovakia was surrounded, landlocked by Romania, Hungary, Poland, Austria and Germany. There was no escape to the sea, just the 430-kilometre river that starts in the west and runs southeast with gathering strength along the hem of the Bohemian Forest before turning north to cross the heart of Bohemia through Prague itself. Both its Czech and German names, Vltava and Moldau, come from the Old German words for *wild waters*.

I have a photograph of Lotar and Zdenka taken on a spring or summer day in 1937. They stand next to each other dressed in matching exercise clothing with the emblem of their local YMCA. It looks as if they have just shared a joke, and they are smiling. They are in the garden at Libčice, probably coming back from canoeing in the waters of the Vltava. Lotar holds her proudly, and Zdenka laughs with raised eyebrows. They do not appear to have a care in the world.

Zdenka and Lotar in the garden at Libčice, 1937.

Yet with every passing week came new laws, fresh restrictions for Jews in Europe. Between 1933 and 1939, fourteen hundred anti-Jewish laws were passed in neighbouring Germany. In 1933, Jews were banned from state-sector jobs in government, law, farming, publishing, journalism and the arts. On 11 April 1933, anyone with one Jewish parent or grandparent was officially defined by German decree as non-Aryan. In 1935 the Nuremberg Laws were passed. In 1935 Poland modelled its own laws regarding Jews on Germany's. Jews and political refugees arrived by the thousands in Prague in the mid- to late 1930s, escaping open hatred in Germany, Austria and further east. Czechoslovakia was then seen as a safe haven, a bastion of democracy in Central Europe. As anti-Semitism metastasized across the Continent, Czechoslovakia remained relatively politically progressive and stable. Many prominent Jews held positions in the Social Democrat government, which was adamantly opposed to Nazi ideology. Czechoslovakia was more receptive to migration than Holland and unlike in France, one could get by speaking German.

I have found photographs of my father's first cousins from the late 1930s. In one, two young women confidently flank a cheerful, middle-aged man wearing a fedora. They are Zita and Hana, Ella's nieces, the daughters of her adored sister Martha. The man is Uncle Richard. The photo catches them mid-stride, mid-conversation, mid-laugh. It is impossible to see anything in it other than happiness. Yet already Richard, who owned the paint factory with Otto, had spoken of leaving and selling his share of the business. He was applying for a visa to join his brother Victor in the US.

Richard Neumann with Ella's nieces Hana and
Zita Polláková in Prague, 1938.

In the box that I received from cousin Greg in California, there is a letter, written in July 1936 to Victor in the US by Rudolf Neumann, one of his older brothers. Rudolf was married to Jenny, with whom he lived in Třebíč, a town southeast of Prague towards the Austrian border. Jenny appears from the photographs to be a large woman with a commanding presence. Together they ran a double-fronted store that sold fashionable clothing in the main square in town. I have traced their granddaughter, who lives in Paris, and she recalls Jenny as good natured and with a hearty and infectious laugh.

Rudolf and Jenny's two sons, Erich and Ota, were ten years older than their cousins Lotar and Hans. Ota, the younger and the quieter of the two, still lived with his parents in Třebíč. Erich, who was more jovial and adventurous, had just moved to Prague and joined the Montana factory to work in sales. I have a photograph of Erich from the late 1930s. He is tilting his round face expectantly towards the photographer. His dark hair, already receding despite his being in his twenties, is neatly brushed back. He wears a striped suit over a shirt that is just a bit too tight around the neck, and a polka-dot tie. Despite it being a passport photograph, his eyes glow with a certain dreaminess. I have a single photo of Ota taken before the war. There are no others in the family albums or boxes. It is a passport photo. Like his brother, he also wears a pinstriped suit and a plaid wool tie. He has high cheekbones, and the corners of his mouth are downturned. His eyebrows are close together as if he is about to frown. His light-coloured eyes are looking down. He seems sad.

In the letter from the summer of 1936, Rudolf explains

that business is not as good as it was, but that the shop is still trading, and his family and brothers are all in good health. He describes a month's holiday in the spa town of Marienbad and anticipates his wife's upcoming trip to Bad Gastein in Austria. He closes by expressing the wish to see his brother Victor again soon.

The general economic climate in Europe in the 1930s explains Rudolf's gloom about the business. Aside from that, his letter seems positive, almost carefree. Below his father's words is a carefully handwritten message from Ota to his American uncle and cousins. His words are much more sombre. Ota, aged twenty-five, wrote:

My dears,

I often remember the wonderful moments that we spent together. I cannot even believe that so long has passed already. I am taking English lessons! Our life is generally still quite good but the prospects for the future are not promising. It thunders everywhere around us and things are especially difficult for us young people, as we are struck with the uncertainty of our future. And yet the situation in Czechoslovakia is better than everywhere else but even here, especially in Moravia, the anti-Semitism is growing. I suppose this is not surprising given how newspapers are reporting on the actions of our neighbours. Enclosed Harry will find a new series of Czechoslovak stamps that I was able to source in Třebíč. I do hope that he will like them.

Warm regards and kisses from your nephew and cousin,
Ota.

Ota was worried about the future. He knew.

The following summer, in August 1937, Jews were officially accused of sacrilege in the town of Humenné, Czechoslovakia. By then open discrimination and even violence against the Jews in Prague seemed to have become a regular occurrence. And yet the Neumann family carried on with their lives. As far as can be discerned from the photographs, they focused on the positive: they worked, studied, spent their weekends in Libčice and travelled and laughed. If they had not before, they must by then have felt it. Otto, Ella, Lotar and Hans must have known that the net was tightening.

In March 1938, the Nazis marched into Vienna, and Hitler annexed Austria in a union known as the Anschluss. Austrian Jews lost their right to vote; they were deprived of legal rights and subjected to systematic public humiliation – made, for example, to scrub the streets with their toothbrushes or consume grass like animals. Hungary too passed anti-Semitic laws, which, like Poland's before them, were similar to Germany's. By the time Hans was seventeen, four of the countries with whom Czechoslovakia shared its borders were openly and officially anti-Semitic.

In October 1938, Hitler occupied the Czech Sudetenland.

At this, Otto's brother Victor wrote from America again, urging his family in Czechoslovakia to leave without delay. This plea was followed by the events that became known as Kristallnacht, the night of crystal, so named for the hundreds of Jewish-owed shop windows that were shattered by Nazi paramilitaries and civilians across Austria and Germany. That November night, ninety-one Jews were killed, thirty

thousand men sent to camps, and Jewish property and synagogues vandalised. In 1938 Germany and Austria ruled that
all people classified as Jews were to carry special identity
cards, have their passports stamped with a 'J' and change
their name to include either Israel or Sara. Across Europe,
people of Jewish heritage, who could, fled.

In almost every photograph of the family in Libčice,
those pictured are smiling. In Lotar's album there are photographs of Ella as a baby, Ella as a teenager dressed up in
a flamenco dress and Ella smiling with her sister. Otto and
Ella can be seen as a young couple, on family holidays, all
of them with their boys at the beach or skiing. Most of the
photographs that fill the album were taken in Libčice in the
1930s. Almost every inch of the album's black card pages is
covered in photographs, some enormous, some so small that
I need to use a magnifying glass to see the detail of the faces.
The boys are playing shirtless in the summer heat. In some
they are wearing shorts or holding a ball. In one picture the
family delightedly cram into an uncle's motorcycle sidecar.
In another they are playing tennis, pristine and smiling in
their whites. In one, Ella is standing in the garden, biting
her lip in expectation as she waits to hit a volleyball. The
family embraces, frolics and dreams. In a few others they
play with the dog, holding him in some or making him
jump. Then there is the tiny photo which is filled with pure
joy. On a hot summer's day, Ella stands in the garden by a
wooden picket fence and pours water over herself from a
large watering can.

You can see the perfect combination of mischief and delight
in her posture, in the way her face is turned up, her eyes are

shut and her lips are open and happy. Elsewhere, Otto and his brother-in-law, Hugo, sit on some stripy deckchairs. They have just stopped to look up mid-conversation and are about to crack a smile.

Ella in the garden at Libčice in the late 1930s.

The only photographs I have in which Otto is smiling are taken in the garden at Libčice. In one, he grins as he reads a newspaper in the sunshine; in another, his customarily slicked hair is a little out of place as he laughs. I am surprised by his happiness and carefree ease. It seems inconsistent with the accounts I have of his character. It is true that one keeps photographs of joyous moments; most family albums are not filled with portraits of people looking worried or upset. And yet these photographs are not posed – they capture natural moments of joy. It seems that even in the late 1930s, in that sleepy town on the Vltava, the family was able to escape, forget any worries and just be.

As I pieced together the life of the family, I was intrigued by Otto and Ella's small oasis in Libčice. Did the house still exist? Should I make the forty-minute drive from Prague, walk down Vltava Street and knock on a stranger's door? If I found it, perhaps the owner could tell me something about its history. I knew that it was so cherished by Ella, by the entire family. Some initial research revealed that while many families lived in the house during the Communist years, it had not legally changed hands since the Neumanns had sold it after the war. A look on Google Maps suggested that the house was now more a cluster of buildings arranged around a courtyard, perhaps a warehouse or a light industrial compound. Magda, the Czech researcher in Prague who has been tracing families like mine for many years confirmed this. There seemed to be little point in going to the house, which would be nothing like it was, modified and stripped of its memories.

And yet I remained curious. I wanted to see what it looked like now, what it looked like then. I tried my luck online. By searching an address and a name from the 1948 Czech property registry, I traced the current owner online. Michal Peřina, more searching told me, is a well-known and award-winning furniture designer. Facebook revealed a smiling man on a sailboat, with kind eyes and cropped greying hair under a baseball cap. I hoped I had the right person; the address and the last name were the same. I emailed, explaining who I was. Michal replied immediately, confirming that his grandparents had bought the house from my family.

After describing my investigations, I asked if he happened

to have any old documents or photographs of the house that he could share. He replied that if I could wait a few weeks he would send me something; first he had to have it restored. He attached a photograph of piles of papers laid on a surface. I was thrilled to have found Michal, at first simply because he said in his email that he, like my grandparents, loved the Libčice house. In my excitement, I forgot to ask what precisely he intended to restore. I zoomed in on the picture that he enclosed in the email, but all I could see were stained illegible papers on a long wooden table. I expected he would send me a few old photographs, perhaps some house plans, or, if I was lucky, the bill of sale from 1948.

A few weeks later, thanks to Michal, a fourth box to add to those received from my father, Lotar and Greg the Californian cousin, found its way to me. Inside it was a handwritten note from Michal. He told me that, as a young boy, he had wondered about the contents of a mysterious safe that stood in an unused room in his grandparents' house. He had tried all the keys that he had found to open the lock to no avail. At first he had been too young to indulge his curiosity seriously, and during the Communist years it had been too expensive to have the safe opened. However, when he inherited the house and refurbished it after the floods of 2002, he took the opportunity to find a way through the battered steel that had fuelled his childish dreams of secret troves.

I can only imagine his disappointment when the old safe yielded no treasure, just damp and crumbling papers. The names mentioned in them meant nothing to him. Yet he had kept them out of an attachment to his boyhood imaginings and because they were part of an important period in history.

Perhaps the fact that the carefully typed correspondence had survived at all gave it a sense of value, a feeling that it must be important to somebody, somewhere. This was why, when my email came out of the blue, Michal took enormous satisfaction in sending a photograph of the tattered sheets of which he had been custodian for so long, and insisted that they be professionally restored before they could be shared. When this work was concluded, they arrived at my home in London, carefully protected in acid-free tissues within a vellum portfolio.

Michal's box was filled not with photos or plans but again, extraordinarily, with documents belonging to my grandparents. Otto and Ella had left them behind in their home in Libčice. These papers had survived in a safe for eighty years in a house that no longer had anything to do with my family. They had been locked away throughout the Second World War, forty years of communism, its fall and even the dreadful floods that had for weeks submerged the house and much of the Czech Republic. I travelled to Libčice the next May, to the building which Michal had lovingly restored, to thank him personally. He walked me though the house as it was, the room that held the safe, the other areas, the outhouses, the tiered garden. We sat under the old flowering trees on the same wrought-iron garden furniture that had been there in Otto and Ella's time. Michal's mystery had been solved, and the documents' journey was complete.

These were my grandparents' papers, a mass of them, which they had deemed important enough to guard in a safe. Against all odds, they were now in my hands. Some were fragments, some had lost any trace of ink or writing. A snapshot of their lives, catapulted across the distance of place and time. Many of the documents delineate a tedious paper trail of a normal life, bank statements, share certificates, newspaper clippings. But there too, among the administrative familiarity, falls the shadow.

In between the carefully restored papers, protected by the crisp white wrapping, lay their applications for immigrant visas to the US. That winter they had not just been planning the holidays. They had not just been laughing in Libčice. Hans, who was seventeen at the time, had submitted his papers to the American consulate in Prague on 23 December 1938. Otto, Ella, Lotar and Zdenka had handed in their applications two weeks later, on 7 January 1939. The entire process had been preserved in Michal's safe. Envelopes addressed to the Hon. John H. Bruins, American consul in Prague, letters from US banks and employers in Washington D.C. and Detroit, Michigan, signed and notarised, certifying that Victor owned a house, had a job and enough funds in the Bank of Detroit to support his European family. Documents with the United States of America seal, dated 1936 and 1938, set out the application rules for those seeking visas as students, as tourists, as immigrants, as refugees.

In every faded, water-stained document bearing the heading 'US State Department', one can clearly see handwritten circles or underlinings in red pen, again and again, around one term: *Non-Quota Immigration*. By the end of June 1939, some 309,000 German, Austrian and Czech Jews had applied for visas in this way and awaited a reply. America had established quotas in the 1920s to curb immigration from people deemed undesirable. Many, like the Neumanns, faced a portcullis of unyielding arithmetic. Only 25,000 visas per year would be made available under the quota. These three words, *non-quota immigration*, were the simple bolt that had slid shut for my grandparents behind the last door that led to safety.

Now I knew beyond any doubt. Even the wild waters of the river flooding the town in 2002 had not destroyed the evidence that Otto and Ella had kept locked in the basement safe. Their laughter in Libčice was real, but so too must have been their fear. Of course, they did not know how far it would go, but they knew enough. They dreaded it enough to want to leave behind the life they had built. All four of them tried to get out. But they could not. There was a quota. The US had restrictions on immigrants, on refugees, and specifically on Jews. There was a slim chance that they would fall within the quota and be allowed to migrate, but it was dwindling. So it was despite the fear of what might be coming, and despite the frail hope that they might be allowed to move to America, that they continued to focus on their daily lives.

The first piece of evidence that the family was trying to work the system, to somehow evade the scourge of anti-Semitism boiling up across Europe, comes from January 1939. Lotar and Ella were baptised by Josef Fiala, a priest at the Basilica of St James, in the centre of Prague's Old Town. The priest was a friend of Lotar and Zdenka and was eager to help the family. I now know that Fiala aided many and even risked death by providing shelter to a Jewish man during the war. After Ella and Lotar, Hans followed suit and was baptised on 24 March 1939, soon after he turned eighteen. But not Otto; he had refused. 'I would rather listen to Gandhi's words than the advice of any rabbi or priest,' he had declared. He never stated a religious affiliation on any official document. On each form that I have found in archives, that line was left blank. I will never know whether this was out of some ideological conviction or fear of discrimination. What I understand from the stories and documents is that Otto believed that religious institutions and zealousness too often brought out the worst in people.

In any case, baptisms were futile as, for the Nazis, Judaism was not a choice but a 'race' determined by your grandparents. What you believed or practised did not matter; what was important was your genetic makeup. The Nuremberg Laws had provided a clear definition that enabled persecution. Anyone who belonged to the Jewish community or was married to a Jew fell within the parameters if they had at least two Jewish grandparents. People who were not registered in the community or had intermarried needed to have three Jewish grandparents. With four Jewish grandparents, all the Neumanns clearly fitted the definition.

And on 15 March 1939, the thunder finally became a storm. As the day dawned at five a.m., Prague radio broadcast a message from the Czechoslovakian president:

> The German army infantry and aircraft are beginning the occupation of territory of the Republic at six a.m. today. Their advances must nowhere be resisted. The slightest resistance will cause unforeseen consequences and lead to the intervention becoming utterly brutal. Prague will be occupied at six-thirty a.m.

4

A NEW REALITY

On 16 March 1939, a triumphant Adolf Hitler was photographed waving from the alcove window of the castle that sits atop Prague and that had filled Kafka with dread thirty years prior. Czechoslovakia, the Führer proclaimed, had ceased to exist. Its territories had been divided into the Slovak Republic and the Protectorate of Bohemia and Moravia. Prague was the capital of the German-administered Protectorate, and this was all part of the Nazi realm, the Reich.

By then, Lotar had long since abandoned any dreams of drama school. In the autumn of 1936, just as his father had wanted, he started to study chemical engineering at the Czech Technical College. One morning at the end of March 1939 he walked into his classroom and found an envelope addressed to Der Jude Lotar Neumann. Inside was a letter informing him that he must leave the school. It was not an official note – the decree that banned Jews from schools and universities did not come until a few months later – but it was enough for Lotar to feel threatened. Halfway through his degree he stopped attending his lessons and started work in the relative safety of the family's paint factory. Otto had been left alone at the helm of Montana when his brother Richard had received his visa and moved to the US earlier that year. Lotar's presence at the factory provided Otto with another much-needed and trust-worthy pair of hands. It also meant that Lotar was receiving a salary, which gave him the added momentum to ask Zdenka to marry him.

Months passed before Zdenka mentioned the engagement to her family. Her family had told her over and over that it was madness to date a Jew. She was beautiful, educated, rich. She could have her pick of anyone in Europe.

'How is it possible?' Zdenka's cousin related that her father had exclaimed in despair. 'With all the boys who like her, why would she choose to be with a Jew?'

It was not that Zdenka's family was anti-Semitic. They had met and even liked the Neumanns. Her mother adored Lotar, who would visit her every week, always bring her a bouquet of violets and show her his photographs and make her laugh. But as charming as he was, this was her eldest daughter, and times were difficult enough for everyone. Zdenka's mother had tried to reason with her: 'He needs friends, Zdenka, not love. You both have to use your heads, especially now, with all that is going on. If you really want to help him and his family, you can do more as a friend.' The family folklore is that even her grandmother, who constantly championed Zdenka's inde-pendent spirit, had on this occasion been stern: 'In these awful times, it would be folly to be led by one's heart.'

Zdenka had no doubt that her family would be opposed to the marriage, and her instincts, as usual, were correct. She and Lotar therefore arranged it all quietly. It was about being together; they had never wanted a big affair. They met with the friendly priest at the Basilica of St James who once more agreed to help. On hearing the news, Otto had been dismissive, while Ella laughed and wept with joy – she had expected it all along. Despite Lotar's protestations, Zdenka had thought it best not to inform her father about the wedding at all. She waited until the last minute to tell her mother – the Saturday morning of the wedding itself, once her father had left for their country house in Řevnice. Humming with fear and excitement, she stormed into her mother's room with the news. Her mother almost fainted with shock. Zdenka had not given her enough time, she said, and she could not possibly attend the ceremony. And when Zdenka told her grandmother, who at all times was supportive and loving, the reaction was similar. She also could not attend the ceremony, she said, not if Zdenka's parents were not there. But as she cried with her granddaughter, she yielded and offered to host a large celebratory dinner in her house at 20 Podskalská Street that evening. She immediately enlisted her maids, Růžena and Anežka, to make preparations and then rushed to Šafařík, the confectioner downstairs, where she bought half of their display of desserts and cakes.

And so it was that on Saturday afternoon, 12 May 1939, at the Basilica of St James in the centre of an occupied Prague, Lotar and Zdenka became husband and wife. The Neumann family and Zdenka's sister, Marie, accompanied them. They were married by Jozef Fiala, who had, a few months prior, baptised Lotar, Ella and Hans. That evening there was an elegant party attended by friends and some family from both sides. Zdenka's mother and sister joined them at the dinner after all. Everyone close to the couple was there except Zdenka's father, who had been told what was happening over the telephone and had refused to return from the countryside.

Lotar and Zdenka at the dinner after their wedding, 12 May 1939.

Every account of the day suggests that the new couple exuded such happiness that it suffused all those around them. For all those present, Zdenka and Lotar's love was so evident that no one that evening even entertained the thought that it was insane. It was obvious, when you saw how they looked at each other, that they belonged together.

Nevertheless, the torrent of new restrictions scuppered their plans for the future. Their intention had been to buy a home in which to start their lives together, but in the face of the general uncertainty, the prohibitions affecting Jews and their efforts to make the move to America, Lotar and Zdenka decided to live in the Prague apartment by the factory. The family's live-in maid had moved to the house in Libčice to help Ella, so they had space to enlarge Lotar's room. They had repainted it in a brighter colour to reflect the morning light. Lotar had specially built wooden shelves to allow for Zdenka's book collection to be combined with his own.

The family left them alone for a week together in Prague. That clutch of stolen days was the extent of their honeymoon, but they loved it all the same. They were tourists in their own city. They drifted through the cobbled streets of Prague as if they did not know them. They discovered new corners in which to hide and embrace. They fed the swans by the riverbank and hiked up to the Strahov Monastery through the steep gardens that overlook the city, and across into the castle grounds.

Lotar took dozens of portraits of Zdenka, and they used his Kodak 8mm cine camera to film each other as they explored the city anew. Zdenka was always elegant and smiling, Lotar so happy and proud. They went to the movies at the cinema on Karlova Street. They let time slip by as they sipped drinks and watched the crowds drift past. They spent delicious hours in the quiet of the apartment, reading poems, dancing, singing and laughing, always laughing. Lotar had long dreamed of going to India. He wanted to visit the palaces that he had read about with Zdenka and to take photographs, but that trip would have to come later, when things were calmer, more certain.

Zdenka, photographed by Lotar, 1939.

As happy as they were, May 1939 was not a time for romantic trips, not if you were Czech, and particularly not if you were Jewish. By then Jewish lawyers and physicians had had their licences revoked, and a law had been passed in March banning the sale or transfer of Jewish property.

Life seemed to be pressing in on them in other ways too. Shortly after the wedding, Zdenka's grandmother had been taken to the hospital with acute pains and was diagnosed with terminal cancer. Zdenka adored her. Her grandparents had raised her for the first five years of her life, when her mother had moved to be with Zdenka's father, a soldier for the Austro-Hungarian Empire who was stationed near Budapest. Zdenka had a difficult relationship with him, absent as he was from family life, and while she loved her mother, the strongest family bond was undoubtedly always with her grandmother. It was she who had taught Zdenka to sing, empowered her to manage her own finances from a young age, given her the responsibility of freedom, and later encouraged her to study law. She had also, of course, been the one to throw them their wedding party. Zdenka wanted to stay close to her, especially now that she was suffering. It made sense for the newlyweds to stay in Prague, taking care of her, working and hoping that their papers for emigration to America would come through.

Ella had already decided to spend her days at the house in Libčice. She had always found Prague overwhelming, but now, with the arrival of the Germans, everyday life there had become torturous. Hans was still studying at the Technical College and lightening the gloom by attending Prankster Club meetings and spending weekends playing at the Libčice house with his beloved Jerry and Gin, the new fox terrier puppy. Family correspondence reveals that in addition to writing poems, Hans had also decided to try his hand at sculpture. He wanted to be an artist and attended school only to appease his father. He spent most of his free time in the city with Zdeněk and Zdenka's sister Marie, who was a few years younger. Together they formed a little gang: making their own movies, discussing art and books, cycling everywhere and playing pranks. Zdeněk and Hans deployed their knowledge of chemicals to create sulphur bombs and firecrackers to startle German soldiers in the crowded main streets.

In the meantime, Otto and Lotar were busy trying to keep Montana afloat as the threat of a Nazi takeover loomed. Otto, Hans, Lotar and Zdenka made an unlikely foursome and spent most weeknights in the apartment by the factory.

Oskar, one of Otto's brothers, had been fired from his job and had to leave his rented home, so Otto and Ella had suggested he move with his wife and little boy to their house in Libčice. Oskar commuted daily to Prague to help in the factory. Each passing week brought news of the difficulties affecting family members and friends. By July 1940, more than half of the Jewish men in the Protectorate of Bohemia and Moravia had no income. And so it was that Ella managed a full house in Libčice while Zdenka managed one in Prague.

Zdenka, it transpired, later wrote down her recollection of the first morning in the Prague apartment with the family. Breakfasts were always early – so early, in fact, that even the punctual housekeeper arrived after they had finished. Zdenka, independent and resourceful as she was, had never been in charge of a household, and certainly not one catering to the needs of three men who were used to being taken care of. Her mother and grandmother had always overseen such matters and had staff to help, so Zdenka had never had to think about practical details. So, when Otto stepped into the dining room at seven sharp the first morning, the breakfast table was not set. He was unimpressed. Otto disliked change, and his morning routine had hitherto been inviolable. He prized punctuality. He had expected Zdenka to be up before he was to prepare things, so he haughtily left her to do so while he listened to the radio in the living room. Zdenka set the table a few minutes later, boiled water and sliced some bread. When Otto returned to the table and asked Zdenka for his tea, she cheerfully handed him a cup of plain black tea. Now, Otto took his tea with lemon, and he scanned the breakfast table for the small plate of lemon slices that Ella always ensured was there. Otto liked to choose his slice with care and use the spoon to squeeze a little of the juice before allowing the lemon to float in his cup. That morning, there was no plate. Worse, he soon found out, there were no lemons in the kitchen.

'Ella must have told you that I have lemon with my tea in the mornings?'

'She must have and I must have forgotten,' replied Zdenka too gleefully. 'Would you like some milk and sugar instead?' Her charm unfailingly got her out of trouble. As she smiled broadly at her severe father-in-law, she suggested that perhaps what was really needed was a bit of sweetness. But her charm did not work here, and Otto left stony-faced to have his breakfast at the Café Svêt on his way to the office. When a startled Lotar joined her in the kitchen, they laughed so hard at Otto's bad temper that they woke Hans. Zdenka, instead of being cowed, took her relationship with her father-in-law as a challenge.

The next morning, when Otto emerged, a surprise waited

for him: Zdenka had laid out a feast on the polished wooden table. She had arranged a platter with cold meats, cheeses and Otto's favourite pâté, next to which she had placed a basket with warmed rolls. At Otto's usual place, she had set out a plate of lemon pieces, some thinly sliced, some quartered. As her father-in-law entered the room, she pronounced formally: 'Here, dear sir, is your breakfast. And, of course, your lemon selection.' She bowed slightly.

Otto could not help but smile back. 'Oh, I know what you are doing. You are trying to fatten me up to kill me,' he returned, completely deadpan.

That was opening enough for Zdenka to tease him about his previous outburst. It was unusual for anyone to joke with Otto. No one dared. Up until that day, his wife Ella and his brother Richard had been the only ones in the family brave enough to do so. For the next few months, until the family was forced to move to the house in Libčice, Otto came to cherish his chats with Zdenka while he had his breakfast. It must have been during those early breakfasts, as he sipped his lemon tea, that their bond was forged. It was then that Otto, just like Lotar, Hans and Ella, began to love Zdenka.

I have a letter written in two parts by Otto and his brother Oskar in August 1939 to their eldest brother in America. It describes the family's new conditions.

Dear Victor and children,

I wish to thank you so much for all your efforts so far on our behalf despite the lack of success. The point is to request a visa from any overseas country. It is only once this has been obtained that one may apply for a departure permit from the Gestapo, requiring certain formalities to be met — a return is, of course, out of the question. It is best if the person wishing to depart has in hand or receives a travel ticket from friends abroad, given that one is not allowed to purchase them here. The process on this side is nearly insurmountable.

I continue to work in the family business, albeit with some limitations, so our income is taken care of. Living is really only a question of strong nerves. I do not know in which conditions you will receive my letter. After all, in the insanity of the Europe in which we live, anything is possible.

It is also very hot here. We leave every afternoon for Libčice, where we recover soon but only to be able, the next day, to face all the unpleasantness and attacks upon ourselves. So far, this is bearable and you do not need to worry. Nevertheless, it is interesting how different people deal with their fates in very different ways. The carefree type seem to fare the best but, unfortunately, the Neumanns are not of that disposition.

Yours,

Otto

Dear Victor and boys,

You cannot imagine how often, in the past days, we have wondered if there would be a letter from you. I have wanted to write before, but I have not been in the mood for it. Please don't think it is out of laziness.

Today, your letter finally arrived and we are writing back immediately. First of all, thanks for your efforts. One day, I hope I have an occasion to reciprocate. Also, thanks for the holiday postcard, the effect of which you cannot imagine: your freedom makes me envious! It just seems incredible, for instance, that one *can travel freely to the seaside without having to take into account the religion of one's grandparents!*

It seems there is going to be a war. Staying here, under the current conditions, unless things were to change, will be impossible for Jews. So far, we all have something to make a living from . . . we are therefore lucky and can wait.

Next Monday, I will move with my whole family into a one-room apartment where we will wait for things to come. I am not sure whether our boy will be able to attend school but will find out in the next days. I thought you would not be familiar with the definition for 'Aryan', but I see from your letter that the word is even known to you. That is something, isn't it? It's the kind of world we live in.

With war in the air, sadly all is irrelevant. We are going to have to wait and see what the future brings. I can only say that I could not consider waiting somewhere abroad for my turn to emigrate; I need to earn something. Whereas, for the young men it is different, I have a family to support. One's love for family is all-encompassing . . . how would I feel if I could not feed my own boy? My son is a beautiful six-year-old boy and I would do anything to keep him safe and fed until he is at least older or able to earn a living on his own. Still I remain optimistic and hope that all turns out well for us.

You are correct when you say that, so far, we have somehow managed and hence we will continue to do so. So far, and I hope this remains true for the future, we have not lost our nerve. We have been living quietly and have been lucky. I hope this luck holds.

I wanted to let you know that the newly married Lotík and his young bride, Zdenka, are very happy, they have a really beautiful life together. She is very kind, sweet, clever and beautiful. It's a joy to watch them together! They are only, like all of us, longing for a little peace. I do not know when, or if at all, it will be possible to write to you again. Just know that we will not give up easily and that I hope that we all meet joyfully in the New World.

Victor, stay healthy and well along with your sons.

Goodbye for now,

Oskar

As it became apparent that migrating to America would prove difficult, Richard and Victor travelled to Cuba numerous times in 1939 and 1940 in a futile attempt to organise visas for the family to escape Europe via the Caribbean. Their efforts are still visible today. A file stored in the Czech Ministry of Exterior Affairs discloses that the consulates of the Czechoslovak government in exile in both America and Cuba requested information about the Neumann brothers from Prague.

Every week that passed brought more laws against the Jews. As I read them now, I am struck by how petty and arbitrary some of them were. As one apparently ridiculous order was added to the next, the process of separation and dehumanisation emerges. In dizzying increments, the rules become devastating in their absurdity, in their horror.

In May 1939, Jews were banned from holding gun licences; in June, Jewish pupils were expelled from German schools; and by July, there were laws stating that Jews were banned from the judiciary, from being lawyers, teachers or journalists. In that same month, a decree was passed that non-Aryans must register their belongings: their houses, their cars, their bank accounts, their gold, their jewels and their art. In July, laws were passed restricting Jews to restaurants with separate Jewish areas. In the coming weeks they were excluded from swimming pools. They were not to enter parks, cinemas or theatres. They were not allowed to travel without a permit. They had to surrender their driving licences – and, eventually, their cars and bicycles. Their radios. Their cameras. Their stamp collections. Their sewing machines. Their umbrellas. Their pets.

The family was not just affected by professional and logistical restrictions created by the laws. The consequences went far beyond the multitude of everyday activities that they specifically forbade. The laws emboldened those with a racist agenda, who were now organised into groups like the Czech fascist association, Vlajka. Individuals too were now empowered to voice their hatred and to act, unpunished, on their prejudices. Racism and violence were being normalised. Every day of May and June 1939 saw the burning of a synagogue in the Czech Protectorate. The laws had another, subtler effect. They generated an enormous amount of paperwork and bureaucracy that increasingly wearied the thousands affected and served further to alienate and differentiate.

The restriction on Jews in schools impacted the Neumanns' younger cousins on both sides of the family. Věra Haasová, Ella's niece, was eight years old in 1939. Věra was the daughter of Ella's brother Hugo and his wife, Marta Stadler. Věra and her parents lived in Roudnice, above a shop owned by Marta's father. They hosted Haas family reunions and usually visited Libčice in the summer to spend time with the Neumanns.

An only child, Věra had attended a German school, and now she, like the other Jewish children in the town, was banned from attending classes. The Czech schools would not accept Jewish children, so Marta's parents put some wooden chairs and tables in a few unused rooms at the back of their shop and created a clandestine place for the children to learn. Marta's father, who had retired, taught maths, science and German, while others volunteered to teach geography, poetry and the humanities.

At the beginning, the children were taken outside to do sports, play, cycle and have picnics, but by 1941 laws had forced them to stay indoors. Nonetheless, the school seems to have been a refuge for the children. In a picture taken in the summer of 1941 that I found seventy-five years later, all the girls hold hands as they beam at the camera. Věra is the tallest, wearing a chunky necklace. Mr Stadler, Věra's grandfather, stands by the doorway in the back with a serious expression. The tiny school likely preserved a little peace of mind for these children, providing a haven of normality until 1942, when the Roudnice Jews were deported.

Children at the clandestine school behind the
Stadler shop in Roudnice, 1941.

We know all of this today because one of the pupils in the clandestine school later gave an account that can be found in the archives of the Jewish Museum in Prague. She donated notebooks and other pictures of the pupils. One of them shows children around a table covered with books and pens. In another, boys and girls are sprawling on picnic rugs in the grass. Bicycles lean against trees, and a guitar lies on a blanket at one side of the picture. Everyone seems relaxed. There is nothing that could lead the viewer to think that these photographs were taken during a war, during a persecution.

The woman who gave the account and donated all the documentation is named Alena Borská. Just like my cousin Věra, she was born in 1931. Alena is now eighty-eight years old and lives in Roudnice still. She does not use a mobile telephone or the Internet. Alena can be seen in the photograph. Dressed in white, she smiles broadly as she stands to the right of Věra.

She speaks only Czech, which, sadly, I do not, so I contacted her by letter with the help of my Czech researcher friend. I asked whether she had any recollection at all of Věra. She answered thus: 'I have been hoping for 70 years that someone would come and ask me about Věra. She was my best friend. We were just girls, and often laughed together.'

She enclosed one more photograph for me, now crumpled and scratched, that she had kept close since it was taken in the autumn of 1938. The picture shows Věra and Alena just before the war. Two chubby-cheeked children in matching coats among leafless trees. The photographer captures Alena smiling broadly, while Věra seems in a more sombre frame of mind.

Věra Haasová and Alena Borská,
both aged seven, 1938.

Hans was able to continue with his studies, as Jews in technical schools were not yet affected by the prohibitions. The only
evidence I can find that the invasion sobered his personality is
an improvement in his grades during 1939. I am told that he
continued to spend his days with Zdeněk and his friends at the
college. After school, they would cross the road to U Fleků,
where Zdeněk's mother would welcome them with a big hug,
usher them to a corner table by the kitchen and sneak them a
couple of plates of the dish of the day. She did this for as long as
she could, despite the ban that had been in place since August
1939 on Jews being in restaurants. By September 1939, Jews

had a curfew of eight p.m., so Hans was forced to cut short his evenings with friends.

By October 1939, Otto and Hans had to stop living in the apartment near the factory. Since the German invasion, Ella had chosen to stay in the country house in Libčice and had seldom returned to the capital. She maintained that life was easier there, and this felt even truer now that war had been declared. There was more space and also, it seemed, fewer threats. When it was announced that Jewish families were not allowed to have more than one abode, the Neumanns declared Libčice to be their home. Otto and Hans were initially obliged to obtain permits to drive into Prague. When they were then forced to surrender their driving licences, they needed permits to travel by train and tram.

As a 'mixed marriage' couple, Lotar and Zdenka were initially registered to live in Prague at the apartment by the factory. The members of the family who still worked at Montana met to have lunch together as often as they could. Zdenka's aunt had a large farm, and its produce, as well as her newly acquired friends in the black market, meant there was always plenty to eat.

By November 1939, there were so many prohibitions in effect that a journal cataloguing the new rules was published each week to ensure compliance. By then the Germans had closed all Czech universities, so even Zdenka had to stop her legal studies. As Jews had been banned from working in most professions, many were now enrolled in programmes to retrain as manual labourers. By February 1940, Jews were compelled to surrender all stocks, bonds, jewellery and precious metals. They were allowed to keep only wedding rings and gold teeth.

In March 1940, the Judenrat, or Jewish Council of Elders of Prague, was established. It was one of a number of versions across Europe of Nazi-imposed Jewish 'headships'. Since the Middle Ages, Jewish communities around Europe had run self-governing municipal bodies, often associated with specific synagogues and ghettos, which kept birth, marriage and death records and carried out various administrative and charitable tasks. Now all Jews, as defined by the Nazi racial laws regardless of whether they practised or not, were forced to enrol and pay membership fees to such Councils. Each one gathered and stored information on all Jewish people in their region. The Prague Council was also created as an umbrella body to manage smaller regional Councils across the Protectorate. Those in charge were compelled to oversee, organise and enforce the implementation of all decrees affecting Jews. All these bodies in the occupied territories were headed and staffed by influential Jews, usually rabbis or leaders within their communities, and operated under the direct Nazi command. They had no authority of their own. The leaders were called Elders.

The initial belief was that it was all part of a structure set up to coordinate the emigration of Jews from the Protectorate and other occupied areas. The Neumanns had a good friend who worked in the Council in Prague. Štěpán Engel, nicknamed Pišta, was the son of a friend of Otto and Ella's. He was a few years older than Lotar and Hans, but they had known him since they were young. He also had become part of Lotar and Zdenka's group of friends. In 1940 Pišta was appointed as chief secretary to the Elders. While he had little, if any, influence in decision-making, Pišta acted as a gatekeeper of sorts and had access to information in advance of its general release. He passed on some of this information to the Neumanns, which allowed them a little more time to prepare. Time became crucial, and advance knowledge would eventually prove invaluable.

As 1939 became 1940, rumours abounded that property owned by people married to Jews was to be confiscated. This meant that Zdenka would lose all her buildings and the revenue from her tenants. Everyone around Lotar and Zdenka told them to divorce. They vehemently protested, but even Pišta confirmed their fears. Initially, they refused. But when Zdenka's grandmother died, leaving more properties to her, the need for this precaution became more acute. Both their families implored Lotar and his beloved wife to sign the divorce papers. The Neumanns expected the Montana factory to be taken over any day. It was only a piece of paper; it would preserve the ownership of the properties, and it was the only way to guarantee an income for them all.

So only nine months after their marriage in February 1940, still promising to keep their vows, Lotar and Zdenka reluctantly signed their petition to divorce. All accounts indicate that they were devastated. And yet they were pragmatic and understood that they were giving up a symbol and not their love. Zdenka's grandmother's advice, now that she was gone, resonated even more in Zdenka's mind: these were not times to be led by one's heart; it was one's head that was crucial. The divorce was granted immediately, and Lotar was ordered to return to live in Libčice. Nonetheless, after a few months of quiet encounters at Montana, they decided to defy the prohibitions, risk punishment and live together in one of the buildings owned by Zdenka's family. For the sake of the neighbours, they posed as brother and sister. Only the caretaker, who had known Zdenka since she was a girl and had helped her prepare the apartment, knew the truth. She had watched Zdenka grow up and was loyal to the family who employed her. She kept their secret.

In 1940, as the Neumanns had expected, Montana was taken over by a Reich-appointed *treuhänder*, or trustee, who held legal ownership of the company. He was a man called Karl Becker from Berlin. Becker tyrannised Lotar and Otto as the head of what had been the family business for seventeen years. A letter from Becker of July 1941, written on the company stationery, reprimanded Lotar and stated that if he did not show up for work, Becker would have the Gestapo summon him to face the consequences. Otto and Lotar had no choice but to quietly accept whatever treatment they received.

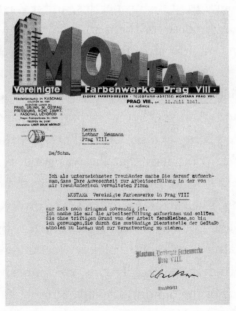

Letter to Lotar on the family company's letterhead
threatening to report him to the Gestapo.

In Libčice, Ella worked hard to maintain normality in what was clearly no longer a normal world. Her family, in-laws and friends had lost employment, belongings, homes. They were scattered and separated by travel restrictions. Her youngest nephews and nieces were attending a clandestine school. Her eldest son had been made to divorce his beloved wife and was risking his life by defying various prohibitions. Somehow the only member of the family who seemed to lead a relatively unscathed life was her youngest son, Hans.

In May 1940, Ella wrote to Richard, who had started his new life in America. She shared the news that, despite all that was happening, *This week, Handa graduated from the Chemical Technical School.* Her letter ends: *Here in Libčice the trees have blooms so beautiful that it almost makes the events around us seem unimportant.*

5

DROWNED LIGHTS

The pages of Lotar's album are carefully tiled with pictures of all sizes. Some are clear, posed portraits of my family in military uniform, elegant clothes or costumes, taken in a studio, the name of which is embossed on the thick handsome paper. These stand proud in the collection and mark milestones like births, marriages or coming of age, but the majority of the pictures are small and casual. They tend to be of groups of people and candidly capture everyday life.

One of the larger photographs stands out. It is not a formal photograph, and yet it sits framed by a white margin on stark black paper. It has a page to itself. It is a portrait of Hans in his late teens. He wears a pinstripe collared shirt and a sweater. He is bespectacled and his hair is neatly parted and brushed to one side. He is holding a Kodak 8mm film camera, many of which were produced in the 1930s for the Czech market. The photograph must have been taken in 1939 or 1940; he seems too grown up for it to have been taken earlier, and by the end of 1941 Jews had been forced to turn in photographic equipment. I do not know if the Neumanns complied with this law, but I know enough about them now to be sure they would not have taken the risk of creating evidence against themselves. In the portrait, Hans appears to be filming, looking down, his face partially hidden by the device. I recognise his hands, his long fingers, his grasp. His way of holding things frequently struck others as awkward. He was double-jointed, so it was perfectly natural to him. I know this because I am also double-jointed. My three children, like Hans and me, have joints that bend more markedly. We hold things oddly too. Activities like riding a bicycle, catching a ball, cradling a pencil and arranging your body in a chair, or your thoughts in a narrative, pose an additional challenge. I never would have noticed, but the teachers at my children's elementary school pointed it out and suggested exercises to improve their motor skills. So now I know that Hans's odd way of holding objects, and probably his propensity to fall off a bicycle, is part of an inherited condition, related to double-jointedness, called dyspraxia. I do not think Hans ever noticed that there was anything awkward in the way he held things.

I cannot be sure who took the shot of Hans with the camera. In all likelihood, it was Lotar. Hans seems unaware of the photographer.

Hans as a teenager, holding a cine camera.

There is a stillness in this picture that comforts me. Hans is perfectly absorbed by the task, his right eye fixated on the view through the lens, his left eye closed. It brings me back to him as he repairs watches in that long room in the corner of my childhood memory. It is the same absorption with which he would sit, many decades later, seemingly for hours on end, gazing through the magnifying lenses and calibrating the tiny mechanisms in his watches. Unaware that he had any motor skill issues, he willed his fingers to pull the tiny pivots and chains to ensure the accuracy of timekeeping. He was also oblivious then to my questioning gaze as I peeked through the crack in the door to that windowless room at the back of our house. This very still and controlled Hans is the man whom I spied on. The Hans who has emerged from my research, this 'unfortunate boy', invariably late, carefree, chaotic and whimsical, bears little resemblance to the father I knew.

There was more than letters and albums inside the boxes from my cousin's house. Among the papers were poems written by my father and Lotar during the first years of the German occupation. Lotar's were more in keeping with the times, full of darkness and dread. One of his verses depicts a family seated around a table, waiting for someone to walk through the door. It is ominously entitled 'A Song of Death'.

My father's verses, on the other hand, deal mostly with lost love, women and heartache. They have titles like 'Florist Girl', 'Evening Stanza', 'Hollow Embrace', 'Sonnet of Spring'. I read them in translation, and even then, despite my partiality, I am afraid that they are not very good. Some of the lines sound clichéd, evidently the work of a teenage boy. *Since you left me, I am no more, I am no longer anything when you are not close by . . .* I read them and cringe a little. I cannot help but find them endearing in their corniness. Despite all that was going on around him, Hans still found the time to write bad poetry and plan pranks with Zdeněk.

After many years of searching, I found Zdeněk's son, who is also named Zdeněk Tůma. He wrote to me recounting some of the anecdotes that his father had told him of his youth. Once, on a summer afternoon in Libčice shortly after the German invasion, Hans and Zdeněk were tasked by Ella with buying a chicken for supper. Returning home late and empty-handed, Hans and Zdeněk had concocted a story and pretended to have lost the money. They had, instead, spent it on wine. I hope Otto was not at home that weekend. I have no doubt that he, unlike Ella, would have seen through their game and despaired.

But I also have evidence that Hans took some things seriously. His graduation report states that he finished his chemistry degree in June 1940. The regime was at that time forcing Jews to retrain and take menial jobs in factories or in agriculture. The Nazis had confiscated a 200-hectare farm near the village of Lípa as part of the seizure of Jewish property. It had been owned by the Kraus family for over a hundred years. They were the only Jewish family in the area. Julius Kraus, the largest employer and the richest man in the town, had built a railway line and station to ease the movement of goods and people. It had been a commercial and social enterprise benefiting the entire region. Precisely because of this railway, the Nazis chose the Kraus farm to set up a 'retraining centre'. It began functioning as such in July 1940. It became known simply as Lípa and was what we would call today a labour camp. The Nazis' declared intention was to teach four hundred young

Jews discipline and agriculture. Initially, the Jewish Council and its branches in the Protectorate were charged with finding healthy unmarried and unemployed men between eighteen and forty-five to send to Lípa. They were to work long hours in the fields every day for months with little nourishment or reward. The camp was guarded by two Germans and a number of Czech gendarmes. From mid-1941, most inmates there were confined indefinitely. Some young Jewish men who were unemployed and destitute went voluntarily, propelled by the prospect of work and some, if nominal, remuneration and shelter. But for most, the prospect of long hours of physical work and enforced separation from their families was daunting. The Councils struggled to meet the numbers demanded by the Nazis, and soon the criteria were expanded to include men who were employed but had no dependants. After being called by the Council, the chosen men had to be examined by their family physician to ensure fitness. They were then to be checked by a second doctor, who worked for the state and to whom the selected men would have no connection.

On 26 August 1940, less than two months after his graduation, Hans received a registered letter in Libčice from the Jewish Council. It contained the following instruction: *We call on you to come on Wednesday, 28 August 1940 to the apartment of Mr Viktor Sommer in Kralupy, for a medical examination, at 9 o'clock in the morning.*

Hans was to be examined there, with four other men from the area, by a Dr Mandelik, who would attest to his fitness for the camp.

Councils were coerced to fill the places in Lípa. The surviving records show that on 30 August 1940, a representative of the Jewish Council in the town of Kladno in central Bohemia urgently telephoned the Council in the city of Slaný which had authority in Libčice. They requested the names of five men who were needed immediately for work in Lípa. These five men were to report to the Lípa labour camp the following day, Sunday, 1 September 1940. The conditions of the selection process were unchanged.

Hans met all the criteria. He was the correct age, without employment or dependants. A mere 412 Jews of both sexes and all ages lived in the area of Slaný. Only a few dozen were men of the right age. To complicate matters further, there were only six Jews in Libčice, a married couple with a young daughter, and Otto, Ella and Hans.

Hans was the only eligible one. There was an obvious onus on the authorities in Slaný and the doctors to deem him fit for work and send him to Lípa. And yet Hans seems to have obtained a medical deferral from this roundup of the very few local young men. The papers indicate that he would have had to attend a further examination in November 1940, but, some-how, he does not appear on the list of those obliged to report to Lípa on 1 September.

Perhaps the family took the huge risk of bribing the doctor, or Hans feigned a mental illness, or there was indeed some physical disability that he played up and subsequently outgrew. I have photographs of him playing volleyball and skiing as a teenager, so the medical issue that proved his salvation on this occasion was clearly not terribly marked. Possibly his double-jointedness, his then unnamed dyspraxia, played a part and helped him escape the forced labour. The records of his medical examina-tion did not survive to tell us how he evaded Lípa.

Meanwhile, in early June 1940, the Slaný Council asked Otto to represent them as a trustee and take charge of the Jews in the town of Libčice. A trustee was the most junior position in the hierarchy of the Council. The role of the trustee was to distribute information and orders from the superior Jewish Community Council at a local level and to ensure that these orders were carried out. While they had no actual power or authority to make decisions, trustees were engaged with maintaining order and reporting those who were not obeying the decrees to the Central Jewish Council.

Otto resisted this appointment.

A letter to the Council from Otto has survived in the archives of the Jewish Community in Prague all these years. In it, Otto politely but firmly refused to take on the role:

> *Even though there is no abjuration to this appointment and I willingly acknowledge the utility of appointments of trustees, I would nonetheless like to express a differing opinion as toward the competency of my person for the contemplated position.*

He went on to explain that he was too busy to take on the role. He also pointed out that he did not know many people in Libčice, as he had lived and worked in Prague for many years. These were just excuses. The family had spent most of every summer in Libčice for years and knew most of the families in the town of three thousand people. I know that they were friendly with the other Jewish family in the town, as it is mentioned it in his letters.

However, Otto, who had always disliked clubs and considered himself something of an outsider, did not want to be part of the system. I do not know to what extent it was a moral stance, but he clearly did not want to comply. He may well have sensed that to be cast in even this limited role in the new hierarchy of power would serve no purpose other than to make him an unwilling accessory in the deepening persecution.

His letter to the Council was answered immediately with a note that summarily dismissed the points that he had raised. Otto thus found himself appointed as the trustee in charge of his own family and the other three Jews in Libčice. He was consequently to be held responsible for ensuring that each carried out the required tasks, obeyed rules and promptly filled out forms correctly. However, despite this official role, Otto's name, along with Hans's, appears on a Council document dated July 1940 listing people who had not filled out their obligatory migration papers on time. This did not signify any desire to stay. It seems instead part of a considered strategy to delay the grinding bureaucracy and, above all, to disclose as little information as possible. By mid-1940, it was obvious that the migration maps and forms were simply a ploy to induce families to declare all their assets and economic interests. Nonetheless, to drag heels remained a risky approach; however, experts assure me that it offered the best chance of evading the teeth of the system. And so the Neumanns played for time.

At the same time Hans was being called up to Lípa, there was a further letter from the Council in Slaný requesting that the Council in Prague *do something about this Otto Neumann of Libčice who is not performing his duties and is exasperating everyone.*

They requested that the authorities in Prague deal with him directly to ensure compliance. Otto was too disciplined a man to have taken the stance for any reason other than as part of a broader effort to distract and resist the real issue, the Council's instruction that his son report to Lípa.

Hans's first cousin Ota, who in 1936 had written to his family in America expressing his concern about rising anti-Semitism, was a single young man of twenty-nine, also without useful employment or dependents. He lived in Třebíč and, like many other Jews, had been fired from his job months before. His brother Erich, on the other hand, could prove that he was needed at the Montana factory in Prague. No such reason for delay could be found for Ota. He was duly summoned for labour at Lípa on 14 December 1940.

One of the letters mentions that my grandfather Otto arranged to have food parcels sent to his nephew in Lípa. Ota's parents had named him after his uncle, and Otto had always felt a close bond with the young, thoughtful Ota. In February 1941, my grandfather neatly listed in his notebook the items that he had sent to Ota: salami, cinnamon biscuits and oranges. It is unclear if Ota ever received them.

Otto's 1940 letters to his brothers Victor and Richard in America catalogue the tightening restrictions in the Protectorate. But they are also filled with assurances that the family was well and healthy despite the difficulties that they faced.

Otto had written in October 1940 to thank the American family for their letters and good wishes and to summarise the general situation: Erich was still working in Montana. On Ella's side, the Pollak and Haas families were managing fine. All were separated and unable to travel, which made life difficult. Luckily, Zdenka could move around freely, visit the elderly relatives and relay messages, money and supplies to those in the family who needed it. All the employees at the factory were taking the changes in their stride and showing the Neumanns nothing but kindness, except the eldest worker, who refused to greet Otto on account of the new laws.

Otto expressed his frustration at the lack of opportunities to *learn anything*. But his letter retains an upbeat tone. He asked that his brothers not worry too much about the family: *the men were working, the women helping and the children still playing*. Ella, he said, was a *veritable fireball taking impeccable care of the stomachs and the hearts and minds of all in Libčice*.

To judge from the papers that have emerged from the archives, it is clear that by 1940, nineteen-year-old Hans was becoming more responsible, more organised. With the guidance of his brother and his father, he was tentatively navigating the system. He signed up and took a course to retrain as a mechanic. He managed to remain in Libčice despite being included in four separate call-up lists for Lípa. He assembled the necessary paperwork to secure a job at a factory called František Čermák, which was involved in the war effort and was conveniently around the corner from the Montana factory where Lotar and Otto spent their days.

And yet he still clung to his desire to be a poet. In December 1940, as his cousin Ota began his forced labour at Lípa, Hans self-published a pamphlet containing six of his poems. There was a copy of this booklet in Lotar's box. Hans had either lost his copy or had decided it was unimportant; there was no poetry book among his files.

Ota was interned in Lípa for six months, until 13 June 1941, when he was allowed home to Třebíč for a short break. During that interlude, on a hot summer afternoon, he decided to make the most of the sunshine and freedom by taking his ten-year-old cousin Adolf for a bicycle ride and a swim. That day, 8 July 1941, a Czech gendarme named Pelikán followed Ota and Adolf as they rambled. He later reported to his superiors that he had seen Ota, a Jew, cycling carelessly and bathing in a part of the river that was forbidden to Jews.

Nine days later, Ota was taken from his home and interrogated at the Gestapo police station in Brno, the Moravian capital. Every detail of this encounter is available today in the local archives. Thorough witness statements were written up and indeed later formed the basis of the prosecution case against Pelikán when he was tried for treason after the war in 1946.

Ota was a popular figure in Třebíč. He was a kind, polite and rather shy young man. His long weeks at Lípa had not changed him. He had always been careful and conscientious. During the interrogations, Ota protested his innocence. He stated that upon his return to Třebíč, he had explicitly enquired of the District Office as to where he, as a Jew, might bathe in light of the new rules. They had specifically advised him to bathe outside the town's boundary. He had followed these instructions, he believed, to the letter. He had even checked a map. Ota argued that the authorities themselves had provided incorrect information.

Ota was initially released, but this was to be a short-lived liberty. He was re-arrested by the Gestapo a week later and taken for interrogation. His was a minor offence for which most people were not even reported. However, the law encouraged and compelled people to notify the authorities of all offences committed by Jews, no matter how trivial. Ota was, therefore, at the mercy of the Czech gendarme, who, eager to advance himself, had filled out the forms detailing the offence of swimming in an area not designated for Jews.

Ota was now helpless within the system, trapped in the Gestapo machinery. After his interrogation, he was not allowed to return home. In his file, the Gestapo officials called this three-month incarceration 'Protective Custody'. On 21 November 1941 Ota was deported directly to the camp at Auschwitz. Auschwitz then was small and had only one functioning section. Further sections, including Birkenau, where most of the mass gassings took place, were just being built. On arrival, Ota was assigned the number 23155 and placed in Block 11 with all those who had been accused of crimes.

The Auschwitz archives hold the only other remaining picture of cousin Ota.

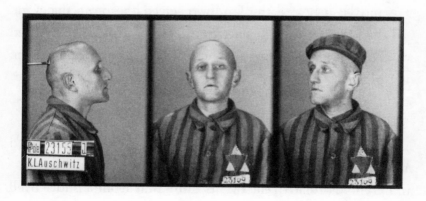

The mortality rate in Block 11 was very high. It was the penal unit, and prisoners were horrifically tortured. Even among the litany of atrocities that took place in Auschwitz, Block 11 stood apart. Holocaust historians have written numerous accounts of the conditions. While the Neumanns were aware that Ota had been sent from the prison in Brno to Auschwitz, I do not think they knew that he was in that particular block. I do not know precisely to which horrors my cousin Ota was subjected.

All I know is this.

On 8 December 1941, Ota's number 23155 was entered in immaculate copperplate in the register of the Auschwitz morgue. They had killed quiet cousin Ota, a young and fit man. They had murdered him in a mere seventeen days.

Among my letters of Otto and Ella is a very short one, just two lines written in uneven lettering. Signed by Ota's parents, Rudolf and Jenny, it reads: *With indescribable heartache we have to inform you of the horrendously upsetting news that we received by telegraph yesterday. Our son Ota has died in the concentration camp at Auschwitz.*

A few days before the family received the news that Ota had died, his brother Erich was forced to abandon his job at Montana and was placed on the first transport to the camp of Terezín.

As I compile the timeline of my father's life during the war and juxtapose it with the events unfolding around him, I find it hard to reconcile the deepening shadows with his pranks and poetry. Somehow this first suggested a man to a degree insensitive to the world in which he found himself, inconsistent with the measured and judicious man I knew as a child. I reread his teenage poems. Amid the lovelorn lines, I encounter some that had escaped me on first reading, ominous and foreboding:

> When you learn it is possible to die, for the sound of a
> word uttered a century ago.

This takes me deeper into the verse and leads me to another poem, which concludes:

> It is not the sound of the Angelus Bell,
> It is only tears ringing an alarm.
> Voices stammered, fitful crying
> And the night smells of chamomile.
> Good-bye.

During my later reading, I realised that the translator of my father's poems had not dealt with the title page. I wrote asking her for it, and the response, by email, arrived almost immediately.

My father's collection had a two-word title.

Drowned Lights.

6

A VIOLENT YELLOW

It was a morning like many others, except that the elusive spring sun shone in abundance on London. I have lived in Britain for the best part of two decades. That day I had followed my usual routine: taken out our lazy basset hound and feisty terrier, overseen my children's breakfast, battled to ensure that teeth were brushed and school uniforms donned, homework packed into the unicorn-adorned backpacks.

I walked my children to their school down the sycamore- and cherry-tree-lined lanes of our neighbourhood. I chatted about exams and play dates with other parents at the school gates, picked up a black coffee at the Italian café by the underground station, and wandered into the park, tugged along by our eager dogs, both straining to chase squirrels and sniff out evidence of nocturnal happenings.

On my return, I found the postman approaching our house. He greeted me and handed over a small bundle of letters. I enjoy getting old-fashioned paper letters. There is a moment of connection in receiving an object, a physical link, that is lacking in the virtual instantaneity of email. I like to hold something that someone else has touched, unsealing the envelope that they have sealed, feeling the paper, reading the words they have formed in haste or with care. There is a ritual moment of anticipation and relish, an appreciation of the tiny decisions that led to the words reaching their destination in their own way. The colour of the ink, the choice of stationery. I always look for the handwritten envelopes first and leave the tedious bills and notices until the end.

There was only one handwritten envelope that day among a sheaf of everyday commercial correspondence, and I recognised my cousin Madla's even and rounded script.

At that time, I had already been researching my family history for a few years, with a view to collating an account of some sort. My early enquiries had naturally included a request of my cousin Madla for any relevant stories or papers to add to the materials I was assembling from other sources. She had already sent me the box with the letters and Lotar's album, which her mother had kept after he had died, but she seemed to have found some more loose bits and pieces here and there in unopened desk drawers and forgotten boxes in the attic; she had mentioned in an email that she was sending them to me. Madla and her husband, a retired immunologist, are keen sailors, and she had said she would post them before embarking on one of their expeditions. I had assumed she meant more photographs or papers, but the envelope felt oddly bulky.

As I carried it up the steps to the front door, I squeezed it. It contained something other than papers, something soft. I went inside and sat down at my desk by the window and moved the computer back to make room. I opened the envelope carefully and pulled out a disk and a postcard. I knew the disk would contain scans of papers, since much of the material, in particular the older letters, was too fragile to post. The picture on the postcard was a melee of blues, ochres and greens, an oil painting of a seashore by Edvard Munch. As I took up the card to read it, a piece of fabric fell from the envelope to the floor.

As I write, I recall that I was struck by the brutality of the colour. I did not make a sound or catch my breath, but I touched the fabric, and instead of bringing it up to my desk, I felt the need to move from the chair and take it with me down to the floor. There I sat cross-legged, in the spring light that poured through the windows. I stretched out the crumpled fabric so I could read the black words that I knew were there.

Jude.

Jude.

Jude.

I counted ten stars. All in rows, and within each was printed this word in a loping black script. Two sides of the cloth were straight and the rest jagged, angled where stars had been scissored out.

The thick weave of the cloth and the dissonant colour were unexpected. The fabric is thickly woven, presumably to be more durable. The colour is a very dark yellow, almost orange. It is the most strident and rude shade of yellow imaginable. It made me think of the sulphur yellow of New York City cabs. Obvious, glaring. Unmissable against any background, noticeable in any light. There were two pieces of this coarse fabric in the envelope, each covered in the stars bearing the stark words. Reminiscent of the dress templates for my daughters' paper dolls, around each star's border were small lines showing where the user was to cut. Someone had taken the time to design this, to make sure that whoever excised them had enough fabric left around the edges to be able to stitch them on, to make it easier for the designated wearers to label themselves for identification, exclusion, deportation and far worse.

The shade of these stars was harrowing in its undeniability, its ugliness and intensity. I held the creased cloth, the same that my grandparents, uncle and father had held, and realised that I too would have had to cut along those dotted lines and wear a star. As would my children. I would have had to sew one of these stars above the red unicorn on each of their school jumpers.

On 1 September 1941, all Jews in the Protectorate of Bohemia and Moravia were compelled by decree to identify themselves with such stars. A fortnight later, the first batches were distributed, and all Jews were given three days to comply with the order. They were expected to wear a star whenever they were outside their home. They were warned that failure to bear the mark could result in a fine, a beating, imprisonment or death by shooting.

As trustee, Otto would have been tasked with handing out the stars in Libčice. He would have had to collect the money, as the stars cost a crown each. The majority of Jewish families were not allowed to work and were living in miserable conditions, but they were still made to pay for the stars.

Lotar himself wrote later about the stars in a letter to his uncle in the US:

Then came a further landmark in our lives; ignominious label-
ling with a yellow star. This was such a ghastly humiliation
that many took their own lives rather than move among others
differentiated and disgraced in this way. It gave every black-
guard an opportunity to spit, slap or kick you. And it was as if

the German SS men had found a new sport, that of throwing
the Jew out of the moving tram. They would watch and laugh
and wait to see whether the poor wretch would break a rib or an
arm or a leg. The worse the break the louder the laugh. It was a
prelude to what would come a month later in October 1941, the
transports.

Apparently, the public labelling also fostered further anti-Nazi
sentiment in the Protectorate. Some Czechs tipped their hats at
Jews with the insignia, a sign of solidarity with the Jews and an
open demonstration of defiance to the German invaders. These
gestures of rebellion were sufficient to ensure that Nazis wasted
no time in passing another law that any sign of deference to a
Jew was henceforward considered a crime.

Initially, it struck me as strange that anyone would choose to
keep this cloth. Then I realised that pieces like these had been
stored in cupboards and packed in boxes and that those who
survived had seldom opened them again. How could they bear
to? Over seventy years on, even I, an inhabitant of a different
world, could scarcely stand holding the thing.

The box that held the crumpled stars had also contained a
pipe and a metal ring. Madla later told me that her father had
shown them to her when she was young, but she had never seen
the stars again until she found them, a few days before sending
them to me.

I try repeatedly, but I cannot picture it. Not in colour, not
in shades of grey. Otto, Hans, Ella and Lotar – all with their
yellow stars. I have very few photographs from this time, and
although they would have had to wear them, the stars cannot
be seen. They would certainly all have been forced to wear

them outside their home, at work, as they travelled. Ella would have had to wear one each time she left the house in Libčice. If she had not worn it she would have been unable to run errands and would have had to stop her riverside strolls. Lotar would have had to wear one as he walked around Prague, to his job and back.

Jews had been prohibited from leaving their place of residence since 1940, but Hans, Lotar and Otto had obtained permits that allowed them to travel on the public transport system to work at Montana. A document issued in January 1941 is addressed to Becker, the despotic Nazi-appointed head of the family company. It is a permit, issued by the office of the senior Nazi representative for the Protectorate, the Reich Protector, allowing the 'Jews Otto Israel Neumann and Lotar Israel Neumann of Libčice to travel by train to work. Though these Jews must be replaced as soon as possible by Aryan workers.'

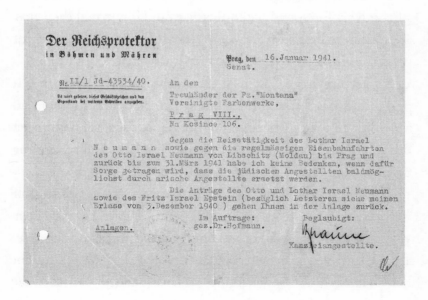

Every morning from September 1941, Otto and his two sons would have taken the train and the tram, and then walked in the grey commuter throng, with their strident yellow stars, the size of a fist, sewn onto their coat just above their heart.

Otto and Lotar travelled to the Montana factory. Hans went to his job at the steelmaking plant of František Čermák. The proprietor was friendly with the Neumanns, as their businesses were near each other, and they had worked alongside each other for almost two decades. Steelwork was a crucial part of the war economy, and this prized job afforded some hope that Hans would not be sent to Lípa or elsewhere. Judging from my archive of documents and letters, it seems that Hans' efforts to take things more seriously had led him to apply himself to his job, working as many extra hours as he was allowed. An official letter on the Čermák company letterhead of April 1941 stated that he was a crucial member of the workforce and had quickly attained a managerial position despite being only twenty years old.

In the autumn of that year, Hans was instructed to deliver order letters from Čermák to another nearby factory. He walked in and met the owner's daughter, Míla, who was working as a receptionist. A timid nineteen-year-old with curly hair and heart-shaped lips, she had Rilke's *Book of Hours* open on her desk. Hans handed her the Čermák envelope and, noticing the book as well as the girl, managed to hold her gaze and muster a line by the poet: 'Nearby is the country they call life'. Míla explained to her son many decades later that it was precisely at that moment that she fell in love with Hans.

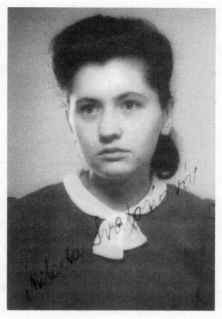

Míla Svatonová in Prague, 1939.

He would have been wearing a star when he walked into Míla's office and wearing one when he met her after work. They took strolls around the streets of the industrial area – the park, cinemas and restaurants being out of bounds to Jews. Míla loved to cycle, but Hans had been ordered to surrender his bicycle in October. A romantic atmosphere must have been elusive for the gentile girl and the Jewish young man with a yellow star on his jacket as they meandered between apartment buildings and factories. Yet Hans persevered and found flowers to bring along as frequently as he could. He spent his lunchtime breaks from work with Míla. They approached each other cautiously, and their connection germinated gradually. Many years later, Hans said to a friend that his relationship with Míla had started 'at a time when anyone who indulged in the luxury of feeling emotion was a dead man'.

Amid it all, Hans also found time to spend with Zdeněk and his friends from college. Nevertheless, the constant pressure of battling with the daily commute to Libčice, holding down his crucial position at the factory and scrabbling together the black-market supplies to support his family always took priority. There no longer was room in his life for Prankster Club meetings or writing poetry. Altering his behaviour was not enough, Hans was also forced to suppress emotions. Even feeling those had become perilous.

Although Lotar continued to work in Montana legally, he availed himself of a false identity card without the bold 'J' that was a required stamp for all Jews. With the help of Zdenka, Hans, Zdeněk and their underground contacts, they had secured a 'lost' identity card. This allowed him to spend time and live with Zdenka in Prague, unhindered by the pro-hibitions and anti-Semitism. In the black market that rose out of the occupation, one could source foods that were scarce to all or forbidden to Jews, items that could be used as bribes or things that could just lessen the strain: sugar, coffee, alcohol, cigarettes, foreign currency, medicine, even poisons, or official documents. False documents were costly and difficult to come by, and anyone caught with them could be shot on the spot. Yet they managed.

Hans and Zdeněk and a few students from their class in tech-nical school had obtained the necessary chemicals to erase the original details on the lost card. They met Lotar in Zdenka's apartment and spent days testing the solvents and carefully altering the document. They inserted a picture of Lotar and used an official stamp lent by some friends with a contact in the civil service.

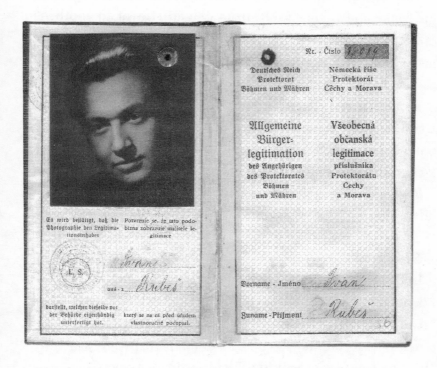

Experts have remarked that this forgery was superbly well executed. Now, over seventy years later, the chemical treatment is fading, and the original owner's details seem to be re-emerging. But, then, it served its purpose perfectly for the time that it was needed. Lotar's fake identity card bore the name of Ivan Rubeš, a suitably non-Jewish friend from university who bravely gave his blessing to the scheme. Lotar knew Ivan Rubeš well. If needed he could easily recall his birthday, his hometown and details about his family. He could pass himself off easily as his friend. It was imperative that Lotar not be seen on the street together with his friend Ivan as gendarmes or Germans could ask for identification papers at any time.

Whenever the neighbours started to ask too many questions Zdenka and Lotar moved from one apartment to another in Zdenka's buildings. They moved at least six times between 1940 and the beginning of 1942.

In March 1942, Governmental Decree 85 was issued to complement the Reich legal code. The second paragraph forbade any citizen of the Protectorate to enter a marriage with a person of Jewish origin. The fifth paragraph went as far as to criminalise sexual relations between Jews and citizens of non-Jewish or mixed origins. Contravention of any of these rules was deemed a crime.

Fortunately, rumours of these prohibitions reached the Neumanns a few weeks in advance. In the early part of the year, Lotar was advised by many, including Pišta, his friend at the Council, that he should remarry Zdenka whilst there was still time. The marriage might offer a chance to avoid, or at least delay, deportation.

The fear of jeopardising Zdenka's property persisted, especially as access to her assets provided a much-needed lifeline for the entire family. The deadline loomed. Lotar, Zdenka and Otto were reassured by those in the know that the risk to property owned by gentiles in mixed marriages had lessened. It appeared that the Nazi administration's focus had shifted from expropriations to segregation and transportation. The advantages of being married seemed to outweigh the threat to their finances. Above all, Lotar and Zdenka wanted to be with each other.

So it was that on 25 February 1942, just a few weeks before

mixed marriages were banned altogether, Lotar and Zdenka quietly remarried. They were now legally allowed to live together once more. However, despite the technical legality of the union, the pressure on mixed couples to separate continued to mount. There was no celebration of the marriage this time. There are no photographs of that day. Public discrimination and everyday hostility also made life difficult. Lotar often resorted to using his fake papers to avoid the abuse and to lessen the impact of prohibitions in his daily life. By then so many laws had been issued against Jews that he was not allowed to go to a tailor or a barber, drive a car or ride a bicycle, use most trams, enter Wenceslas Square, visit libraries, walk in parks, sit on benches or go to museums, theatres or town squares. Whenever he was with Zdenka, he avoided wearing the star if he could.

Lotar did not have a permit to leave the city limits. Nonetheless, I know from the recollections that he and Zdenka on occasion illicitly travelled to the country house to see Ella, who was, of course, confined to Libčice. On 11 November 1941, Ella, still hoping that the US visas for the family would come through, wrote to the family:

> I live here completely secluded from the world, like a nun. For months now I have not gone outside the front door. I am not proud of the badge, I am too modest. But what hurts me the most is the separation. You know me, my life belongs entirely to Otto and my boys.

Lotar would not have worn the star on those trips to visit his mother, as it would have attracted attention to his illegal movement. Instead, he used the card in the name of Ivan Rubeš. His safety, even his life, depended on evading detection. Lotar's anxiety about the perils of arrest for breach of the increasingly nightmarish mesh of laws became such that by 1941 he had secured on the black market several small vials of cyanide that could be easily broken with the teeth. A single dose could kill in seconds. To Zdenka's dismay, Lotar began carrying two vials, one for each of them, in his jacket pocket at all times.

People in the small provincial town of Libčice knew the Neumann family. Otto and Ella had first come to Libčice in the early 1920s as a newlywed couple to work there for a few years. They had then gone to Prague to start the Montana factory but had returned some years later to buy their beloved country house. The townspeople had watched Lotar and Hans grow up. Like everyone in the Protectorate, they would have known about the directive and about the stars. The Nazis constantly reminded citizens that Jews who had left their designated residential area would be punished with death; the same penalty applied to anyone who came to their aid. This included providing them with shelter or food, giving them money or transporting them in vehicles of any sort. It was the duty of all Protectorate residents to report Jews who were committing crimes and any non-Jews who helped them. On 28 February 1941, German Radio in Prague warned that anyone seen as friendly towards a Jew would be considered an enemy of the state and punished accordingly.

And yet not one of Libčice's three thousand people said a word. No one reported the tall young Jewish man who arrived from Prague on most weekends between September 1941 and May 1942, even though he was not wearing his star.

My parcel contained so many stars because they were intended to supply not just my family but also the other Jews in that sleepy town by the Vltava. They were intended to identify them, to label them all, without exception.

Them, the others.

My father never said he was Jewish. I am not sure he ever said it before the war, but he certainly never said it afterwards. He was not a great believer in clans or clubs. I cannot be certain whether this arose from some philosophical conviction, fear or a deeper trauma. I suppose, like most tenets in life, it came from a mixture of ideas and experiences. Throughout my life, he repeated that it was up to each individual to choose who and what he or she was. I heard him label himself only once, and that was to say that he was Venezuelan.

Yet, growing up in Venezuela in a firmly Roman Catholic culture, attending a school run by Ursuline nuns, I felt out of place but never quite understood why.

I was the only child in my class who was born of a second marriage, whose parents had been divorced. A classmate once solemnly pronounced that I was the product of sin. With equal solemnity, I told her that she was the product of imbeciles. As I grew up, I thought that was the extent of it. I was different because my mother and father had defied Venezuelan religious mores. I had unconventional parents. This both irked me and made me love them even more.

The fact that my parents were perceived as liberal, that my father was an immigrant and that my mother worked full time all served to compound the issue. And the matter of my parents' house being filled with enormous sculptures of naked women and alarming canvases of deconstructed bodies did not help.

My father had no great love of organised religion and particularly disliked Mass with sermons. I thought this was, as he always explained, because he objected to men affecting to have a direct line to God. In fact it was my mother, who came from a traditional Catholic family, who refused to take me to church. It occurred to me that this further segregated me from my contemporaries, who dutifully observed the Catholic calendar. Like most children, I wanted more than anything to be like everyone else. I distinctly remember one Ash Wednesday during my first year in the Ursuline school when I was ten. My maternal uncle and aunt had taken me to church. I was thrilled to have the grey cross thumbed in ash on my forehead. I tried desperately to keep it intact for school the next day. In the bath that night, I kept my face away from the water. I took cushions from the room next to mine and placed them all around me on my bed to stop me from rolling over and inadvertently wiping the ash from my forehead in my sleep. I wanted to show them I belonged. This was the evidence needed that I was just like the other girls at school.

The ash did nothing to further my cause. No one else appeared at school with a dusty forehead the next morning. The problem was more intrinsic. I was set apart because those children and their parents determined that, somehow, I was not one of them. I know now the reason that some of the girls sniggered as I sat silently during the Monday discussion of the Sunday sermon, was not because my mother had not taken me to church to hear it but because they suspected that I, like my father, was a Jew.

All of this I have discovered in recent years from classmates, family and friends, who have given me their candid recollections. I was absolutely oblivious to it as a child. I never heard the word 'Jewish' uttered by anyone in reference to me, my father or anyone else. My time with the Ursuline nuns in Venezuela did not last long. At thirteen I asked my parents to send me to boarding school and, as their marriage was falling apart, they thought it best for me to study abroad. The secular American school I went to in Lugano in Switzerland had girls and boys representing over fifty countries and of all religious affiliations. The sense of not belonging disappeared. In that melting pot of cultures I was relieved to find that no one cared whether your prayers were directed to Jesus, Hashem, Allah or someone else entirely. And nobody visited my home to be shocked by my father's peculiar taste in art.

In fact, I was first called Jewish by a complete stranger in an auditorium at Tufts University when I was an undergraduate.

It was the end of the orientation process for international freshmen. The university had invited us to arrive a few days early to meet others in the class and familiarise ourselves with American campus life. I, together with hundreds of others, had duly complied.

As I left one of the talks, I was approached by a slight young man with short brown hair and intense eyes. Unlike most of the other students present, he had a rather formal manner, not least because he was wearing a jacket and tie. He spoke to me in Spanish and introduced himself as Elliot from Guadalajara.

'I was told we should meet,' he pronounced benignly, 'Because we are both good-looking, Latin American and Jewish.'

He beamed. I was baffled.

I have never been good at witty comebacks, but I was pleased to manage: 'I am sorry, but you are mistaken. You see, I am not Jewish, and you are not good-looking.'

'You need glasses,' Elliot responded cheerfully, undeterred. 'But you are Latin, and, of course, you are Jewish. With a name like Neumann, you have to be.'

'Wrong. I was raised Catholic.'

'Where is your father from?'

'He is Venezuelan, but he was born in Prague,' I answered.

'You can call yourself what you want, but you must be Jewish. Many Jews left Europe before and after the war; your father must have been one of them.'

I had genuinely never thought about it until then. Was my family Jewish? Was my father a Jew? Was I? What did that even mean? Is one's identity predetermined by inheritance? Or are you who you choose to be?

My roommate had brought her treasured telephone from home and connected it to a socket in our freshman room. It was in the shape of a laughing Mickey Mouse. To emphasise his laughter, one white-gloved hand was placed as if he was holding his belly just above his red shorts. The other held a plastic yellow receiver. The buttons were set out by his yellow boots. I used Mickey to call my father and tell him that all was well after my first week.

'Something funny happened the other day,' I added. 'A Mexican boy I had never met before, all dressed up in a suit, came up to me saying I was Jewish.'

My father was intrigued and asked who he was. I told him and explained that Elliot had said that Neumann was a Jewish name.

My father's initial laughter quietened.

'He said I must have Jewish blood.'

There was a pause.

His voice now came through, coarse and tremulous. He was upset. I had seldom heard my father upset. 'Jewish blood. Jewish blood? Do you realise what you are saying? You are never to use that expression. Do you hear me? Never. That is what the Nazis said about us.'

Without further explanation he hung up. I do not know if I started to cry before or after he did so. I stared at the enormous frozen smile on Mickey Mouse's face, his tongue sticking out, and put the bright yellow receiver back in his white-gloved hand. I called back, kept pushing the buttons by the yellow boots, but all I heard was the continuous beeping of a busy line.

7

A SPRING MORNING IN PRAGUE

In May 1990, two years after we spoke about Jewish blood through the Mickey Mouse telephone, my father and I travelled to Prague. The Berlin Wall had fallen on 9 November 1989, and this was followed by peaceful student protests in Czechoslovakia. By December of that year, the country had peacefully transitioned into a parliamentary democracy led by the playwright Václav Havel. A cathartic winter had given way to a gentle spring. The city's buildings and cobbled pavements were still blackened from years of neglect and economic stagnation. The restaurants and shops were almost empty and devoid of variety, their frugal offerings bearing the mark of the austerity that had settled like dust during forty-one years of stark communism. In contrast, the people of Prague seemed to buzz with ideas and possibilities as they became ever more emboldened by the success of their quiet revolution. The May sunshine heralded the first democratic elections in many people's lifetimes, set to take place that summer. On almost every pavement, students perched on stands made of old wooden boxes, distributed pamphlets and vociferously exercised their newly acquired right to free speech. It was an exciting time to be Czech.

Earlier that year, the Czechoslovak ambassador in Caracas

had visited my father. He bore an official letter of invitation from the new government, which was trying to engage and draw successful émigrés back to their native land. My father had initially refused the offer to return to Prague even for a visit. At that time, paradoxically, he was working with the Venezuelan government to bring skilled European immigrants to Venezuela. He had been planning trips to other Eastern European cities, but his itinerary avoided Prague.

When I heard about the invitation I pleaded with him to accept it and take me along. My father lived alone in *Perros Furibundos*. He had been divorced from my mother for many years by then, and if we flew there during the summer holidays, I could be his travel companion without missing any classes. I was curious to find out more about my father's family, and I thought that going there, especially as things were changing, might open something inside him that had been sealed for decades. At that stage I knew nothing of their fate during the war. More importantly, I also did not know who or how many they were. I imagined that he would show me the places where he had lived, tell me stories of his youth and finally open up to me about his family and his past. He reluctantly agreed to the trip.

Instead of the emotive journey I had envisaged, we spent three days being led ceremoniously around tourist sites. Wenceslas Square with its darkened museum, Old Town Square and its fifteenth-century mechanical and astronomical clock, the imposing castle on the hill, the half-forgotten baroque churches, the fabled Charles Bridge with its statues standing sentinel in the fog, the gilded and hand-painted libraries in the Strahov Monastery were all intriguing, but seemed entirely unrelated to me or my father. Whenever we were alone, my father was more interested in discussing Kafka's novels than he was in his own past.

Pavel, our guide, was a rotund, balding and slightly nervous government official with whom my father insisted on speaking English. Pavel's English was rudimentary, and my father's was itself weighted with a heavy Czech accent, which made it even odder that they should not speak in their mother tongue. If Pavel understandably reverted to speaking Czech at any point, my father would just stare at him blankly and wave in my direction. For my father, Pavel with his crinkled suit and thick round glasses was a character straight out of the pages of *The Trial*. As for Pavel, I cannot imagine where he thought my father hailed from, with his fashionable suede jacket and Adidas tennis shoes. As Pavel determinedly showed us each landmark of their shared homeland's history, my father insisted on quizzing him about Communist-era bureaucracy and expounding on the natural marvels of Venezuela. Pavel dutifully persevered.

It was not until we were left alone on the afternoon of the second day that I realised there was more to my father's behaviour than just obduracy. He simply could not remember the streets of his old city. This amazed me. Although he had recently turned seventy and had been away for over forty years, Prague had been his city for his entire youth. His mind worked perfectly, and he remained sharp and focused, so I knew that it had nothing to do with age. It was odd, as if he had never been there before. We would amble around in circles in the centre of town near our hotel, losing track of what should have been familiar routes. He scarcely spoke as I ushered him through the streets of Malá Strana, the Old and New Town. He just firmly held on to my hand. I had dozens of questions, but it was clear to me that he could not answer them. So instead, I asked him to teach me Czech words. I only knew a handful: *nazdar* (hello), *papa* (goodbye), *děkuji* (thank you) and *hubička*, an old-fashioned way of saying 'kiss'. As I carefully repeated each word, my terrible pronunciation made him chuckle. When he laughed, I knew my father was there with me. The rest of the time he was far away, lost in some distant corner of his mind. As we walked alone, there was a freshly marked frailty to him, hitherto unseen and transmitted through the bony grip of his hand. This scared me and made me realise that he needed me. We wandered the streets, and for the first time I felt our roles had reversed. My remarkable father, the powerful Renaissance man, was not guiding me through the cobbled streets of Prague. I was leading him as I would a child.

Despite my awful sense of direction, my brief perusal of some guidebooks on the flight over seemed to have left me with the better, albeit limited, sense of the city. We became so lost trying to find the Basilica of St James that we had to stop and buy a map. Only some of the names had changed, but clearly my father had entirely wiped the web of Prague's streets from his mind.

He had arranged our trip to coincide with the fiftieth reunion of his class from industrial school. On our last night in the city he was collected from the hotel by a friend who would take him to the celebratory dinner. I offered to accompany him, but he said that it made no sense, as I did not speak Czech and no one there would understand any language I knew. I spent a quiet evening alone at our hotel.

At breakfast the next morning, my father seemed unusually

tired. When I asked about his reunion he simply said it had been fine, without much further elaboration.

'Just old people, some interesting, some not,' he proferred.

'And the man who picked you up?' I asked. 'Who is he?'

'Zdeněk. He is a friend. A good friend,' he answered. 'He saved my life.'

'He did? How? What do you mean, saved your life?' I had never heard the name Zdeněk before.

'It's a complicated story,' he said quietly. 'One day I'll tell you. But not now.'

His hand trembled as he stirred his coffee with a minuscule spoon, and there was such sadness in his eyes as he spoke that I just could not ask more. We ordered our breakfast and talked about summer plans.

Selfishly, I had been looking for answers that my father was not able to provide. I suspected by then that many in his family had died during the war, and I had innumerable questions. I wanted to know the details, hear anecdotes. But it was clear then that it was wrong to ask more. Witnessing this newly emerged frailty, seeing his quivering hand, I felt guilt at having asked him to bring me to this city that he did not recognise.

That last morning in Prague, as we left the breakfast room, he announced that he wanted to take a short car ride to the place where the family had lived. We would have just enough time before heading to the airport.

He seemed thrilled to have remembered the address. So we set out in a taxi that morning to the industrial area of Prague called Libeň. We approached what seemed to be a group of largely commercial buildings set within a gated development. My father and I got out of the car and entered on foot. My father stopped by a detached house, set apart from the more industrial buildings, surrounded and separated from the road by tall trees. It was a three-storey nineteenth-century building divided into apartments. We stood outside together, before a wide front door.

'The family lived there,' he stated plainly. He pointed up at the first floor.

Taken aback, I suggested we ring the bells by the door. My father refused.

'We had a factory called Montana that was just around the corner.'

I thought he had made a mistake. 'Montana like your paint factory in Venezuela?' I asked.

'It was also the name of the paint factory here. The one my father started.'

I was astounded not to have heard this before. 'Did you work there with your father?' I asked tentatively.

'No, I never worked with him.'

'And were you happy when you lived there?' I pointed up to the window.

'Yes,' he uttered after some thought. 'But we were happiest in the country house in Libčice.'

'Why don't we go there?' I urged, encouraged by this unusual outpouring of information.

'Libčice is far, and we don't have time.'

'Shall we try to find the factory?'

'No,' he said, 'there's no time. It won't exist any more. You asked where the family lived, and now you know. There's no time for more. We have to go back. We can't be late.' And then, rather tersely, he added, 'Sometimes you have to leave the past where it is – in the past.'

As we headed back to the hotel, my father noticed something through the window. He spoke quickly in Czech to the driver who halted the taxi. All I could make out was a lot of Czech thank-yous and a name that my father said a few times. Bubny? Bubny. We had stopped in a part of town that, as far as I could tell, seemed deserted and almost derelict. We were still outside the centre of Prague, and the beautiful landmarks were far away. 'What is this?' I asked.

'There's a place here that's important, a station.'

He pointed at a building some hundred yards away. All I could see across the unkempt grass by the side of the road were train tracks leading up to a group of brown and grey buildings. We were not at the entrance but to the side of the station. The tracks were edged with wire-mesh fencing. There was no way of getting closer, no gap in the fence as far as I could see in either direction.

'Important?' I asked him, puzzled.

My father seemed once more to be lost with his memories as he stood next to me. The driver had hung back by the car and was leaning against it, smoking a cigarette. As I studied the map in search of a way forward to the buildings, I noticed that the fence was swaying. It was shaking. My father's fingers were clutching through the wire diamonds, and he was sobbing silently. He could only mutter, between short gasps of breath. He mumbled, over and over, that this was where he had said goodbye. I did not know what to do. I called him Papi, as I had always done, but I did not think he could hear me. I gently unclenched one of his hands from the wire and stood between him and the fence. I held him and reminded him that I was there. For an instant he leaned the side of his face on my head. We stood there frozen, holding each other, him petrified by his memories and me terrified of the monsters that I sensed were lurking there, unseen.

He quickly regained his composure and whispered: 'Thank you, Coquinita. It's fine. I'm fine.'

I tried to catch and hold his gaze while I told him I loved him. I realise now that there are sorrows that cannot be conveyed, wounds with which you learn to live but which never completely heal. I was nineteen at the time and thought that words and love could assuage every sadness. I ventured that I was there to listen if he ever wanted to speak. He never did.

The transports began leaving for Terezín in November 1941. Initially some Jews – those in mixed marriages, or their children under fourteen, and those employed by the Jewish Council – were kept off the transport lists. The Central Office for Jewish Emigration decided the date and number of between twelve and thirteen hundred people for each transport. The lists were then sent to the Jewish Council for each region, who compiled the actual names and were then compelled to send a summons to each individual deportee.

Those deported from Prague and its surrounding towns left from the Bubny station, on the other side of that wire fence my father had clung to.

Summonses were delivered at night. Those served also received details of timings, assembly points, documents and belongings they were to bring. Families were usually deported together. Those from Prague and its outskirts were called to some makeshift buildings near the old Trade Fair building or in

Czech Veletržní Palác, close to the Bubny station. The premises
consisted of dirty and poorly ventilated shacks with no heat or
sanitary facilities at all. They were guarded by Czechoslovak
gendarmes outside and SS men inside. Deportees were assigned
a piece of floor as their 'living area'. Each spent a minimum of
three days filling out forms and being questioned by SS guards
about every aspect of their lives and belongings.

Most of the deportees were sent first to Terezín, the camp
northwest of Prague. Established as a walled garrison town in
the eighteenth century, it was home to fewer than four thousand people by 1940, after the dissolution of the Czechoslovak
army. In the Autumn of 1941, all of them were moved out to
transform the town into a detention camp for Jews.

On 27 April 1942, the Central Office for Jewish Emigration
in Prague sent a transport notice to my grandparents' house in
Libčice. The family members were to report to the Veletržní
Palác near the Bunby train station in Prague on 4 May at eight a.m.

I found the document in one of my boxes.

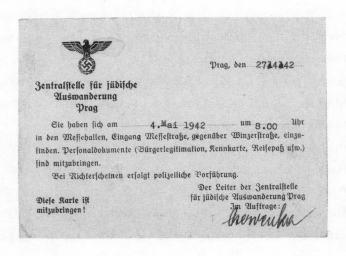

The summons is a double-sided card, headed with the black eagle atop a swastika. It neatly lists the names of Otto, Ella and Hans. Otto's name has a line through it, removed by someone at the Council who decided, persuaded by the family friend Pišta, that as the head of the paint factory he was important in Prague for the war effort.

The Neumanns knew the importance of avoiding being transported. Every month since the autumn someone in the family had been deported. In November 1941, cousin Erich, Ota's brother and a salesman at the factory had been sent away; it was believed he went to Latvia. In December of the same year, cousin Hana Polláková had been taken. In January 1942, Rudolf Pollak, who had been married to Ella's late sister, had been sent to Terezín, together with his daughter, Zita, his wife and their fourteen-year-old son, Jiří. Hugo Haas, his wife and their little daughter, Věra, who had attended clandestine school, had been transported in February 1942.

Many of those deported were thought to have been sent to

Terezín, but communication from the camps was precarious. The only person from whom they had clear news was Otto's brother Karel. He had been transported in March. Amazingly, a few weeks later the family had received a letter from him stamped in Lublin, Poland. He begged the family to send food, as he faced starvation. Through black-market connections and friendly gendarmes, the family managed to dispatch a parcel to him.

They never heard whether it found Karel or received any further news of him.

The consensus at the Council was that the only possible strategy was to delay departure and stay in Prague for as long as possible. The Neumanns now faced an appalling challenge. They had five days to get Ella and Hans off the list.

Hans pleaded with his boss at the Čermák factory to help him out. By then he had proved to be a hard worker, and after a few months his boss had decided to appoint him as deputy. Otto wielded what little influence he had left and spoke to, telephoned and wrote to anyone he knew who might potentially help. Lotar drew on every contact he had.

Their efforts were not fruitless. Hans secured a letter from František Čermák stating that his work was crucial to the factory. A few days before the transport date, Hans was taken off the list. This small victory spurred them on. More calls were made to Pišta, the family friend at the Council in Prague. This was followed by more pleading with anyone who might be able to tilt the scales in their favour.

But try as they may, no one could get Ella off the list.

Ella was to be deported alone.

Zdenka drove to Libčice with Lotar and helped her pack for her departure that Monday in May.

Otto, Ella, Lotar, Zdenka and Hans. The five of them spent that last weekend together. The Sunday night before she left, they sat down for dinner together at their home in Libčice, as they had so many times before, but now with Ella's bag packed and waiting. I have nothing to reveal about how the hours passed beyond my own horror in contemplating them. No one spoke or wrote of it afterwards. I can only imagine the relentless and mounting trepidation that must have filled the house in Libčice that night. Ella's, Otto's and the boys' dread would have been palpable. Zdenka, who had come to love Ella as a mother, must have been devastated. Ella would have had to wrestle with the desperate fear of being separated from her family as the hours crawled by. Otto, his need to control abjectly frustrated, would have despaired. His beloved wife of twenty-five years, the one who drove him mad and kept him sane, the mother to his children, the ever-cheerful Ella, with her smiles and music, warmth and silliness, was simply being removed from their lives, excised, taken away. And he could not stop it. He could not protect her. Hans and Lotar must have felt equally powerless, guilty and afraid.

There is one single relic of that period between the summons of 27 April and Ella's departure. It is a photograph of my grand-parents at home in Libčice. Ella is absorbed in her knitting. Otto is dressed in a jacket, looking down, a cigarette in one hand and a pen in the other. There is a piece of paper in front of him; he could be writing a letter or completing one of the endless official Protectorate forms – it is unclear. On the table is a bottle of wine, glasses, matches, an ashtray and newspapers.

Everything around them is darkness.

At first glance, it is just an unremarkable photo of a couple sitting, perhaps after dinner, at their home. It does not appear to record any moment of importance. The sitters seem preoccupied and are looking elsewhere. It is an odd picture to keep, unless the scene holds some other meaning.

This is the washed-out photograph that always stood on my father's bedside table, the one I had wondered about as a child, the one of my grandparents seated around a table looking old and sad. It was taken that very last week. This greying image that baffled me then is the last picture taken of Ella and Otto, relatively free and together in the Libčice house. Of all the photos in the album, casual playful shots or carefully posed and smiling portraits, this is the only one that my father kept.

Ella had to report on the Monday morning, 4 May, for the same transport as her brother Julius, his wife and their two young children. Otto's brother Oskar, his wife and their eight-year-old son were on it too.

Zdenka drove with Otto and Ella into Prague that morning before sunrise. It was decided that it was best if Hans and Lotar said their goodbyes at home and made their way to work as usual. Only Otto and Zdenka went with Ella all the way to Veletržní Palác.

They were detained before the entrance by the SS guards and ordered to leave Ella to carry her two suitcases and enter the holding area alone with the other deportees. Most Jews had to walk to the assembly point from their homes, hauling their allotted 50 kilograms of belongings, as they were no longer allowed to drive. Ella had been forewarned that often the suitcases never made it to the destination, so it was important that she carry essentials in her handbag. I cannot imagine how they felt, but I presume Otto continued to be stoic and Ella tried to stay positive, as she always seemed to be in the anecdotes and letters. I am sure they found comfort in thinking and saying that this would be temporary and that they would find a way to all be together again soon.

My grandmother spent three days in that transit centre by the station, on her patch of floor with a straw-filled sack for a mattress, with her two suitcases and her carefully packed shoulder bag, filling out forms, handing in belongings and answering endless questions under the watchful eyes of the SS guards. Wearing nothing of value other than her wedding ring, Ella must have watched as those around her were dispossessed of their jewellery and valuables. I pray that her allotted patch was close to her brother Julius and her brother-in-law Oskar and their families. I hope that the children distracted them and made them smile. It comforts me to think that at least during those terrible days of waiting, having left behind her husband and her two boys, Ella was with people whom she knew and loved. They will have cared for her. She will not have been entirely alone.

After the long days in the assembly point came the journey by train to Bohušovice, the station nearest Terezín. One thousand men, women and children were transferred with Ella in the windowless wagons that left Bubny on 7 May.

Otto, Lotar, Zdenka and Hans heard nothing for three months.

In August, Pišta, the family friend who worked at the Council of Elders in Prague, brought news. Ella was alive in Terezín. She had fallen ill and fainted in the train, but she was alive. She had been one of some forty people carried off the transport in the station nearest to Terezín because they were ill. It saved her life.

Julius Haas and Oskar Neumann and their young families were ordered to stay on board while others filed into the already crammed carriages. They travelled on to Sobibor, in occupied Poland. The family never heard from them again.

Not a single one survived of the one thousand souls on that particular transport. There is a record of the departure from Terezín but no record of their arrival at the camp in Sobibor. Virtually all at Sobibor were murdered immediately. It remains unclear whether they were shot on arrival or marched into the gas chambers. A letter from Prague sent to Victor and Richard in America in June 1945 says that the family had found comfort in learning that those few, at least, had been spared further suffering.

As I now reflect on my grandmother's fate, sitting with my own family in my own home, my thoughts inevitably pass to my father sobbing at the station in Bubny on a beautiful spring day in Prague, a day that should have been filled with hope. Exactly forty-eight years before, his mother had left that same station and had been so overwhelmed, so terrified, that she had lost consciousness. And yet I have the letters to show me that she still trusted that the time would arrive when she would be reunited with her family once again.

Despite the departure from Bubny, the wrenching separation from her boys, amid the dread and grief, that May in 1942, Ella still retained hope.

8

ZDENKA

Ensconced among the pages of the family album from Lotar's
house was a loose and crumpled black-and-white portrait
of a striking young woman. I recognised her face from the
many other photographs. After Otto, Ella, Lotar and Hans,
she appears most often in the albums. In some pictures she
is with Otto, in some alone, posing, pensive or smiling; in
many others she is with Lotar, walking or laughing.

This particular portrait was tucked away inside the album, but its condition, its creases and worn corners, betrayed that it had been kept loose for a long time, separate and unprotected by an album or a frame. It was obvious to me that it had been handled often, looked at, loved. Perhaps it had been stowed away in a wallet or a bedside drawer or between the pages of a book.

When I asked my cousin Madla about that photograph, she told me that she thought it was her father's picture of Zdenka.

As I worked my way through all the documents and letters in my boxes, I noticed that everyone wrote about Zdenka. Zdenka the beautiful. Zdenka the clever, the resourceful. Zdenka the joyful. Zdenka the brave. She chose to be courageous when she had every opportunity – and was encouraged by those close to her – to opt for self-preservation. Unlike my own family, she could so easily have taken a simpler, safer path. Nevertheless, she decided to marry Lotar, a persecuted Jew. Her family surely would have been understandably relieved if she had settled down with a different man, one who would bring less trouble upon them. And yet in 1939 she wed Lotar, and in 1942 she did it a second time, just as Jews and everyone close to them were being deported. Many around Zdenka had urged her not to marry Lotar again. They asked her to steer away from danger. Instead, aware and defiant, she headed straight towards it.

She did not have to help her husband or his family. She did not have to risk her life. And yet that is what she did, this is what she chose to do. Over and over again.

Despite this, nobody had ever mentioned Zdenka to me.

I knew Lotar only when he was married to my elegant aunt Věra. They lived far away from Caracas in a hamlet in Switzerland, in what seemed to me as a child to be a fairy-tale castle, complete with an old well in the garden beneath a wide and ancient weeping willow. My uncle Lotar was older than my father, and taller. He was gentler, more softly spoken, with enormous hands and a tentative but very kindly smile. His wife Věra, with her graceful manner and sparkly eyes, was also Czech. She and Lotar had two daughters who were some twenty years older than me – my cousin Susana and her younger sister, Madla, who shared her father's mementos and albums with me. As far as I knew, Lotar and Věra had married young. No one mentioned that he had been married before. When Madla and I first spoke about it during my research, Madla explained that she herself had discovered her father's earlier marriage only as a teenager. She also made it clear that, even then, it was not a topic upon which anyone dwelled.

The brief and rare fragments of my father's story that he managed to share towards the end of his life contained no reference to Zdenka. I suppose this was unsurprising, given that he never spoke about his family in Czechoslovakia either. Nonetheless, her name could, for example, have slipped out during our trip to Prague in 1990, but it never did.

I asked my mother if she had heard about Lotar's earlier marriage. She admitted to a vague memory of a first wife but struggled to remember details or even her name. She did recall my father saying that Lotar had a first love in Prague, before the war, but without any precise context.

'I think I remember your father saying that she was beautiful

151

and clever. But I recall there was something uncomfortable, something vexing about it all, about her story. She survived the war, but no one wanted to speak about her. I don't know why, precisely.'

I asked my mother many times to try again to remember what made any mention of this person troubling, but she simply could not remember anything more. Was it uncomfortable in the way that marriages ending can be uncomfortable? Was Zdenka not mentioned because it was far in the past and everyone had moved on? Or was it something else?

Frustrated by the lack of answers, I pressed my mother on my father's general reticence about the past. While I now understood that my father might not have wanted to burden his child with painful memories, I wondered if his relationship with my mother, whom he had loved deeply, had allowed for a fuller exploration of his life before and during the war.

Yet it had not. I realised slowly that demanding answers of my mother now, after all this time and with all that my research had uncovered, was profoundly unfair. My urging her to revive stowed remembrances in search of something that had been left unspoken demanded she return to a place that she had moved away from long ago. It was to ask her to go on a journey that would at best bring melancholy and at worst bring regret. And yet my mother tried to help me as much as she could. She explained that she too had been curious but that a therapist had once told her that my father's memories were so painful and troubled that they were better left repressed, unexplored.

So my mother in her time, much like I was, had been scared to ask questions. As I dwelled on these thoughts, she added as if it should be obvious: 'Your father always said that life was now, in the present. He did love technology and science fiction; his favourite film was Stanley Kubrick's *2001: A Space Odyssey*. It was about possibilities sometimes, but it was always about the present for him. It certainly was never about the past.'

Perhaps he had told her, like he had told me, that the past should remain in the past.

In many ways, that must have been the correct approach for him. For my father, the past was lost, imperfect and irremediable, unlike his watches with their mechanisms that he could always repair with patience and time and the right tools. This was how he endured and became the man I knew as my father, a strong, hardworking, magnanimous visionary man focused on the present. And yet he had retained and left me mementos of experiences that he had tried to leave behind. Was life for him never about the past? There were moments, perhaps just a mere handful, when the past pushed poignantly through. My mother was aware of them too. The nightmares, the stunted answers, the shaking hands.

'And you didn't focus on those moments?' I asked my mother.

'No, I didn't. I wanted to be in the present with him and focus on what we had. I wanted him to be happy and to bring him joy.'

As I delved deeper into my research, it became clear to me that Zdenka was also a bringer of joy. She was a key part of the family history, a central figure in the mosaic I was putting together. I could not understand how it was that no one had ever talked about her, this fundamental piece of the puzzle. I was determined to learn more about this intrepid woman.

Once more, I enlisted the resourceful researcher who had traced my lost Czech family, but all enquiries of the recent

registers in the Czech Republic came up blank. We could trace
Zdenka Neumann until 1968, at which point she had been living
in central Prague. We knew that she worked as a journalist and
a writer. An article she wrote in 1967 dealt with sexism and the
social inequality of women, characteristically forthright for the
time. We also found that Zdenka, who had trained as a lawyer
before the war, had worked as a lay magistrate. Another writer,
Jaroslav Putík, mentioned Zdenka as one of the people involved
in the demand for reforms in 1968, during what became known
as the Prague Spring. Her independence, political engagement
and courage had clearly outlived the war.

But it seemed that perhaps her and Lotar's love had not. We
knew from the Registry Office in Prague that in December
1949 she had a daughter named Lucia with a man called Viktor
Knapp. For a long time, this single fact was all we knew about
her personal life. As she would have been close to a hundred
years old today, I knew that I would not find Zdenka herself, but
I wondered whether her daughter or maybe a grandchild could
help me piece her story together. Tracing women who have
changed their name on marrying is remarkably difficult. If the
marriage certificate is missing from the archives, the trail fades
away. For this and myriad other societal reasons, unearthing
the lost stories of women is markedly more challenging. The
doughty researcher scoured archive after archive but could find
no trace of Zdenka or Lucia after 1968.

However, my cousin Madla did remember meeting Zdenka
briefly in Switzerland in the late 1960s or '70s. Zdenka had
visited Lotar for a few days at their family home. Madla had
it in mind that Zdenka herself had lived in Switzerland with
her daughter at some point, but she recalled no more. I asked

Madla about Zdenka during each conversation we had about the family in the hope that more fragments of memory would emerge. Occasionally she called to mind a further detail, but it was never significant enough to help us trace her.

'You have to understand that her name was not mentioned in the house, she was not someone who my parents talked about. Any mention of her made my mother uncomfortable. The last time I heard Zdenka discussed was probably in the 1970s, and I was very young.'

Then, one day as we sat over lunch discussing an upcoming exhibit of Madla's paintings, my cousin recalled something new. I had told her at the start of our meal that every attempt to find Zdenka's daughter Lucia had been fruitless. Madla commiserated, but the conversation naturally moved on. Then, all of a sudden, as we sipped our coffee and complained about our stress levels, some apparently unrelated note in our exchange dislodged a fragment of recollection.

Memories, like misfiled documents, are not always where you expect to find them. My direct questions as to Zdenka's story had produced no helpful answers. As I interviewed people about my family's history, I learned that detailed questions often did little to trigger specific memories. People returned to distant facts in roundabout ways, along their own winding paths, which seemed more mapped by emotion than by logic.

As we sat together that afternoon, Madla mused on the pressure of having to finish her paintings to a deadline. Then, undisturbed by my barrage of previous questions, a memory struck her. Even Madla, always eager to help me, seemed startled as she announced: 'Zdenka's daughter had a boyfriend called Jiří, and he had a gallery in Switzerland. I remember! He offered to exhibit some of my oils when I first started, a very long time ago.'

Madla had been extremely touched by this offer, coming as it had at the start of her career. And then she remembered that Jiří's gallery was called '9'. We had to find Jiří at Gallery 9 in Switzerland.

And so that afternoon, having found a website for Gallery 9 in the town of Solothurn, I found myself talking on the telephone to a charming Czech/Swiss man named Jiří Havrda. Jiří is also a writer and documentary film director. Upon hearing my name and learning that I was Lotar Neumann's niece, he announced that he knew exactly who Lotar was.

I did not have to elaborate much beyond telling him that I was trying to learn more about Zdenka. Jiří, who had loved her daughter, seemed to know precisely who my family members were. I liked him immediately. He was forthcoming, passionate and generous. Perhaps my call provided that sense of ease that we sometimes feel with complete strangers and, unrestrained by established patterns and expectations, lets us discuss personal feelings with abandon. Within a few minutes, Jiří was sharing stories of his adventures with the wonderful Lucia, whom he declared to be his first true love.

Jiří described the Prague of the summer of 1968 and life with his beloved Lucia and her bold and beautiful mother, Zdenka. They had all been active politically, meeting and agitating for a freer society and contributing to the growing criticism of the repressive Communist regime. Then, in late August, the Soviets and their allies invaded with overwhelming strength, and the moment of potential change was gone. Jiří, Lucia and Zdenka had fled west and ended up in Switzerland.

Jiří was happy to tell me his story, yet he was reticent to tell me what he felt were other people's stories. He stressed that he believed it was important for me to find Lucia and hear Zdenka's stories from her. This was not going to be easy, he explained, as he regretted that he was no longer in touch with Lucia. They had spoken for the last time by telephone decades before, and he had understood that she was married and raising two boys. He vaguely remembered the name of her husband but not the spelling. Swiss telephone numbers had changed since he had jotted down her number, and we were now a digit short. To complicate matters, Lucia had moved too. Jiří thought she might be somewhere near Bern, but he did not know precisely where. He was not sure what had become of Zdenka either. Nonetheless, Jiří, an unlikely knight in shining armour, promised to help me find Lucia.

True to his word, Jiří rang my cell phone a few days later and announced that he had ploughed through the phone books and telephoned everyone with a name similar to Lucia's husband in the entire canton of Bern. Not all his calls had been well received. 'For a nation of polite people, the Swiss can be so rude,' he said, chuckling, 'but I have been victorious!'

Jiří had found Lucia.

When they finally spoke, he explained my quest, and she had agreed to talk to me about her mother. Buoyed by Jiří's enthusiasm, I emailed Lucia that evening and received a long, open and friendly reply in return. I understood with that first exchange that Lucia had been told so much more about my own grandmother and my family than I ever had.

Zdenka had indeed died some years ago. However, while she herself was gone, it transpired that many of her memories were intact, as she had set down, in writing, episodes of her life during the war. These memoirs were written in Zdenka's native Czech, and over the following weeks Lucia patiently translated them all into English for me. As email after email arrived, my inbox filled with stories and pictures of my grandparents and Lotar, Hans and Zdenka. Zdeněk, Pišta and other names that I had encountered during my own research reappeared in Zdenka's account. Lucia also remembered meeting some of my family and their friends in the years after the war. Her mother had stayed in contact with them despite her departure from Czechoslovakia in 1968. Connecting with Lucia and hearing her mother's voice, directly in her writings and channelled through her daughter, filled me with joy. And all of a sudden, thanks to the kindness of this stranger, I had a clearer vision of my family during the war as missing pieces of the picture were revealed and slotted into place. Details that had initially seemed disjointed or inconsistent all started to make sense.

In 1942, after they had remarried, Zdenka and Lotar lived together again in the apartment that her grandmother had reconfigured for them on the fourth floor of Trojanova 16 in Prague. It was a corner apartment in a tall, ornate building in pink stone, built by her family in the nineteenth century in the New Town area of Prague. At that point, the entire property belonged to Zdenka. It was only a block from the banks of the Vltava river and similarly close to the imposing eighteenth-century Orthodox cathedral of Ss. Cyril and Methodius. The building stood, as it does today, in a quiet residential area. Filled with western light, it was large enough to allow residents a degree of seclusion. Next to the living room, Zdenka's grandmother had set up a darkroom especially for Lotar to pursue his passion for photography. Trojanova 16 provided Lotar and Zdenka with a comfortable, and comforting, refuge during the first years following the Nazi invasion. Within its walls they were able to exist in relative peace.

However, the war found them eventually. In late May 1942, a few weeks after Ella had been deported, Czech commandos assassinated Reinhard Heydrich, the highest-ranking Nazi in the Protectorate, who was the Reich Main Security Officer and deputy Reich Protector for Bohemia and Moravia. He bore various soubriquets, including the man with the iron heart, the hangman and the butcher of Prague, and had been chosen by Hitler and Himmler to control the Czechs through fear. He had three public aims: to 'Germanise' the Czechs, to wipe out any resistance, and to implement the 'Final Solution', settled in December 1941.

Heydrich had shown every sign of delivering his objectives. Five days after his arrival in the autumn of the previous year, he had ordered the closing of all synagogues in the Protectorate. Two weeks later he had started the deportations, personally ordering the first 'evacuation' of five thousand Czech Jews to a camp in Lody. By November 1941 he had coerced the Jewish leaders in the Council to begin the deportations to Terezín. The onset of Heydrich's regime marked the beginning of a markedly brutal campaign against not only the Jews but anyone who refused to cooperate. Thousands of dissidents were arrested, put to death or sent to the camps.

The Nazis were particularly effective in their campaign to dehumanise Jews, fragment society and crush resistance in Czechoslovakia, more so than in other occupied regions. Yet a small team of Czechoslovak army parachutists, marshalled by the resistance in exile in London, had set out to assassinate Heydrich in an operation codenamed Anthropoid. Their effort to ambush his open-top car as it was driven from his home in the suburbs to his office at Prague Castle was not instantly successful due to a faulty machine gun. However, showing remarkable bravery, they managed to injure Heydrich with a hand grenade. Heydrich was taken to a hospital and eventually died from infection to his wounds on 4 June 1942.

The viciousness of the Nazi response was staggering. They were determined to find the perpetrators, to punish anyone who had helped them and to terrify the rest of the Czechs into complete submission. Five days after Heydrich's death, the village of Lidice, the occupants of which had been falsely accused of harbouring the parachutists, was entirely destroyed. Every man over fifteen was shot, and women and children were sent to the camps. To emphasise the finality of these actions, the buildings were razed to the ground.

Two weeks later, a radio transmitter was found in another village, Ležáky. The entire adult population was shot, the children deported and the village destroyed. According to official numbers, 1,331 people were executed in the Protectorate between late May and early July. At that point, General Daluege, who had assumed Heydrich's post, issued an order stating that anyone found promulgating, or even failing to report, hostility to the Reich would face the death penalty. Helping Jews in any way was deemed worthy of similar treatment. Posters to this effect were plastered all over Prague. Daily announcements blared out of radios and public loudspeakers. A reward of ten million crowns was offered for information leading to the arrest of the assassins. This inducement was accompanied by stark warnings that execution awaited not only those who withheld such information but also their families.

The Nazi reaction to the assassination decimated any effective underground resistance movement in the Protectorate. This frightful period was termed by the Czechs *Heydrichiáda*. The Gestapo and the SS literally tore the capital apart in search of the perpetrators and those who had helped them. It was the largest manhunt of the war, with 36,000 homes raided and more than 13,000 civilians arrested. By mid-June, the pursuit was concentrated in the New Town area of Prague, as it was suspected that the parachutists were being hidden in the neighbourhood. Trojanova 16 sat at the heart of the search zone. The streets swarmed with troops. Search parties erupted into hundreds of homes around Lotar and Zdenka. The suffocating atmosphere left an already anxious Lotar paralysed with fear. Ella had been deported only a few weeks before, and they had still received no news of her. While his marriage to Zdenka provided some theoretical legal protection from being transported, Lotar, just like Hans, lived in constant and legitimate fear. The Nazis were outraged by the insubordination of the Czechs, and they needed no legal excuse to shoot or imprison a Jew. Lotar was also acutely conscious that he was still using his fake identification in the name of his friend Ivan Rubeš. If his apartment was searched and he was found to be holding false papers, he would certainly be killed. Zdenka recalled that one night Lotar and she awoke to the din of shouts from the Gestapo in the streets. The stomping in hallways, banging of doors and barked orders seemed closer than ever. The police had entered their building.

Terrified, Lotar dragged Zdenka into the bathroom, where he kept a small leather case holding his glass vials of cyanide. They sat in darkness, trying to remain absolutely silent, but Zdenka could tell Lotar was crying. She comforted him quietly and murmured over and over that they should not give up. They were on the fourth floor and the noises were rattling up from the floors below. It was impossible to tell from which floor precisely, but they sounded close.

'I am not giving up yet. I am not biting one of these. If you want to do it, go ahead, but you are on your own,' she said defiantly.

Zdenka managed to prise the case away from Lotar and convinced him to wait a moment more, until the soldiers were at their own door. The shouting and crashing reverberated around them, echoing through the old building as the two of them huddled alone in the lightless bathroom. Then, as suddenly as it had burst upon them, the storm moved on. The Gestapo had obtained information that the perpetrators were being hidden in the Ss. Cyril and Methodius Cathedral, just yards away, and redirected their forces accordingly.

On 18 June, seven hundred Waffen-SS troops bore down on the handful of parachutists who had been hidden in the church. Any hope of escape disappeared when the Nazis resorted to flooding the crypt where they had been driven to make their last stand. As ammunition supplies dwindled and the water rose around them, the parachutists determined never to surrender. Some shot themselves; others bit into their cyanide vials. The tragedy drew to a close and, once more saved by Zdenka's fortitude, Lotar carefully stowed his own poison.

As daily life became ever more difficult, Lotar, Hans and Otto continued trying to remain as inconspicuous as possible. And yet the boys still took some calculated risks. Despite Otto's ire towards him, and many promises to the contrary, Hans continued to be late for curfews and spend time behaving foolishly with Míla and Zdeněk. Lotar was much more cautious than Hans, but he too was inclined to push his luck. He accepted an invitation from a theatrical friend, Erik Kolár, to help teach in a clandestine school. He revealed these visits only to Zdenka, not wishing to worry his father. The school was on the second floor of a building on Spálená Street, a few minutes' walk from where they lived.

Erik and Lotar taught theatre and poetry to a handful of Jewish children who had yet to be deported. They worked hard to provide their charges with a semblance of normal life and moments of escape from the increasingly grim reality outside the walls of their little makeshift classroom. They even staged a performance of Karel Jaromír Erben's fairy tale *The Three Golden Hairs of the Wise Old Man*, complete with costumes, an act of quiet rebellion that must have provided a momentary distraction.

August finally brought some better news. Ella managed to get a letter out of Terezín. This letter survived. The tone is cheerful and brimming with details. She had managed to gain weight and was adapting well to her new life. She was trying to secure a job that would protect her from being transported 'east' to camps that were known, at the very least, to be far worse than Terezín. She asked for the family to send twenty *bekannte*, a code word for German marks, as well as more clothing and whatever food they could muster. She offered reassurance that all was fine for her and that, above all, they must not worry. However, the impression of a mother offering her family comfort is underpinned by the clearest instruction: Otto, Lotar and Hans must do everything in their power to avoid being sent to Terezín.

Ella's letter gave a much-needed lift to the family's mood, which had been brought close to hopelessness by the terror that followed the death of Heydrich. Together they formulated a plan to communicate secretly with Ella. It was difficult to find the right people, but some of the Czech gendarmes in the camp were open to persuasion or bribes in order to help the inmates, or at least turn a blind eye to what was happening behind the scenes.

The family started to use all the resources at their disposal to send whatever they could to Terezín to supplement Ella's food, keep her warm and provide her with the currency needed to obtain favours and barter. The logistics took time to establish; every link in the chain had to be infallible. Contacts had to have the necessary access to the camp and be willing to take the risk. It took weeks for the family to arrange things.

But Zdenka, being Zdenka, would not wait. She could not be dissuaded from action. As soon as she heard that Ella was in Terezín, she decided to enter the camp and find her. This was difficult, but nothing had ever seemed impossible to Zdenka. She was, at this point, already driving between the homes of various family members and friends, shuttling letters, medicines and currency. She had already helped Lotar with the false identity card. But this idea established a new level of resistance more defiant and immensely dangerous. It could easily have cost her her life.

Zdenka during an afternoon stroll
in Czechoslovakia, late 1930s.

She asked questions of friends and sought advice from people engaged in resistance. It was difficult and very risky for a gentile to access the camp, but it was not impossible. Zdenka discarded her sleek modern skirt suits, covered her hair with a handkerchief, found a pair of comfortable walking shoes and dressed in the plainest clothes she could lay her hands on. She stitched a yellow star onto her oldest coat. She had been told there were two options. She should either look like one of the few locals who entered and left Terezín, employed to do laundry and cooking for the SS, or like one of those interned. She chose the latter.

The easiest way in was to go to just before noon and meet up with the groups of inmates who worked the fields surrounding Terezín. She would then walk with them as they headed back into the camp for their midday soup. The town had two main gates that were guarded on rotation by Czech gendarmes and German SS guards. Yet Terezín was self-administered, and the people responsible for counting inmates in the fields or barracks were Jews. The field workers were led and monitored by a higher-ranking prisoner and usually returned at the time when the SS guards were on their lunch break. They entered via a gate near the gendarmes' headquarters, which, rumour had it, was patrolled by friendly Czech guards. Chances were that the Jewish inmate in charge of the group of field workers would not denounce her, so Zdenka needed simply to blend in and avoid any contact with the SS.

Her knowledgeable friends had shown her a map of Terezín, on which were marked the various entrances and barracks. She managed to locate the group of buildings that, Pišta reported, included Ella's dormitory and workplace. Zdenka knew how to do it; she knew where to go.

She chose a busy weekday and packed an old cloth bag with items that Ella had requested: a black sweater, a wool dress and a small pot of marmalade. She drove her car to the town of Bohušovice. There she borrowed a bicycle from a contact and cycled the remaining 2 kilometres to the fortified town of Terezín. When she spotted the country unit of workers in a field, she hid her bicycle in the nearby shed she had been told about. She donned her jacket with the star and joined them in their labours until it was time to go in for their lunch.

She walked into Terezín with a large group of inmates who pushed handcarts and lugged tools and sacks of potatoes. As if she entered the camp every day, she brazenly smiled when she walked past a gendarme with his bayonet. I do not know why they did not stop her. Once through the ramparts, she found her way towards the buildings that housed the workshops and eventually reached Ella. Zdenka had a limited amount of time to spare before she had to return to the fields with the agricultural workers headed for the afternoon shift. Otherwise, leaving the camp that day would be impossible. Zdenka's written recollection paints her bold adventure as an easy feat. The reality is that there are very few historical accounts of people illicitly accessing Terezín.

Many years later, an elderly Zdenka remembered her encounter with Ella in the camp: *Reunited, we touched each other's hands and faces over and over in disbelief, we held each other and talked and wept. We cried out of joy and sorrow.*

A few days after the visit, Ella sent a letter to Otto and the boys:

This encounter with my beloved Zdenka has brought me so many beautiful memories and such happiness it has shaken me out of my apathy. Today I am back at work and hopeful once more. I miss you all terribly. I live for you and pray that this will only be a short chapter and will not be in vain. I never thought I had it in me to be so brave. I'm on good terms with all and with none . . . I have never found so much evil anywhere before and I fear I will not be able to forget it as long as I live . . . It would be best if you never had to see this human misery . . . but should it come to it, remember to put as much as possible into the hand luggage, food, lard, soap, medicines, warm clothing, etc.

Thanks to the devoted and resourceful Zdenka, who had not thought twice about risking her life, the Neumanns once more had, albeit temporarily, a reason to be joyful.

9

VYREKLAMOVÁN

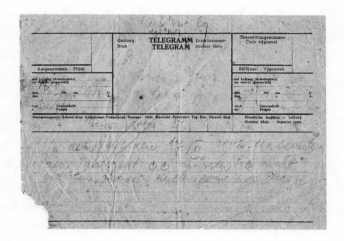

A delicate piece of paper headed with the word *Telegramm* in
neat print was stored in the box that my father left for me. It is
browned with time and missing a corner. To the left it is dated
18 November 1942. The addressee is Hans Neumann. The
faded handwriting, in German, is hard to decipher, but one
can still make out within the body of the message the words
Transport CC and the date 17 November 1942, the day before
the telegram was sent.

Around 12 November 1942, a second transport notice had
been delivered to the house in Libčice. This time Otto and
Hans were instructed to present themselves at the deportation

centre in Bubny on 17 November. Once more, they had less than one week to muster evidence to prove that they were indispensable in Prague.

This time, Otto, Hans and Lotar knew the drill. They dispatched the frantic letters, made the desperate calls and bombarded anyone with the power to help with nervous pleas. Again, Hans and Otto beseeched their employers to provide supportive letters. Hans succeeded in securing one from his boss at František Čermak. At Montana, Karl Becker, the original Nazi-appointed administrator, had left to fight with the German army. He had been replaced by the more empathetic Czech Alois Francek. Eager to help the family, Francek typed a letter emphasising to the authorities the importance of Otto's work. To capitalise on this momentum, Lotar took the letters straight to the Jewish Council offices himself and handed them to their friend Pišta.

However, this time it seemed that their efforts had been in vain and they received no news from the Council. The weekend before they were set to depart, Lotar and Zdenka drove to Libčice to make plans. Hans's girlfriend Míla and his friend Zdeněk also took the train to visit him in the country house. They buoyed him with poetry, jokes and some plum brandy that Zdeněk's mother had procured. As the friends left Libčice they reminded Hans that there was still time to get off the list and they promised to visit him wherever he ended up, as if he were off on an army posting.

But Monday passed without any word from the authorities. The Neumanns had heard that the young and strong fared better within the Nazi system. The vulnerable were cast aside. It was important to appear hardy and capable of hard labour. That last evening, Mr Novák, one of the managers at Montana, arranged for his cousin, a hairdresser, to visit Libčice. He was to dye Otto's thick silver head of hair a dark brown in the hope of making him appear more youthful than his fifty-two years. Otto and Hans bore in mind the instructions from Ella's first letter from Terezín. They packed their bags with warm clothes and put the most useful things in their hand luggage, including, in Otto's case, a small bottle of hair dye that the hairdresser had given him.

Otto and Hans headed to the assembly point first thing on the Tuesday morning of 17 November 1942. They carried their bags along the shortcut of empty paths between their house and Libčice's station. They showed their Nazi-approved work travel permits and boarded the early train to Prague. Zdenka and Lotar met them in the city, and the solemn quartet made their way to the annex near the Trade Fair building at Bubny, where months before Ella had said her own farewells.

Otto forbade Lotar and Zdenka to even approach the entrance. They had heard stories of the SS guards at the doors bundling those who escorted the deportees along with them to the camps. I can imagine my uncle Lotar watching from a distance, supported by Zdenka but stricken with grief and guilt as the figures of his brother and father became submerged in the throng. Lotar would have been struck by the unnatural changes. Hans' characteristically easy saunter would have been replaced by the deliberate step of a frightened man. Otto's hair was now dark, and his commanding bearing was bowed under the weight of his bags and his trepidation.

Lotar was inconsolable, but the next day brought merciful news from Pišta, their friend at the Council. Miraculously, they had succeeded in taking Hans's name off the list. He could be *vyreklamován*, 'reclaimed', from the transport. There was nothing, Pišta explained that the Prague Elders could do for Otto. He was simply too old to be deemed sufficiently important to the war effort. Otto would have to make the journey that they had all worked so hard to avoid, but Pišta himself would collect Hans from Bubny.

The telegram that I had found had been sent from the Jewish Council to Libčice on 18 November 1942, the day after Otto and Hans had registered at the assembly camp near the Trade Fair building. It was stored in my father's box along with an official document from the Reich Ministry of Armaments in Prague stating that the work at Čermak of the Jew Hans Neumann was deemed crucial to the war effort.

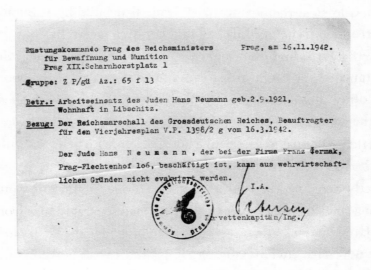

Armed with this official document to retrieve Hans and a handwritten note for Otto, Pišta went into the assembly area by Bubny Station. In his note, Pišta encouraged Otto to try to find strength in being reunited with Ella. He assured him of his friendship and wished him well in facing the road ahead. He concluded by writing that above all, Otto must keep his faith in him. He signed off 'Pištek', the affectionate moniker that Otto had always used for him. When I found this note in one of the boxes over seventy years later, it was clear, even out of context, that the writer was consumed with a desperate regret at his helplessness.

After I pieced together the episode at Bubny I told Ignacio, my older half-brother from my mother's first marriage, about it. It brought to the fore a childhood memory of his with my father. Ignacio recalled distinctly that, one day, when he was in his early teens, my father had taken him into his study and shown him a handgun. Venezuela at the time had seen a slew of kidnappings, and I remembered that in addition to stationing more guards around the house, my father had also taken to carrying a small gun in an ankle holster. Ignacio had been startled when Hans explained that the gun was not there just to fend off criminals. He had looked intently at his stepson and quietly explained that he was to tell no one, but that the gun held a special bullet for the guard who had separated him from his father at the station in Prague. The weapon and, even more so, this remark were entirely incongruous with my calm and measured father, a man who never raised his voice. Ignacio at the time had not understood what Hans meant and, scared of the gun and this strange disclosure, sensed that it was best not to pursue the matter. He obeyed his stepfather's instruction to keep the secret and, over the decades, more or less forgot about it. When I mentioned this story to my mother, she remembered that my father had also told her something about being saved at the station. She thought it had been traumatic for him and she had not dwelt on it as she felt it compounded his terrible feeling of guilt.

Hans and Otto had been ordered to turn up at the assembly point at eight a.m. on 17 November. They had registered with the authorities at Bubny that morning, queued at the desks and started to fill out the dozens of forms required for deportation. Hans had spent the day and night with Otto and the thousand others in the same transport in the grim conditions of the hall. At some point after the telegram from the Jewish Council was sent the following day, Pišta had travelled to Bubny with the official Reich Ministry of Armaments *vyreklamován* notice and the handwritten message for Otto. Pišta was not allowed to enter the area where Otto and Hans were seated with their belongings, so an SS guard had delivered the news. The guard did not allow time for embraces or lengthy goodbyes. He hurried Hans into gathering his bags and escorted him out. Hans would have had no choice but to comply, bundle up his things and tear himself away from his father, who would be deported alone.

Hans was saved and Otto stayed behind at the station. That evening the four of them, Hans, Pišta, Lotar and Zdenka, sat down and took what little comfort was available in the discussion of practicalities. Lotar was protected for now by his marriage to Zdenka, but it was unclear how long this dispensation would last. He could continue to work at Montana. They reckoned that if Jews in mixed marriages were to be transported, the friendly *treuhänder* Francek might succeed in making a case that, because of his youth and expertise, Lotar was crucial at the factory. Hans would be sure to work the longest hours possible and maintain his position at Čermák. He too needed to make himself indispensable. They would all take care of each other. They would keep a low profile and behave sensibly in daily matters. They would live on their wits and trust only the very close chosen few. Together with Zdenka, they would arrange for parcels to be sent into Terezín, and they would use every contact to prevent Ella or Otto from being sent east.

The family now battled on two fronts, ensuring that the boys stayed in Prague and that Otto and Ella were kept safe and fed in Terezín. Lotar reminded Hans of Otto's words of caution uttered a few weeks earlier. Any deviation from the rules could cost their lives and those of others. It was imperative that Hans particularly understood this, given his tendency to flightiness. Otto had always been the one to be stern with his younger son, but now it was Lotar's turn to try to talk some sense into him. Hans was fortunate to still be in Prague. Despite the positive noises to date from Čermák, it was critical that he stop fooling around with his friend Zdeněk. He must resist the temptation to take any unnecessary risks.

Somehow, on the back of the note that Pišta had written to him, Otto managed to scribble a message to his boys and get it out of Bubny on 19 November:

So far all is well. We have loaded our luggage onto the train now and will depart tomorrow. I have managed to identify someone in Terezín who will help. It will be another sleepless night as it is simply impossible to sleep here. I hope it will be

better in Terezín. Please don't worry at all about me, I will
adjust to everything. I kiss you with all my heart.

Otto was transported from Bubny to Terezín the next morning.

As my own research was drawing to a close, I decided that I
had to go to Terezín. Initially I felt I should go alone, but was
grateful when my husband and children insisted that they
would accompany me for support. My mother, who lives in
New York, announced that she had to be there for her grandchildren. Her sister, my aunt, who had worked with me on the
family letters and knew as much about Otto and Ella as I did,
clearly had to come as well. Dr Anna Hájková, a professor at
Warwick University and an expert on Terezín who had helped
me with my investigations, offered to guide us so we could find
the places where my grandparents lived. Her partner, an architect who had never visited Terezín, joined for good measure.

This disparate band of French, Venezuelan, American,
British and Czech travellers, ranging in age from twelve to
seventy-six, assembled in Prague early on a foggy Sunday
morning in October 2018. We drove out of Prague to Terezín,
each of us a little sleepy but apprehensive for our own differ-
ing reasons.

After just under an hour on the motorway, we followed the
country roads that lead to Terezín. We passed along an access
road over the old moat and through one of the entrances built
into the red-brick fortified walls. The early mist had cleared,
and an unseasonal sunlight poured onto the caramel stone of

the eighteenth-century buildings. We pulled up and set off down a quiet street on foot, with Dr Hájková leading the way.

At first, Terezín seemed like any one of the countless historic towns that dot Central Europe, with a formal square outlined by rather grand buildings arrayed around a church, complete with bell tower and a town hall. The square was covered in lawns, a little dry after a long summer, but well tended. As we adjusted to the scene, it became clear that we were almost alone. The streets were empty and the windows dark. Apart from the occasional passer-by and the few patrons of the only small café open, which offered a lunch of stew or fried cheese, the town was more or less deserted.

When Terezín was a detention camp, the church was locked and its bell silent but the town was far from quiet. It was obscenely swollen with people, every room and attic crammed with confined humanity. This square had been hemmed with barbed wire and tented in canvas to provide an additional roofed area as a workplace for the prisoners, who hammered, sawed, scrubbed and sewed within. These perfectly perpendicular and silent streets thronged, and the metal bars on every darkened window would have framed the faces that craned for a view of life beyond the stifling rooms.

In the stillness, we walked as Dr Hájková spoke and my children took turns holding my hand. Overcrowding, disease, hunger and misery were most of the factors that led to death. Originally a garrison town built to accommodate 4,000 people, by September 1942, Terezín housed nearly 60,000 souls. More than 140,000 Jews were sent to Terezín throughout the war. Over half of them were from the Protectorate of Bohemia and Moravia, the rest from Germany, Austria and other parts of Central and Northern Europe. Only one of every ten survived the war.

As one ventures around the perimeter of the town towards its cream and grey crematorium, or the area known as Small Fortress which housed a Gestapo prison, there are sculptures commemorating the victims, a stone menorah, a field of graves around a Star of David, stark reminders of the many who died there or passed through on their way to death camps further east.

Two of the buildings now serve as museums, and here the visitor can view re-created barrack rooms, with crude bunks tightly serried as they would have been. Photographs and examples of the deft artworks produced by Terezín inmates are on display in glass cases. Each charcoal sketch evokes the events that took place there and that left the streets deserted for all these decades after the war. The works invariably portray a teeming, overwhelming desperation. And yet all this is punctuated by incongruous notes of solace, the musicians still playing, even composing, the poets somehow still finding inspiration and the artists drawing and painting it all. It is ironic that the horror of Terezín was captured through art. The human spirit fought on and continued to produce poignant works in a place that was designed to numb, silence and dehumanise. Norbert Frýd, a Czech theatre director who was deported to Terezín in August 1943 and survived the war, wrote:

If Terezín was not hell itself, like Auschwitz, it was the anteroom to hell. But culture was still possible, and for many this frenetic clinging to an almost hypertrophy of culture was the final assurance. We are human beings and we remain human beings, despite everything!

It is unsurprising that many of the local families who had made Terezín their home before the war went elsewhere and that no others replaced them. Official figures suggest that there are a few thousand residents left today, yet when we visited it felt emptier. All but a handful of the buildings are uninhabited and neglected. The place feels mostly soulless, depleted. And yet as I walked the gravel paths between the buildings where my grandparents were housed, I could almost hear them utter the words in their letters. They were not mutterings of despair. What survived and resonated were their dreams, the descriptions of moments of happy respite or mundane frustration, titbits that seeped through enough to give me a glimpse of who they were, of how they lived, of how, despite all, they still hoped and loved.

That day in Terezín, as I looked up at the unwavering stone buildings, it seemed to me that I saw silhouettes, delineations of their figures looking back from the depths of the windows, behind the bars. I maintained the gaze for a yearning second before reminding myself that the light plays games and creates shadows, especially as it finds its way through years of accumulated dirt on the glass.

Terezín was a concentration camp, another tier in the carefully constructed Nazi strategy. The first tier had been to exclude the Jews from society, the second to concentrate them as a segregated temporary workforce in places like Terezín, and then, finally, to deport them to extermination camps further east. Terezín was not itself a death camp, like Auschwitz or

Dachau. Sometimes it is also referred to as a ghetto, but this word fails to convey the heinous crimes committed there. It had no gas chambers, although thirty-four thousand people perished from disease and starvation within its overcrowded confines. It is referred to as the 'model' camp, because Terezín was used for Nazi propaganda. It incorporated a bank and a post office, and it had a working hospital. Nevertheless the inmates were malnourished and frail. This, together with the overcrowded and unhygienic conditions, meant that illnesses proliferated. The hospital functioned and was staffed by superb doctors from all over Europe who had themselves been deported there. The bank and post office, on the other hand, were mostly a charade. Inmates nominally had bank accounts and were paid for their labour, but Terezín banknotes, complete with an image of Moses, had almost no value other than for buying tickets to concerts or plays put on by inmates. The post office could be used to receive some letters and small packages which were checked, but only postcards could be sent, and they were read by the SS and censored. Solely letters that were sneaked out of the camp by illegal methods told the truth about the conditions there.

While the Nazis, of course, retained ultimate control and set the laws, they established a Council of Elders in Terezín to self-administer. As in Prague, the Council was made up of respected Jews who had to organise labour, provide some degree of municipal services, ensure that the Nazi guidelines were obeyed and, ultimately, draft transport lists. This body consisted of inmates and worked in much the same way as the local Jewish Councils did throughout occupied Europe. While taking part might offer some protection to its members and families, it was only temporary. The organisational structure was a clever tactic, since it helped create the illusion that the Jews remained in control of their fate even as it pitted them against one another. Refusal to participate in this sham governing body was not an option. As the majority of Jews from the Protectorate were transported to camps in 1942, the centre of power shifted from the Jewish Council in Prague to the Council of Elders in the camps.

When my grandparents arrived in 1942, Jacob Edelstein was the head of the Council in Terezín. Contemporary accounts say he believed, at least initially, that if the Jews of Terezín worked hard and made their value obvious to the Nazis, they would be allowed to live. Everyone between the ages of sixteen and sixty-five was required to work. Men found employment in one of the workshops or in construction or in the nearby fields or mines. Women tended to work in agriculture, food preparation, in the clothing warehouse or as nurses and cleaners. There were hierarchies to these positions and a few were prized, especially those that allowed some freedom from the constant watch of the SS, a little privacy, access to food or some protection from being on a further transport list.

My grandparents hoped that Pišta in Prague could put in a good word with the Terezín Elders. Like them, thousands of other inmates hoped to attain a favourable nod from the Elders that might convey some form of sanctuary.

In 1942, with both Otto and Ella interned at Terezín, the family established a connection to smuggle clothes, food and other useful items into the camp. They managed to secure the services of a Czech gendarme and a local woman. Each time a parcel went in, a letter or two was smuggled out of the camp.

Unlike 'official' correspondence sent from the post office, which served for propaganda purposes, Otto and Ella's letters were not limited in length or censored. Yet there was no guarantee that their letters would have been read only by the intended recipients, so they were guarded and coded with nicknames or initials often used for people or contraband. *Bekannte*, the German word for acquaintance, was clearly a reference to German marks. There were constant references to the fluctuating price of 'Robert' or 'Roberty', most likely a foreign currency, perhaps Swiss francs. The letters returned time and again to the treasured parcels, the supply of which kept them fed, enabled them to help others in the camp and gave them the means to barter. The letters often mentioned the 'kind gentleman', in all likelihood a friendly Czech gendarme, and 'Mrs Rosa', a laundress who could enter and move freely around Terezín. In order to safeguard the couriers, their real names were never disclosed.

These letters, and Zdenka's account, indicate that the family's usual method of supply was to deliver a parcel to Bohušovice Station, 2 kilometres from Terezín. From there, a trusted intermediary would bring the parcel, suitably concealed, by wheelbarrow to the camp. This incurred great risk for all involved. If Mrs Rosa or the kind gentleman had been caught assisting inmates in this way, they would have faced severe punishment. The consequences for Otto and Ella would have been far worse.

In January 1942, nine men had been publicly hanged in Terezín. Their crime had been to smuggle letters out to their families. The SS staged these public executions to set an example and show their sovereignty. Sending anything in or out of the camp was a risk for all concerned. Yet it was also an important emotional and physical lifeline for the family. Lotar, methodical and thorough, kept a record of the contents of every parcel that was sent to my grandparents in Terezín. The box that Madla gave me, that Lotar had stored for decades, contained the inventory for each of the eighty parcels: smoked meats, sugar, Ovomaltine, butter, soap, flashlight batteries, shoe polish and chocolate bonbons all appear regularly. Lotar's box also contained the dozens of pages of letters written by my grandparents to their boys, which were smuggled out in return. The letters burst with their thoughts, emotions and practical details of life at Terezín, as well as requests for food, clothing, currency and messages from other inmates to their families outside. As a contemporaneous record, they provide an unflinching first-hand perspective on the conditions within the camp. For me, they also offer an intimate glimpse of the personalities of the grandparents I never knew.

An October letter from Ella to her boys, her *golden ones*, sent reassurance that her living conditions were better than those of many others, to the point of arousing envy, in fact. She wrote that she was lucky to have found a job as a housekeeper for a Czech man who belonged to the higher echelons of the Terezín hierarchy by virtue of overseeing the woodwork workshop. This role allowed her to benefit from his somewhat better circumstances and degree of influence and, critically, allowed room for the hope that *all would be fine except for those excursions to the East*. Most inmates of Terezín did not know until later the precise consequences of those journeys east, but rumours abounded. My family members were certain that they must avoid these journeys at all costs.

Ella cleaned and cooked for Engineer František Langer, or *Eng. L*, as she referred to him in the letters. He lived alone in the camp and had use of some rooms by the workshops. This meant that Ella could keep some of her belongings away from the desperate occupants of the bunk rooms, to which she had to return each night. The workshop rooms allowed her some precious privacy. A third letter from Ella, of November 1942, described her surprise at seeing Otto, joy at the reunion and heartbreak at having to watch as he too endured the misery. She herself felt stronger and better able to handle their appalling circumstances, having been already introduced *into those terrible secrets*.

Ella announced that she had secured a greatly fought-over certificate, *with much effort*, to enable Otto to work as a chemical engineer, which might reduce the likelihood of the dreaded transportation east.

Some of Ella and Otto's family were also interned in Terezín that fall. When Ella arrived, she had encountered Rudolf and Jenny Neumann, Erich and Ota's parents. Rudolf Pollak, the widower of Ella's sister Martha, was there with his daughters, Hana and Zita, as well as his second wife Josefa, and their teenage son Jiří, a young poet. Some of Jiří Pollak's poems can be seen today in the archives of Terezín and the Jewish Museum in Prague.

Finding and helping one another cannot have been easy among sixty thousand, segregated by age and gender, but perhaps there was a little comfort to be had from the sight of a familiar face in the sad loneliness of those crowds.

Otto's first letter, written in December, was markedly negative in tone and recounted that, while the journey to the east was still postponed for the time being, Ella had a police

Weisung, a pending criminal deportation order, hanging over her. *Weisungs* were issued for offences like smoking, possessing prohibited items or absconding from a transport, and had to be avoided at all costs. Rumours were they meant certain death on deportation. Otto added: *We don't see each other much. I miss her.* He carefully catalogued all the things that he needed: Roberty in every form, lighter, batteries, clothing, shoe polish or hair dye, soap and, of course, food. His letter warned them:

> . . . *not to expect sensible news . . . this is one crazy mess . . . there is barely enough food to half feed you and he who does not have a way to supplement will die of hunger, unnoticed. Housing and hygiene conform to that of antiquated POW camps . . . Here, man becomes a hopeless, selfish animal that does not care about anything else but, at the expense of a fellow sufferer or even the closest relative, to gain some little advantage.*
>
> *In the short time since our separation I have somehow forgotten all that I left behind with you, what used to be important seems now inane . . . I know you will not understand me as I, myself, nowadays, do not understand the life I left with you . . . It is all like a terrible dream . . . 'Live life well', this can only be appreciated by someone who has sunk so low into humiliation as I have . . . You don't have to worry about me . . . I am quite active, in order to get out of the — hopefully — initial difficulties and to adapt to the unreal local circumstances. Please be patient with me, brain cells do not work with the same accuracy as in normal circumstances. If I were not to write, it would be out of fear and nothing else. Think of me as little as possible . . . Life from 14 days ago has disappeared into darkness.*

Lotar and Hans must have felt a profound sadness at reading Otto's first letter from the camp, one that echoed across the years when my father's sobbing rocked the fence near Bubny nearly half a century later. Those few words Hans could manage in 1990 – 'This is where we said goodbye' – allowed me a glimpse of the separation and the sorrow of the months that followed. Yet the full meaning of the words was not clear to me for another twenty-five years.

There was a small rectangle of very thin paper among the others in my father's box. At 8.5 cm by 6 cm, it is by far the smallest item. The letters 'CC' are inked in red in a black box. On the line below is my father's name. Three large black digits, 449, are printed above.

This tiny relic was an official transport ticket, the slip of paper that a deported person would hand in to the officials just before boarding the wagon to a camp.

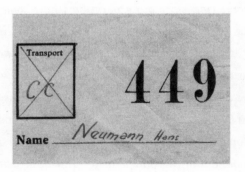

I know now that Otto's transport was CC and his number was 448. Spared this journey with his father, Hans held on to his transport ticket. He could have torn it in pieces, burned or crumpled it in relief at his reprieve. But Hans had done no such thing. Amid the dozens of typewritten A4 documents, official identity cards and photos, this wisp of yellowing paper stands out, minute and immaculately preserved. Perhaps a reminder of his survival. Perhaps a hallmark of his guilt.

10

THE SHADOW BENEATH
THE CANDLE

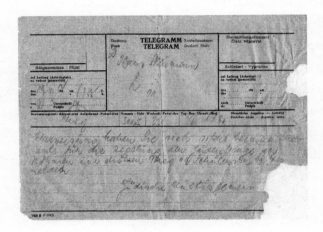

A second telegram arrived for Hans on 18 November 1942, hours after the message that had been his salvation from the transport. This new missive demanded that he report at once to the 'Central Office for the Regulation of the Jewish Question in Bohemia and Moravia'.

This entity, originally known as the Central Office for Jewish Emigration, sat atop the SS command structure in Prague. It had been established and led by the notorious Adolf Eichmann, who held ultimate responsibility for the logistics of the Final Solution, the plan to exterminate the Jews.

In November 1942, when my father was asked to report there, the department was led by Hans Günther, who managed a staff of thirty-two SS men and reported directly to Eichmann, by then back in Berlin. The office oversaw all the activities of the Jewish Councils in Prague and in Terezín and remained tasked with the deportation of the Jews from the Protectorate. It was uncommon for a Jew to be summoned to the Central Office, and my boxes and archives offer no evidence that might explain the summons.

Nonetheless, each document in the box was kept for a reason, sometimes sentimental, often practical and, on occasion, both. Each paper yields a story, a reason for its inclusion as a memento or clue to the puzzle that was my father's life during the war. Hans would have had some purpose in keeping this telegram. The document itself or the event it recalled must have been important to him. Perhaps he believed that proof of that visit might be useful later. The consensus among the experts with whom I have spoken is that the most likely explanation is my father was called in to pay a bribe. This might have been agreed upon for his retrieval from the transport or perhaps was settled in the hope of sparing his parents' lives.

Whatever the reason for the meeting, Hans must have attended that SS office quite alone, utterly shaken by his time at Bubny and his father's departure just hours before. He had to muster the courage and calm to handle whatever was presented to him by the SS officer in charge of his case. It must have been a risky and delicate encounter, carefully transacting with people who held his fate, as well as that of his parents, in their hands. Though the SS officer had the power, he too must have been apprehensive, facing chastisement, demotion or worse if his actions were discovered.

Hans and the SS man would likely have trodden this strange and frightening path together. Hans could not afford the slightest error of judgement. If he uttered the wrong word, if he hinted at insubordination, if his composure slipped, if he refused whatever was asked of him, it could have been disastrous. We can only assume from the lack of repercussions that Hans conducted himself with perfect deference and concluded his business without incident. The man who gave this performance was not the unfortunate and chaotic boy prankster who was always late. This Hans was punctual and punctilious, at the mercy of the world about him but entirely in control of himself. This was the man he would have to become in order to survive the war.

In a letter dated 1 December 1942, Ella wrote to her boys:

Jointly we will get through anything. Distance cannot separate us. I have the strong will to last at any cost. You too, my golden darlings, have to use your head and give up all sentimentality. We have won the first two rounds and as we approach the final, the stronger we need to be.

Hans, at twenty-one, was certainly finding a new strength and maturity. But he was far from being led solely by his head. He refused to stay in Libčice now that Otto had been transported. Jews were required by law to reside in their registered abode, but Hans did not. In Libčice he would have been alone in the large house, heavy with memories. He would have been away from Lotar and Zdenka and his friends in Prague, without radio, telephone, bicycle or car. At the prospect of this isolation he decided to ignore Ella's plea for steely rationality and risk breaking the law.

He determined to spend weekdays in the city. He arranged

for a friendly Libčice neighbour, Pajmas, to visit the house daily. Pajmas had also been caring for Gin, the fox terrier who had outlived their beloved older dog, Jerry. In July 1941 the Nazis had prohibited Jews from keeping pets but the neighbour had agreed to declare the Neumanns' fox terrier as his own. Hans travelled back to Libčice at weekends, sometimes driven by Zdeněk, Míla or Zdenka but often alone by train. Lotar, by then remarried to Zdenka and officially registered as living in the city, did not have a permit that allowed him to travel by train.

Zdeněk and Míla had both offered to help hide Hans during his days in Prague, but he did not want to endanger them further. Things with Míla were difficult; her parents were worried about the risks created by a relationship with a Jew and were doing their best to persuade her to spend less time with Hans. Zdeněk had, along with other Czechs of his age, just received a summons to report for war work, in his case to a factory in Berlin. Zdeněk would not be able to help Hans in Prague for long. The evenings and weekends when Zdeněk and Míla sat with Hans laughing, reading poems, drinking and smoking were already dangerous enough.

Lotar and Zdenka took him in. A small apartment of Zdenka's, a little way from the centre of town, had just become vacant, and to keep him safer, Zdenka and Lotar moved in with Hans. They pretended to be a family of three, two brothers and their older sister. Despite increasing difficulties, Zdenka had managed to purchase another set of identification papers on the black market. Zdenka, Zdeněk, Lotar and Hans worked on changing the name and the photograph. They chose the fictitious name of Jan Rubeš. Lotar's own faked identity was in the name of his friend Ivan Rubeš, so the fabricated identity was created to pass Hans off as Ivan's younger brother.

The caretaker of the building had been happily employed by Zdenka's family for decades. She did not ask questions and was trusted to keep their secret. I do not know how they came and went, whether they wore their yellow stars as they entered the building when they returned from work, passing into a hidden world, or if they took the risk of not donning the stars. There are no photographs from this period. The documents left behind reveal little, indicating only that Hans lived in secret with his brother and sister-in-law at an apartment in Prague 5.

Zdenka later recounted one memory of her time living with Hans in 1943. He had been left alone in the apartment, as she had to go to the farm and Lotar had been called in to Montana. Zdeněk had already been despatched to Berlin. Míla was away with her family.

Hans had two days off from work and had promised Zdenka that he would be quiet and behave responsibly. It was a very cold day, and the heating in the apartment suddenly broke down. Hans was freezing but did not want to attract attention by asking the caretaker for help. He decided to fix the heating himself, starting with the kitchen radiator. He had never been very good at manual tasks. As he grappled with a valve, it broke. Water poured from the radiator onto the wooden floorboards and seeped down to the floor below. Hans grabbed all the sheets and towels from the bedrooms and bathroom and threw them down in an attempt to staunch the leaking.

Zdenka returned to find Hans completely drenched, on

his hands and knees. She called the caretaker and went downstairs to offer her apologies to the neighbours for their cracked and dripping ceiling. Her younger brother had just arrived from the countryside, she explained, and was not used to modern plumbing. Always charming, she offered to pay for any repairs. She presented them with a bottle of plum brandy and, for good measure, added some black-market bonbons that had been intended for Otto and Ella. When she was satisfied that the risk of suspicion was removed, Zdenka went back upstairs and instructed a shivering Hans to change into his warmest clothes. She affectionately wrapped him in a thick wool blanket and admonished him. As Hans warmed his fingers by nursing a cup of tea, instead of being angry Zdenka teased him: 'I always knew it was risky to live with two Jews but never imagined that it was because one of them was going to flood the building. I now see why they call you the unfortunate one.'

Zdenka and Hans both laughed in relieved amusement. Lotar was less entertained by the occurrence and fretted for days that the flood had aroused speculation about the unusual trio among the neighbours. His anxiety turned out to have been unfounded, and had Zdenka not written it down many years later, this incident would have been forgotten.

As the Prague winter took hold, life continued for the three of them, their efforts focused on keeping their heads down and working. The days revolved around obtaining goods for the illicit packages for Otto and Ella and ensuring that they were delivered. News from Terezín trickled out both through the Council in Prague and in the letters. The boys learnt that their uncle Rudolf Neumann had died of heart trouble and that his wife, Jenny, had been ordered on to Auschwitz, beyond the reach of parcels and letters. Uncle Josef, with his wife and two children, had been sent further east as well.

In early December, Otto and Ella's names were included in a transport list for Poland, but Lotar and Zdenka did everything they could to ensure that they were removed. Lotar would later write that their efforts to keep them near Prague in Terezín were 'superhuman'.

In reality, this meant sending parcels with a surplus of food and currency for bribes and also beseeching Pišta for help from the Elders. It is not clear whether it was thanks to their efforts or down to luck, but the transport to Auschwitz was postponed, and Otto and Ella spent their first Christmas in Terezín. Letters from the camp started arriving almost weekly in December, and while Otto reported that the contents of many of the parcels had been looted in transport, what reached them was enough to keep them fed and protected. Otto and Ella were delighted to receive the packages and described how they used the food, clothes, items and money for themselves and to help others. Their letters were filled with news of family and friends inside the camp, to be passed on to relatives outside. They were also crammed with requests for more food, more currency and all the everyday household things that were so crucial – dark shoe polish or hair dye, lighter fuel, currencies, sturdy boots, batteries, soap.

Otto and Ella wrote separately. They lived in different buildings, segregated by gender and job. Otto explained that he tried to have dinners with Ella, as she had access to cooking facilities, but this was not always possible.

The new distance between them was not solely physical;

they also differed in their attitude towards their surroundings. In the senseless world of the camp, they coped differently, and the words in their letters reflect this.

Otto was dour. He persisted in being appalled at the conditions, outraged and burdened by the immorality and inhumanity of the place. He wrote that, even after a short time in the camp, the typical inmate had

> grown numb and was like a chased animal that only seeks food and rest. It will be difficult for those who return from here to recover any sliver of their humanity. No one reads or engages in conversation, it is all bitter arguments about places in queues. All feelings of emotion, sensibility or sexuality have been extinguished. Women here suffer from early menopause and the men are rendered impotent.

And yet he tried to maintain a degree of positivity when he added, *But it all seems like paradise compared to the alternative in Poland.*

In another message, Otto implored Hans and Lotar to *love each other, that is the only way you will be able overcome the evil that lies ahead.*

Otto managed to keep his sense of irony, despite it all. He wrote of his happiness at being assigned a bunk bed and no longer having to sleep on the floor. He was thankful that his dormitory, *unlike the ones infested with bedbugs and fleas, housed only fleas.* A later letter says: *Oh Zdenka, how you would laugh! I queued up for a dumpling for lunch and it fell to the ground but the new me nevertheless ate it with delight. It did make me miss dear Mrs Novakova's dumplings at Montana. What an artist she was!*

In her communications with the boys, Ella continued to be more optimistic than Otto and was also pragmatic about life in the camp. This was perhaps due to the fact that her living conditions were marginally better, but it was also her nature to take a sunnier view. Her letters were brisker, more concise, less descriptive and critical of her surroundings. They were heartfelt and lacked irony. She worked to remain positive about both her environment and her ability to withstand it. She concentrated on an imagined future together with her boys and on practical ways to attain it. She wrote that she was working hard to obtain better jobs and protection from the transports to the east for both her and Otto. She remained focused on ensuring that Otto stayed healthy and did not lose weight. Ella also asked for supplies but emphasised that her strength was holding up and the parcels should not be sent if doing so presented a risk. *I have lived here for so long without anything that I can do without it all for a while longer.*

In early December 1942 she remained hopeful that this would be the first and last holiday that they all spent apart.

The letters continued regularly throughout the winter months and were filled with advice, pleas and mundane detail. Ella asked for pickles and vanilla extract. Otto explained that he needed work boots and longed for gingerbread biscuits and Christmas cake.

I have no record of the boys' holidays during that winter of 1942. There are no documents, no photographs, no subsequent written recollections, but it seems doubtful that there would have been many celebrations. I do not have the letters that were sent to Otto and Ella, but the replies tell us that Lotar worried and sought Otto's counsel about handling things at the factory.

On 19 December, Otto advised Lotar not to fret excessively about business matters at Montana. *Here, one looks at things differently. There are between 80–100 corpses per day.* Their oldest terrier, Jerry, he wrote, *had received a better burial than the dozens that died daily in Terezín.* In reference to Lotar's gloom, he opined: *I don't quite understand Lotík's remark that life is not really worth it any more. It is a strange comment for us to hear as we think of the life outside these confines as more than a paradise. Everything is relative, so I am asking you Lotík – please don't despair. Don't give up!*

At the end of December, Otto had to inform his sons that Ella had fallen ill with stomach ulcers but was being taken care of by *great medical experts* at the Terezín hospital. He urged his boys to have a good time and raise a New Year's toast.

The brothers struggled despite the relative freedom and safety of their life in Prague. Lotar, always the more conscientious of the two, bore the weight of it all, of the parcels, the endless requests to Pišta. He became physically ill with worry and some days could barely function at all.

Hans wrote less often than Lotar. His parents' replies do not show a concern about his state of mind. If he was depressed, I imagine he kept it to himself. In fact, Otto and Ella wanted to know more about their younger son and asked specifically for him to write with news.

The winter bore on and turned to spring. At the beginning of March 1943, yet another deportation notice arrived at Libčice. For the third time, Hans had been designated a transport, this time the day before Lotar's twenty-fifth birthday, on 9 March.

On this occasion, they wasted no time with work letters and

calls to the Council. Pišta had already warned them that letters attesting indispensability were no longer even being read by officials. He could not be taken off the transport list this time. The brothers had learned enough from the Terezín letters to know that Hans had to avoid deportation altogether.

There was only one option. Hans would have to abscond.

Lotar turned for help to their trusted manager at Montana. Frank Novák, whose wife was the creator of the dumplings that Otto dreamed of in Terezín, had always been Otto's right-hand man. He was loyal, courageous and, above all, practical. Lotar and Frank devised a plan to hide Hans. They would construct a false wall in a side room at the factory, concealing a few square feet of floor space, just enough to accommodate him. The secret chamber could not be reached from inside the factory. Machinery would be installed in front of part of the new wall. The rest of the surface would be hidden behind a stack of paint drums, originally two deep but now consisting of only a single row. Access was just about manageable from the outside by scrambling through an old half-submerged window frame. The grille could be removed, allowing the occupant to crawl out into the garden. Keeping this arrangement secret could not have been easy, with some forty-five people still working at Montana. Most would have, in more normal circumstances, supported the family. Few could be trusted now, given the penalties faced by those harbouring fugitives and the rewards on offer to informants.

Frank, Hans and Lotar built and disguised the compartment over a weekend. Then they waited. The change seemed to pass unnoticed by the workers who clocked in on Monday morning. It was decided that Hans should remain silently in the cavity during factory hours. As soon as the staff went home, food and clothes could be brought to him and his bedpan cleaned. When the factory emptied and it was dark, Hans could crawl out of the window into the shadows and breathe the crisp air. He could then access the factory to use the shower in the changing room and heat up food in the kitchen next to the dining area, but he was to do so only at night and without turning on a single light. It was vital that neighbours remain oblivious to his presence. He was to keep things immaculate and perfectly untouched. It was critical that there was not so much as a coffee mug out of place when the workers arrived each morning. Hans was provided with a blanket and a mattress, a torch and candles. He would have to remain in this makeshift secret room until a more permanent place could be found.

They recognised that the key to hiding was not to stay in one place for too long, to move before people noticed the inevitable signs of another person's presence. Montana was the obvious place for the Gestapo to look for Hans, so obvious that paradoxically it seemed to them all, at least temporarily, the best place to hide. The local people knew the Neumann family and the boys by sight. Frank, the Montana manager, once again arranged the services of his cousin the barber who had dyed Otto's hair before his transport. He visited at night and bleached Hans's hair a pale ash, so that if anyone glimpsed him around the factory he would not easily be recognised. Just before dawn on 9 March 1943, instead of heading to Veletržní Palác near Bubny, the newly blond Hans entered his secret room.

That same day the Gestapo received notification that Hans

Neumann of Libčice had not registered at Bubny for his transport. He had officially absconded and was duly placed on the SS wanted list in Prague. Hans's citizen's registry card can be found in the archives in Prague today. It still has a scribbled note, from April 1943, to the effect that any attempt by this man to register his domicile anywhere should be reported immediately to the Gestapo.

Lotar would linger after the last workers went home every night. Zdenka and Míla took turns delivering food and helping him with cleaning chores. Mr Novák would arrive particularly early to ensure that Hans was safe and that any indication that someone was using the facilities at night had been removed.

Frank Novák and Marie Nováková in Czechoslovakia, 1940s.

Frank Novák took an enormous risk helping Lotar and Hans. His wife, Marie, was, understandably, deeply worried about the consequences for the family if he were discovered helping to hide a Jew. Jana, Frank's stepdaughter, who was seven at the time, still remembers their numerous and impassioned debates on the subject.

I reached Jana through an organisation called Memory of Nations, which collates the memories of witnesses of the war. She had told them her story. Jana and her younger half-sister, Eva, agreed to meet me and my family during our Czech visit in October 2017. We met outside the old Montana factory building, which still stands in Libeň. It comprises now, as it did then, two buildings, a rather elegant and modern 1930s white and grey office block built onto the side of a more rugged nineteenth-century yellow brick warehouse.

It is no longer a factory and has seen many occupants over the past fifty years. Most recently, the building has been used as a disco and rented out as a space for concerts and parties. Still, much like it was when Montana was in existence, it is surrounded by other factories and offices. When we visited, a crew of painters and builders was busily redecorating. There we stood, Jana and I, with no language in common, both of us raised by men who had risked their lives together in this place, one to save the other.

My children, husband, mother, aunt, Eva, her husband, Mr Nedvídek, and Magda, the diligent Czech researcher, made up the party. Magda and Mr Nedvídek acted as translators as Jana and I pieced together our shared moment of history.

Jana and Eva were eager to share what they remembered and did their best to answer the dozens of questions we had for them. It struck us all at that moment that my children and I really owed our own lives to Mr Novák's extraordinary bravery, without which my father was unlikely to have survived. When I thanked them, Eva grabbed my hand, looked at me, her eyes brimming with humanity and grace, and uttered some words that Mr Nedvídek translated, 'Please stop. Your thanks are not due, because my father did not do anything extraordinary. He only did the correct thing. Simply, he did what everybody should have done. We should all, as a country, have behaved like Frank Novák. And it is us who apologise to you that we did not.'

We must have seemed an odd and disparate bunch to the workers repainting the building in Libeň. Eleven people of all ages and heights, some with walking sticks, a couple hunched in teenage awkwardness, all attempting to understand and be understood, pointing at and asking questions about an empty disco, while some hugged and a few wept in that industrial estate on a Tuesday morning.

As one walks to the right of the building, the low-lying window by which my father entered and left his secret room is visible. He sat inside for days on end in silence, reading his books, writing his letters. Míla brought him puzzles and stitched him a small doll for company and for luck.

My father kept the handmade good-luck doll in the box that he left me. Time has softened its colours and erased the inked features of its face. The details of the dress and the delicately knitted red and cream bonnet still evidence the care with which it was crafted.

In early April, when Zdeněk returned for a few days to Prague from his job in Berlin, Míla brought him to visit Hans late one evening at Montana. The three friends sat in the gloom of the night-time factory, happy to be together again, their simple supper dimly visible in the candlelight. Zdeněk talked about his life in Berlin. He explained that he was working for a paint manufacturer called Warnecke & Böhm, making industrial lacquer for the Luftwaffe, the German air force. Most young and able German men had joined the army, and the factory was understaffed. Zdeněk was so busy with work that he had little time for anything else.

'We need good chemists. I wish you could come and help me, Handa. Life would be easier then!' he joked.

But Hans did not laugh. Absorbed by the candle's flame, he simply murmured an old Czech saying: '*Pod svícnem bývá největší tma.*' The darkest shadow lies beneath the candle.

Míla did not understand, but Zdeněk, who knew Hans so well, grasped the meaning instantly. 'Not in this case it isn't! It is an insane idea, Hans!'

'That's where you are wrong,' Hans replied evenly.

The Gestapo were looking for Hans Neumann in and around Prague. They would never think of looking in the German capital; no one on the run chose to go there to hide. The searchlight scorched Prague, and they would undoubtedly find him if he stayed there. If he travelled to the centre of it all, to Berlin, to the heart of the Reich, just beneath the candle, where the darkness was greatest, the Gestapo might never find him.

There, he would hide in plain sight. He would give himself a new name – Jan Šebesta, like the fellow who got out of town in an old nursery rhyme from their childhood: '*Jede, jede Šebesta, jede, jede do města . . .*' Go, go Šebesta . . . He would become someone else entirely, so that in reality he would not be hiding at all. He would go to Berlin. He would not have to remain invisible any longer. 'You have gone green, Zdeněk, don't fret. It was all your idea, and it is a good one. It really is the ideal place. I will come and work with you at the factory in Berlin.'

Míla initially thought that Hans was joking. Zdenka, for whom daring was second nature, agreed that it was a perfect plan. Lotar fretted about every detail and was anguished at the thought of allowing his younger brother to travel on his own to Berlin. However, the simple fact remained that it was only a matter of time until the Gestapo came looking for Hans at Montana. Eventually, even Lotar reluctantly accepted that there was no alternative. They all agreed to the plan. No physical characteristic prevented Hans from living among the Germans. Otto, never a follower of religious dogma, had refused to have the boys circumcised; his fastidious obstinacy, as Ella always referred to it, had in this instance proved an unlikely blessing.

Together with Míla and Zdenka, Hans and Lotar went to work on constructing a cover for Hans. They needed to make another identity card, as the one in the name of Jan Rubeš was about to expire. Lotar thought it would be best to use an entirely different name anyway, in order not to expose his friend Ivan to further risk. The name of Jan Šebesta seemed unremarkable and gentile enough. In the weeks they had to prepare, Zdenka could not source another identity card, not at any price. Míla volunteered her own card. It had been issued by the Protectorate in 1940, so the text appeared in both Czech and German. As she was a gentile, it lacked the stamp with the 'J' for Jew. She managed for weeks without it and then reported it lost. The report from 1943 can be seen today in the police archives in Prague.

Lotar and Hans armed themselves with magnifying glasses and solvents and carefully erased Míla's name without damaging the paper fibres. Hans's handwriting had always been illegible, so Zdenka, the better calligrapher, carefully penned in the name Jan Šebesta and his fictional details. They listed his place of birth as Stará Boleslav, a small town northeast of Prague, known as Alt Bunzlau in German. His birth date, which he would have to remember easily, became 11 March

1921, the year of Hans's own birth and two days after he should have disappeared in the transport to Terezín. Perhaps 11 March was the precise day when Zdeněk and Hans had, in the dark confines of the cubicle, first devised Jan. Maybe the date was just chosen because it was the day after Lotar's birthday. This remains a small mystery that I will probably never solve. The other particulars – the height, face shape and hair and eye colour – were all Hans's own: 182 cm, oval, chestnut, green. Finally, Míla's photograph was removed, burned and replaced with a head shot of Hans, and Jan Šebesta's identity was complete.

Forgery of the second key piece of identification needed for travel, a passport, was an altogether tougher proposition and beyond their resources. A passport was needed for the journey Hans was to make, as his card was from the Protectorate, so he would have to use Zdeněk's. It was settled.

On his return to Berlin, Zdeněk asked his boss for a special permit to visit his 'ill' mother in Prague in early May.

Hans remained in his hiding place, terrified that he would be found before he could enact his plan and only marginally less afraid of the plan itself. Eager and anxious, he endured a month of waiting for Zdeněk's return so that he could escape and leave his identity as Hans behind. As the hours crawled by, he continued to be careful and silent in his dark and damp cell.

One day, when I was still a schoolgirl in Caracas and my father sat transfixed by mechanisms in the long narrow room, I worked up the courage to interrupt him. I asked him when it was that he had first looked inside a watch. He swung the light aside, turned to me and raised his magnifying visor so that I could see his eyes. They were mazes of moss and still gently round despite the wrinkles. He called me towards him and put his arm around my back protectively as he spoke.

He explained to me that he had become enthralled by watch mechanisms in Prague when he was a young man. He said that it was during a period when he had so much time on his hands that he felt that time had stopped.

How could time have stopped?

'Because,' he said, 'and you will understand this when you are older, sometimes you just feel that everything around you has come to an end. You feel that you are completely alone, that time is frozen and that you are invisible. At first, you might feel exhilarated by the sense of freedom, but then you'll be frightened that you are lost and you will never be able to go back.'

He explained that when he first felt this, he had been isolated and afraid and had prised open his watch case to verify that time was indeed passing. The rhythm of the watch might have been imagined. Sound was not enough, he needed to see and touch it. It was the first time that he had dismantled a mechanism. The turning wheels, ticking each second away, had reassured him.

It was then that he had comprehended the importance of time.

I realise now that this must have happened while he was hiding in that dark and narrow chamber at the factory. His days alone, caged in the cramped stillness, were a void of timelessness. The ticking on his wrist would have grown louder in the absolute silence of his confinement. This would not have been sufficient. In those endless hours, he momentarily feared that time had ceased.

My father took apart his watch because he needed to ascertain that the noise was not only inside his head, that it was not just his thumping heart; that there was order somewhere, and that time was real and going by. To examine the movement, he used the magnifying glasses that they had brought to alter his papers. He found comfort in the tiny universe of the mechanism, complex and yet perfectly orchestrated. He willed his hands to be steady, his fingers to be precise. He played with the crown and springs of the wind-up and studied the wheels and pivots as they moved. When everything around him seemed frozen and he was lost and invisible, my father oriented himself by learning how those minute spinning wheels worked with such perfect precision that they managed to keep time.

I I

ZDENĚK'S FRIENDS, HANS AND JAN

Zdeněk Tůma *c.* 1942.

Zdeněk Tůma risked his life for my father. He returned to Prague in the first days of May 1943 and let Hans have his passport so he could travel to Berlin. It was impossible to predict which document a border guard might ask for on such journeys. Identity cards, passport, work or travel permit. The demands seemed to shift, perhaps to throw off forgers, and was as much dependent on the rules as it was on the whim of any particular official.

Hans had his false identity card, but the SS, the gendarmes or the German police might just as easily want to see a passport. They might well demand to see both. Hans's new card could not bear Zdeněk's name, as he hoped to find a job with him at the same paint factory in Berlin. There was no alternative. He was to travel with two sets of papers in different names, and he had to take the risk of both being seen together.

Czechs making the journey to Berlin during the war needed an additional travel permit. In Hans's case, it must have been forged, but the document was not among his papers, so I do not know whether it carried Zdeněk's name or that of Hans's new identity. Either would have posed yet another risk.

A cursory review of the physical features listed in Zdeněk's passport, let alone an inspection of the photograph, would have awoken even the sleepiest guard to the fraud. Zdeněk and Hans looked nothing like each other. The barber had been called in once more, this time to darken Hans's hair slightly to match Zdeněk's, but this had not been enough. Zdeněk was much shorter than Hans, with wiry hair swept up and back from a high forehead. His eyes were a light-blue, sharp and narrow, while Hans's were a deep green, gentle and wide.

The risks for Hans would be appalling and immediate, but the danger faced by Zdeněk was no less so. Even giving a cigarette to a Jew was forbidden, so lending a passport to assist a Jew in evading the Gestapo would likely result in imprisonment or death. Zdeněk would have to wait for days, wondering whether his passport would be returned safely or whether he would be asked to pay the greatest price for his dearest friend.

And yet my father had mentioned Zdeněk only once to me, in passing, at breakfast on the morning of his class reunion in

Prague in 1990. Zdeněk was otherwise consigned to that silent space where my father kept his memories. In fact, I realise now that he made only two faltering attempts to tell me about his war at all. His bids happened within a few weeks of each other and raised more questions than they answered.

In the summer of 1992 I was living in Boston, having just finished my college degree. One evening I walked into my apartment and pressed the flickering button on my answering machine. The soft voice of Miguel, my older half-brother on my father's side, filled the room, urging me to return his call without delay. Twenty-three years my senior, Miguel had actually been named Michal when he was born in Prague in 1947. His mother was my father's first wife, Míla. The age disparity between us meant that we had grown closer as I approached adulthood. Miguel was earnest and kind but had always had a difficult relationship with our father.

Their increasingly sporadic conversations tended to end with Miguel losing his temper. They had resorted instead to writing each other letters to avoid the inevitable clash. At the time, Miguel craved approval and a verbalised kind of love, which our father was incapable of providing. Our father in return demanded perfection, precision and a strength that Miguel lacked. As much as it aggrieved them, they simply could not understand each other. Their experiences, expectations and languages were so wildly different that now, looking back, having hoped for anything else seems hopelessly naive.

Miguel's message was followed by one from my father's assistant in Caracas, which explained Miguel's call. She apologised for having to tell me in this way but informed me that Lotar, my uncle and godfather, had died the previous day. She told me that my father was on a business trip in Europe and was headed directly to Lotar's home in Switzerland for the funeral. She added that she was sure he would call me as soon as he had a moment.

Lotar was seventy-six and had been suffering with Parkinson's disease for years. I was profoundly saddened but not surprised that my father's beloved and tender older brother had died. We had lived on different continents for most of my life, but he had always been an affectionate, softly spoken presence, with a benevolence that was somehow enhanced by his great height.

I called Miguel immediately, and he explained that he had wanted to reach me personally to tell me about Lotar. He had assumed, correctly, that our father would not telephone with the news. We had a long chat that day. We reminisced about our uncle and cheered each other up by exchanging memories. Miguel regaled me with funny stories about the holiday he was having with his wife in Aruba. I told him that I was hoping to start a job in September at a publishing house in Italy. We had not spoken in a while, and it felt like an easy if overdue catch-up. We joked about how remarkably balanced we had both turned out considering our father's inability, for all his brilliance, to deal with anything emotive.

My father had always been close to Lotar. Their personalities contrasted sharply, but the fondness between them was obvious. Throughout the war and afterwards they always depended on each other. They created a business and rebuilt their lives together. Hans was deeply upset by his older brother's death, but Miguel and I knew that he was incapable of expressing emotions of sorrow or anger. He could be affectionate and loving, though sometimes a little mutedly. It was as if there were a concrete wall around his feelings, and he feared that even a trickle of emotion would be the prelude to the dam bursting.

Two days after my chat with my brother, I was awakened before dawn by the telephone. It was Miguel's wife, Florinda. She was distraught. Miguel's heart had stopped and he had died during the night. He was forty-four. On the day when our father was attending his own brother's funeral, I had to call him in Switzerland to tell him that he must return to Caracas at once, because his only son was dead.

Still stunned, I arrived in Caracas and spent that afternoon and evening with my brother's widow at the funeral home. Early the next morning, I crossed the awakening city to collect my father from the airport by the coast. Together we drove to Miguel's funeral through a torrential rainstorm that bowed the strongest palms and roiled the mangoes, ceibas and oaks. At the graveside, we leaned into each other under our umbrella and watched the handfuls of dirt being tossed down onto the glistening wood casket. I scarcely dared look at my father, and when I did glance up I could see only his tearless profile deformed by grief. I clasped his hand and tried to steady it as it shook with the same force that had swayed the fence at Bubny. I have never witnessed a person in such torment. As we headed back home in the car, I told him I would pack my things in Boston, cancel my plans and come back home to be with him. There was nothing more I could say.

After a fitful night, I found my father standing at the foot of my bed.

'You are always asking questions, so here you have some answers.'

I sat up startled but still half asleep. He handed me a clutch of white pages and sat down on the edge of my bed. It was a typed translation of a letter addressed to *My dear ones*. It was signed by Lotar.

Bewildered, I read through it. There were references to Hans, Otto and Ella, but the pages seemed filled with the names of countless other people and places, none of which I had heard before. I tried hopelessly to make sense of it. All I could discern was that most of the people mentioned had not survived the war. My father, ashen, looked at me expectantly.

'It's a letter that I brought back from Lotar's house. He wrote it after the war. Do you understand now?' he said almost defiantly. 'Do you understand why I cannot talk about it?'

Before I had a chance to answer, as suddenly as he had appeared, he swept the pages from my hand and left the room. I scrambled into the first pair of jeans and T-shirt I could find and went out to look for him. I walked from room to room, calling out, past the huge jagged paintings in the hallway, onto the chequered terrace edged with sculpted nudes and abstracts in bronze and limestone. The garden door was still locked, so he had not gone further. I headed to the kitchen to ask if they had seen him there and was told that he had taken his car and left for the office. It was seven o'clock on a Sunday morning.

My father never showed me that letter again. I looked for it that day, but he had not left it on his desk in the library or on the counter in his study. I wanted to ask questions about it, but it was clear to me that day that showing it had not been an opening. It was an attempt to close a door on my questions.

I lived in Caracas for the following months so that I could be with him. I worked as best I could but spent most of my free time at home with my father. Even when he was not at the office, he buried himself in work. He was always busy with business issues or new projects or research for something he was writing. When he was not writing or on the phone, or being visited or interviewed, he was alone with his watches in the long narrow room.

Although we lived together in the house, we each faced our sadness in quiet solitude. Occasionally, we would stir ourselves to respond to the invitations that arrived from well-wishers. I would accompany him to the opera or a concert or drinks party. The latter were a little embarrassing because, on my father's insistence, we always arrived perfectly on time. Venezuelans always expect guests to show up about an hour after they are invited. It is an unspoken but unbreakable social rule. Despite his fifty years in Caracas, my father still refused to adapt to the more relaxed Latin American timings. He was relentlessly punctual. So we would arrive at our host's house as the clock turned seven and would bide our time in an empty living room. My father and I would sit on our own with matching highballs, listening to the piercing songs of cicadas and frogs until our flustered hosts eventually appeared. My initial embarrassment gradually faded. I grew to enjoy these moments of quiet rebellion and complicity with my father as we marked time together, alone in other people's houses.

The evenings when we stayed at home and he did not have guests for dinner, we resorted to our usual habits while spending time with each other, solving word or number puzzles or discussing books, art or the news. We never really spoke about personal matters. He seldom asked about my life outside our shared routine, and as a result I never really asked about his. Perhaps this was his objective.

My father's second effort to draw back the curtain on his past came a few months later. He had asked about my plans. I explained that a creative writing course that I had taken at university had led me to think that I wanted to be a writer. He reacted with his characteristically cool scrutiny, carefully testing my thinking rather than expressing a clear view. Then he did something different. Without a word, he disappeared into his office and returned with a single sheet of paper. For a moment I thought it might be Lotar's letter, but when he handed it to me, I saw that it was a typed page in Spanish, his fourth language.

It told the story of a train journey to Berlin.

He said he had not finished it. I read rapidly down the page and noticed immediately a reference to his friend Zdeněk, the man he had met up with on our trip to Prague. My father had written many articles on social issues, government and economics for Venezuelan newspapers but never anything like this, never anything that was remotely personal.

He explained that he was thinking of writing his own story of the war and rather solemnly asked me to help him. I asked if I could keep the document to edit it, but, taking the page back, he said that he would give me the whole manuscript once he had finished it. At that point, all I really knew about his experience of the war came from my glimpses of Lotar's letter and that typed page. A train journey to Berlin, the loss of many lives in his family and, above all, a sense of abject despair.

He showed me only that first page and never again raised the subject of the others. Whenever I asked him about this memoir, he always replied that he was working on it and would let me read it one day. Time passed, and the pages never appeared. He had a first stroke some years later that paralysed his legs and an arm, and I assumed he had not written any more.

A decade later, after his death, I found a clipped bundle of papers at the bottom of the box he left for me. It was a retrospective diary of his escape to Berlin, written in 1991 and 1992. The first page was the one that he had shown me. This was the story he had asked me to help him write.

These reminiscences must have been wrested from wherever they had been buried by the man I thought I knew so well. They represented my father's first and last articulation to me of what had happened to him. They gave a voice to the 'unfortunate boy' whose carefree youthfulness had been sacrificed so that this new and tirelessly disciplined man, Jan Šebesta, might survive.

I now know that my father took the night train to Berlin on 3 May 1943, the 'Elite 147' train that departed Hybernské Station in Prague at one-forty-four a.m. and arrived in Berlin nearly eight hours later, at nine-twenty-three a.m. In the spring of 2018, I travelled alone along the same route. It takes four and a half hours today, and there is no longer a night train. Even if there had been, I would not have been brave enough to take it. I bought a ticket for the noon train on a May morning.

The tracks trace the same path out of Prague as they did in 1943. To my surprise, as the train finally left the suburbs behind and curled along the wooded banks of the Vltava river to my right, I passed through the town of Libčice. From the large carriage windows, I could clearly see the roof, balcony and casements of my grandparents' country house. The train then headed north, weaving along the course of the river, and came within a kilometre of Terezín itself before crossing the former Czech border and pushing on to Dresden. Then, finally, it reached Berlin. I followed my father's route, seventy-five years after his journey, almost to the day, clutching copies of the papers that he had left me.

As I made that pilgrimage, I hoped that the night on which my father travelled was moonless and that, in his fear, he did not notice his parents' house, unlit, as the train rolled onwards. That he did not know how very close he was to them in the blackness, just south of Terezín. I hoped that he felt me cradling him, holding his hand, across the worlds of time and experience which then and now lay between us.

This is what my father wrote about that journey:

The train did not illuminate the tracks. The carriages were dark. The dim light of the aisles only allowed you to see the coming shadows, the delineations of figures moving, the shells of bodies slumped. I could hear the sound of the train incessantly rumbling and churning. There were five others in my compartment, their faces hidden, like mine. The darkness is why I chose this train, this hour. It must have been close to dawn, four hours since we had left Prague. Passengers sitting and swaying with the move-ment of the train, our faces shrouded by our coats that hung from bronze hooks. The others might have slept, but I couldn't. I was too afraid.

We were close to the German border now. I checked my doc-uments again: the ticket, identity card and the passport. I had destroyed my old false identity card under the name Jan Rubeš. I kept the picture but ripped it up in the smallest shreds and burned every one. I still could not believe I was here, outside that room at Montana, on this train. I touched the passport in my left pocket, the one with the permit to cross the border that Zdenka sourced. In my other, I had the identity card that Míla gave me. We had used a chemical to carefully erase the names and mixed the inks to match the colour of the rest of the text. It now read 'Jan Šebesta, Chemist, born in Alt Bunzlau on 11 March 1921.' Only the passport had the name Zdeněk Tůma.

I could still see Míla, her intensely grey eyes that looked at me without tears. I felt her brush her lips against my chin as she hugged me awkwardly and turned away to look at me no more. I knew she had not wanted me to see her anguish.

I sat in a first-class carriage. In front of me a sign read 'Official Personnel Only'. There was nothing official about me, but people see what they expect, and seated here I hoped they would think me trustworthy. I tried to look important, unfazed, as I boarded the train.

I prayed the identity check would be quick in this compartment – a swift formality. I owed Míla the passport also. She was the one who finally convinced Zdeněk. Things were awful enough, no one wanted to take unnecessary risks, so to have this passport was a miracle. On arrival, I was to post the passport back to Prague so that Zdeněk could use it to travel back to Berlin in three days. Helping me meant that they were both risking their lives. Zdeněk had not wanted to let me down but he was terrified for his sake and mine. He was scared that I couldn't pull it off. My main worry was the photo in Zdeněk's passport.

Zdeněk's face was much thinner and more angular than mine. His eyes, like clever piercing darts, were unlike my large green ones. 'You have the dreamy eyes of an artist,' my mother had always said.

The train stopped.

I heard voices that I assumed to be the conductor and the border police. I took the thin glass vial covered in brown rubber from my pocket and placed it at the back of my mouth. I held it between the lower back left molars and the side of my mouth. I was told it would take only a few seconds, a minute at most. Cyanide poisons your nerves so the brain dies first, then the heart. Would death be easy, or would I feel unspeakable pain? 'Passports,' a German voice said. They were not asking for other papers, just passports. Not the papers with the other name. I took a breath. In the darkened carriage, the handheld beam lit up each passport held by every extended hand. Three men had the light flash in their faces, two remained obscured under their hanging coats. I pretended to be asleep. The guard shook me. I kept my face hidden beneath the coat, my eyes half closed. My hand moved the coat a few centimetres to show deference and offered him the passport. He looked at it for a few seconds. I was certain that he must be able see my heart pounding in my chest.

'Danke schoen, mein herr,' he muttered as he closed it and handed it back. I waited a few minutes to make sure they were gone. The train heaved forward and I was able to breathe again. I coughed and spat the ampoule into my hand. I placed it carefully back in my pocket. I could need it again.

I slept until we pulled into the station in Berlin. It was midmorning. I placed the passport in an envelope which I addressed to Zdeněk at the Central Post Office in Prague and sent it through the Reichspost. If I was caught now there would be no more danger to Zdeněk. The warming sunlight shone in between the buildings as I stepped outside. Suddenly my briefcase felt very light. It was a beautiful spring day in Berlin in May 1943, the fourth year of the Second World War.

Berlin. There I was, now Jan Šebesta, a Czech chemist looking for a job and a room to rent.

Jan Šebesta never would have existed without his friend Zdeněk. As the name Zdeněk Tůma is not uncommon, it was difficult for me to find his family. There are thousands of Tůmas in the Czech phonebooks. On Facebook alone there are more than ninety Zdeněk Tůmas. When I started my research, I was not even sure of what he looked like. There were a few photographs in the box that I felt might be of him, but they are old and tiny, and the faces are hard to make out clearly. Luckily, one had his first name scribbled in pencil on the back and looked nothing like my father's first cousin also called Zdeněk. I knew from the Czech archives that my father's friend had moved to the region of Opava after the war. Eventually I found online a hip young woman with blue hair who worked for an NGO in Indonesia, who had the traditional Czech feminine version of Tůma's last name and hailed from Opava. In Barbora Tůmova's picture on LinkedIn, her eyes and smile bore a remarkable resemblance to Zdeněk's.

I emailed her. She wrote that she was travelling in Asia and confirmed that her grandfather was named Zdeněk and had indeed been friends with a man in Venezuela called Hans Neumann. By chance, she was stopping by London on her way to Prague. We met at a coffee shop and chatted for hours. Her uncle, also named Zdeněk, had shared stories about her grandfather and Hans. He too had written down his memories and saved pictures spanning over fifty years of friendship.

I discovered that Zdeněk had made the journey to visit my father in Venezuela three times in the 1960s. My father, who by then had a pilot's licence, had flown Zdeněk to the archipelago of Los Roques and let him take the controls. They had also ventured together out to a Yanomami Indian reserve in the Amazon jungle and slept in hammocks in the communal huts known as *shabanos*. The Bohemian pranksters had reunited briefly in a Latin America that must have seemed a lifetime away from the European past that they shared.

Once again, I realised that my father had revealed very little of this relationship to anyone. My mother, who came into my father's life after these trips, was never told about Zdeněk. She had never met him or even heard of him. When my father had mentioned him to me in Prague, he had disclosed only the briefest details and no sense of the depth of their friendship. It saddened me that he could not tell me about it, that he had kept this lifelong kinship secret for all those years. He could have introduced me to Zdeněk when we visited Prague. I felt that this was a part of his past he could have shared because it was also his present, and joyful. But he could not. He was unable to have the past and the present connect in any way.

Zdeněk's son had accompanied him to that reunion in 1990. He recalled that when they dropped my father off at the hotel, the two men had locked each other in a long embrace. That moment of affection had been their last goodbye. Zdeněk had told my father that night that he had terminal cancer. He died in July 1991, the year before Lotar and Miguel.

Zdeněk's death must have generated the tectonic emotional pressure that was needed for my father to suddenly want to record his past, even if it was a matter of just a few private pages. I understand now that the deaths of Lotar and Miguel, and his return to Prague with me, all played their part, but they were not the catalyst. My father had started to write his Berlin memoir after losing Zdeněk.

On a hunch, after meeting Zdeněk's granddaughter, I called my father's assistant in Venezuela, now long retired, and asked her if the name Zdeněk Tůma rang a bell. She replied immediately, 'Mr Tůma, of course! Your father's school friend in Czechoslovakia. Your father was so fond of him and always made sure we sent him a Christmas card.'

She told me that my father also sent regular parcels from Caracas filled with T-shirts bearing the logo of one of his companies, games, baseball caps, hammocks, roller skates and chewing gum, gifts of one kind or another.

She said, 'Oh, I almost forgot, he often sent presents that were practical jokes. Once it was a chewing gum pack that would snap if you pulled it and some candy that would colour your mouth.'

'Were there other friends he kept in touch with in Czechoslovakia?' I asked her tentatively.

'Oh, no. It was just Mr Tůma. He was the only one.'

I 2

CHOICES

Almost every time I told this story to researchers or curators in London, Prague or Berlin, the initial reaction was disbelief. When I first opened my father's box of papers, I was unsure of what precisely I would find. I attempted to authenticate every detail it contained. I pored over maps, combed archives and checked names and addresses against old phone and address books. Once I knew the narrative was accurate, producing the dozens of documents and written accounts became a familiar part of the story that I told. I explained the facts again and would describe in detail how I had come to learn them. Each new puzzled witness needed to be persuaded, as I had been.

Hans Neumann from Prague had absconded rather than submitting to transportation. He had hidden and assumed a false identity. This was not unusual; thousands of those persecuted had survived by doing the same. It was the rest of the story that, at first, raised the bemused smiles. As his daughter, I was just another unreliable witness telling a story as I wanted to hear it. Their expressions changed as I produced Jan Šebesta's identity documents, permits and letters from Berlin. As they absorbed the dozens of papers, their friendly scepticism became genuine interest and then astonishment.

Perhaps what is so hard to believe is that my father chose to hide in Berlin. He was not sent there as a forced labourer; he chose to go and find work there at a key supplier of the German military. Most of the others who hid had found refuge where they could, in basements, outhouses, convents, anywhere they deemed safe. If they travelled, it was driven by desperation and often towards less populated areas, towards the furthest edge of the Reich with the hope of reaching beyond it. My father struck out in the opposite direction entirely, determined to go the centre of it all. It was a completely illogical choice for either the happy-go-lucky prankster of his youth or the robustly disciplined man he was becoming. It must have militated against every instinct of self-preservation. It was not just unsafe and unusual; even seventy years on, it seems like absolute recklessness.

In 1943 Warnecke & Böhm was the principal manufacturer of protective polymer coatings for the German war machine. The paint technology that they were working on was critical in reducing drag, vital for effective aircraft and missile development. The company was eminent in the field. In 1939 it had been given priority status by the government because it delivered paint and varnish for U-boats and the newly developed fast bomber, the Junkers Ju 88. Their scientists provided the camouflage skin of the Focke-Wulf Fw 190. Their activities were important enough that there is a now declassified British intelligence report from 1945 that studied paints for the Luftwaffe and cites the company in Weissensee as the most successful in supplying formulas for special paint ingredients throughout the Reich.

It was exceptionally lucky for Hans that Zdeněk had been

sent by the Germans to work in a paint factory and knew that they were chronically short of skilled people. It was a stroke of good fortune that, because of the family business, Hans could field some knowledge about the paint and lacquer industry. These two pieces of happenstance gave him a window of opportunity to implement his crazy plan.

My father describes his first moments after stepping off the train in Berlin on 3 May 1943 in the memoir he left me.

The city did not seem to be in the middle of a war. Well-dressed people busily went about their chores, many of them in official uniform. The only obvious sign that something was different was the number of women on the streets. Many had pins and insignia identifying them as members of the NSDAP, the Nazi Party. It was thanks to Zdeněk that I was there although it had been my idea and he, at first, had thought it mad. And yet it was he who planted the seed. He was the one who mentioned in passing that there weren't enough trained scientists in the factory in Berlin. I followed precisely the instructions that he gave me when he visited me in Montana. I took the overground train, the S-Bahn. Zdeněk's scribble on the piece of paper reminded me that I had 1 stop to the first change, then 4 stops east until the next change and then 2 stops to arrive to the northeast corner of the city. From there it was a 5-minute walk. I left the overground station and headed north until I was in front of the imposing grey building.

I was aware that this was it. I tried to marshal my thoughts. I hesitated for a second, took a breath and, before doubt could cloud my resolution, I walked straight in.

This was the place Zdeněk had described in whispered detail, a factory called Warnecke & Böhm. At the door I asked a young man wearing filthy glasses to direct me to the person in charge of employment. I was pointed to the personnel office. The door was ajar, I knocked and greeted a middle-aged woman behind the desk. She seemed pleasant enough and I volunteered a smile and began to talk nervously.

'Good morning. I have a chemistry degree from the technical college in Prague, experience in paints and want to offer my services to your company. Perhaps Dr Högn can see me?'

She seemed a bit surprised and hushed me with the wave of a hand.

'You don't need to tell me all this. I will check if Dr Högn can see you.' She looked me up and down and told me to wait. As she walked away I noticed that her shoes were freshly polished and her greying bun was immaculately pinned to the middle of her head. Not a strand of hair was out of place. She stepped into an office down the hallway. I looked around and rubbed my drenched palms down the front of my trousers. A few minutes later she returned and asked for my name.

'Šebesta,' I said, 'Jan Šebesta.'

'And you don't have an appointment,' she stated, already knowing the answer as she signalled for me to follow her down the corridor. 'Herr Dr Högn will see you.' She took me to a bare office with three metal chairs and a desk by a window. A picture of the Führer on the wall by the large window was the only decoration. I was faint with fear.

'This is Šebesta,' she said to the man behind the desk.

Högn was a bald man with a sweaty, ruddy face and glasses.

'Heil Hitler! Šebesta, I hear you want a job at Warnecke & Böhm?'

I wished desperately that I had listened more carefully to the *endless work discussions between Uncle Richard, my father and Lotar at the table, instead of writing verses in my head.*

'I am qualified in chemistry and while I studied I also worked in the summers in paint development at the Montana factory in Prague.'

I heard Zdeněk's words of caution and added, 'I worked mostly developing industrial paints.'

'And your papers?'

I explained: 'The issue, you see, is I am a specialist in polymers and synthetic paints and my friend said that's what you do here. If I had stayed in Bohemia, I would have been sent with all the men of my age to perform menial work for the Reich. Most of my friends are being sent to work in farms or mines and that would be a waste of my talents.'

'It is true, of course,' I went on with an assurance born of desperation, 'that I am avoiding labouring in the mines or fields, but you have to understand that I came here not just for me but also for the good of the Reich.'

My interviewer looked up at me from his seat with steel-blue eyes that contrasted with the blood-red border of the swastika pin on his lapel. I could tell from the way he held his hands, both index fingers pointing upward, that he was giving my gabbled plea real consideration. I kept my own sweaty clenched hand behind my back and tried to smile.

After a pause, he pronounced, 'We'll give you a try. The problem is going to be getting you a permit from the Ministry of Work. We'll have to say that we hired you in Prague. But you are in luck, Šebesta. You've come to the right man. I have a friend who works in the ministry. He'll help us out.' He disappeared for a few minutes and then came back saying he would accompany me.

'You have your own mind and I admire that, Šebesta, but you must not use it too much. That's where danger lies.'

We crossed Berlin by train. I tried to make conversation and ask him about the city and about his powerful friends. Zdeněk had been right in saying that Dr Högn liked to appear important; he was buoyed by showing off his connections.

Once inside the ministry, he approached a man in a brown suit. Wary, I hung back a few steps. They looked in my direction a few times as they whispered. From where I stood, I could not hear what they were saying, but I tried to hold on to the fact that both seemed to nod their heads more than they shook them. They came over and asked for my Czech identity card. I tried to quiet my terror as I handed them Míla's forged one. The two barely looked at it as they completed pages of forms for what seemed hours. Then the man in the brown suit took me to present the papers at a teller's window. The teller automatically stamped and returned them. Those were my forms, my proof that I was allowed to work, live and get food in Berlin. I folded the papers and put them inside my breast pocket. I thanked them both profusely and bowed my head deferentially.

As we returned together to Warnecke & Böhm's personnel office to obtain yet more documents, I pushed my luck and asked Dr Högn if he knew how I could find a room to rent.

'I can do better than that.' He smiled. 'I have a friend, Frau Rudloff. She lives here in Weissensee. She is a widow and is look- ing for a tenant for a room. She wants someone quiet and serious.' He called her then and there and told her that a sensible young man called Šebesta would be coming over to talk about the room.

Frau Rudloff's dark apartment was very close to the factory, a minute's walk away at number 108 Langhansstrasse. The widow seemed very old and severe. Her curled lips gave her a sour expression, but she seemed harmless enough and the room was clean and cheap. I unpacked the few items from my bag, arranged the lucky doll and books on the bedside table and collapsed onto the wooden bed.

I was exhausted but trying to sleep seemed unnatural. As my body sank deeper into the mattress, I stared at the shadows on the ceiling and realised that I was shaking. As I tried to calm myself, Frau Rudloff knocked and opened the door. I sat up on the bed and covered myself with the grey wool blanket.

'Do you need something, Herr Šebesta? Can I get you anything at all?' I was startled by the kindness but the sight of her breasts, clearly visible through her nightgown, made me uncomfortable. The scarcity of men was noticeable. I thanked her, told her I definitely did not need anything, and wished her a good night.

My first day in Berlin, and thus far all had accepted Jan Šebesta's story. I had a job, papers consistent with my new identity and a warm room in which to sleep. Miraculously everything had gone according to plan. I gave up my attempts to fall asleep and I sat down at the small desk to write to Míla one of what would be many almost daily letters. I wanted her and Lotar to know that my first day had gone well. I asked her to burn the letter immediately after reading it. I would do the same with her replies. They were coded but still there were risks you simply could not take. It was too dangerous to keep anything that could possibly identify me as a fraud and her as the accomplice of a man wanted by the Gestapo. I finished the letter by writing a short funny poem to cheer her up.

Eventually, I managed to sleep. The next day was to be my first day as Jan, the Czech chemist officially employed at Warnecke & Böhm in Berlin.

Jan Šebesta's certificate of employment, stamped by Warnecke & Böhm.

So Hans was now Jan, and Jan was employed in Berlin. The work insurance card issued to Jan Šebesta that my father left me gives a start date of 3 May 1943, the Monday morning that he arrived by train in Berlin. This would be the first of many official documents that he would amass under his new identity as the weeks passed — ration cards, address registration, tax forms — and that he would eventually leave for me in the box.

Jan Šebesta's insurance card, stamped by the
Reich authorities on 10 May 1943.

231

Hans's absence did not pass unremarked in his parents' letters. Precisely two weeks later, Otto wrote a coded latter to Lotar from Terezín:

> *We can only imagine all you have gone through and how upset*
> *you must have been with H's illness. What a beautiful reward*
> *it is to hear that he recovered like Richard a long time ago. But*
> *you must not keep things from me, you did not relay his greet-*
> *ings while he was sick. I implore you not to hide the truth from*
> *us as cruel as it may be. As well you know, I also write about*
> *unpleasant things when the situation merits it.*

Richard was the Neumann brother who had emigrated in 1939 to America. Otto's words made clear that, ever the patriarch, he was unhappy at not being told that his son had been in hiding during March and April. Nevertheless, he was plainly relieved that Hans *had recovered like Richard* and managed to escape Prague. It is unclear whether my grandparents were told that Hans had left for Berlin. I imagine that Lotar would have spared his parents that detail, which would have only worried them and endangered Hans. Lotar would have borne well in mind their written pleas at the time to *keep safety above all and not to attempt anything where much danger is involved.*

It is evident from their continuing letters that in 1943 my grandparents were becoming accustomed to their surroundings and doing their best to create some semblance of a life. Even the deterioration in Ella's health, resulting initially in hospitalisation for stomach ulcers and then an inflamed gall bladder, did not dampen their hopes that the family would soon be reunited. They missed no opportunity to use the letters to pour out their love and gratitude to their boys and to Zdenka.

At the beginning of the year, Otto's boss had written a *reklamatzia*, an appeal to the Elders of Terezín. Thanks to this, they had managed to obtain a repeal of Ella's *Weisung*, which brought them some relief from the threat of being listed for the next transport to the east and immediate execution. But even without a *Weisung*, the threat of what they referred to as *excursions* to camps in the east remained a daily menace. *If only the monstrous excursions completely disappeared.*

Nonetheless, Otto still seemed to strike notes of optimism. In one letter, he recounted that he caught himself *on the way from work crooning Golem*, a comic song made famous by Voskovec and Werich, a duo of avant-garde entertainers who had been critical of Nazi ideology. The Golem was a mythical creature reputed to protect the Jews of Prague from anti-Semitism in the sixteenth century.

Both Otto and Ella forged new relationships and engaged in helping others in Terezín. They used their network of helpers, the gendarme and Mrs Rosa the laundry woman, not only to receive clothes, food and money but also to get messages to their own and other families outside. Otto established a friendship with Stella Kronberger, a Viennese widow from Prague whose husband had committed suicide the day before their deportation. Otto also 'adopted' a young girl named Olina, whose parents he knew from Libčice. She was alone in the camp, as her father had not been deported by virtue of being in a mixed marriage. However, as a *mischling*, a person deemed to be of mixed race and over fifteen, she had been interned in Terezín. Otto's letters often mentioned both Olina and Stella, with whom he spent time, sharing rations and any surplus he received from his illicit packages.

Ella begged her *golden ones* to write, giving details of their everyday lives in Prague to keep the image she had of them vivid, vital and current. *Not a day, evening or night passes in which I do not think of you. My only desire is to see you again and reunite our family.* She remained focused on the day when they would be together again.

Despite her illnesses and situation, her longing for beautiful things and tendency to coquettishness were intact when the warmth of spring arrived. Ella wrote in mid-April that *the budding flowers on the trees make me dream of Libčice.* She requested her spring coat, her cork shoes, her face powder and some perfume. She complained that many of the parcels' contents had been looted, but clarified that she had received clothing, food, toiletries and the shoe polish that was so crucial to maintain the darkness of Otto's hair. It seems that amid the chaos, illness, overcrowding, hunger and cold, they found a way to carry on. They forged new friendships, managed to relish small pleasures and find moments of relative peace.

They were not the only ones. Ella's niece Zita, the twenty-four-year-old daughter of her sister who had died of pneumonia in 1923, had been interned in Terezín since January 1942, yet she managed to fall in love and even marry in the camp.

I first encountered the name Zita while poring over my grandparents' letters. When Magda the researcher helped me put together a family tree, we discovered that I had living relatives not only in the US but also in France, England, Israel and the Czech Republic. One of them, from Prague, was Zita's daughter, Daniela, born in 1948. We met for the first time one evening in October 2017 at the bar of the hotel where I was staying and talked for hours, a bit in French and a bit in English, about our family. Afterwards, Daniela sent me a few pages of Zita's recollections, together with photos of Zita's mother and father, Rudolf Pollak and his second wife, Josefa; of her sister Hana, and her brothers Zdeněk and Jiří – all of whom were detained in Terezín when Ella arrived. There were pictures of the children lined up in sailor suits and elegant outfits and of Ella's sister posing proudly with her firstborn son. One photo shows Ella's nieces and nephew seated happily around their father; it was taken some months before their deportation to Terezín. Still today I am struck by its depiction of shared affection and a moment of careless joy.

Ella's brother-in-law Rudolf Pollak with his three children: Zita and Hana on the left, and Zdeněk on the right. Teplice, c. 1940.

Rudolf, Josefa and Jiří Pollak had been deported to Auschwitz in September 1943 on Rudolf's 59th birthday, but Zita, Hana and Zdeněk provided some respite for my grandparents in the camp. Otto reported, after one of the many moves of barracks, how relieved he was to have Zdeněk in the same bunk. Ella helped her nieces steal some flowers from the trees for Zita's marriage bouquet.

In her letters of this period, Ella started to refer to Otto as *Grumpy*. Otto had always been cantankerous, and life in Terezín could only have magnified this. Instead of allowing them to find strength in each other, it appears that life in Terezín had begun to wrench my grandparents apart.

Ella's relationship with her employer seems to have been a key catalyst for this division. In her first Terezín letters, she often mentioned *Eng. L. He is very influential. He takes good care of me. He eats out of the palm of my hand.*

In the first weeks after his arrival, Otto was also grateful for Engineer Langer's kindness, which benefited both Ella and him. Otto wrote in early 1943 that he had Langer to thank for his new job, which afforded him some protection from being transported. He suggested that the boys get in touch with Langer's wife in Prague to give her news of her husband. Otto also asked his sons to offer Mrs Langerova the opportunity to use their parcels as a conduit for her to send messages to Langer.

But Langer was also the cause of friction, which stemmed from Otto's jealousy. A mere month after his arrival, Otto was scathing: *Eng. L is responsible for ruining the family happiness, though I blame Ella above all, as she is not behaving like a normal person.* In many instances in the letters that followed, he referred to his *failed marriage.* Ella repeatedly denied any romantic involvement with anyone and wished Otto could find better ways of expressing his love for her. In March 1943, she wrote about Otto's jealousy: *though he has no reason to be jealous he simply cannot stand that some men with power in Terezín like me and play into my hands. So in this respect I do what I can, my only mission here is to survive at all costs, if it wasn't for my influential friends we would either be dead or have long been deported far away.* She criticised Otto for being *petty* and *senseless* and suggested that he should be more focused on important things, *such as surviving.* In June 1943, she begged her children to not take *Otto's news so tragically,* and asked Lotar, especially, not to fret about their relationship. *There are no circumstances in which you could imagine what life is like in this madhouse.* She wrote, as she often did, that her only goal was for her and Otto to remain alive, while also clarifying that *how I achieve this is not irrelevant as I don't want to return to life outside crippled physically or mentally.* While she remained focused on surviving, there were limits to what Ella would do to ensure this survival. This clarification to her boys implied that having an affair fell beyond those limits.

Nonetheless, over and over, she expressed a deep appreciation of Langer for taking care of her in what she described as a *movingly fatherly fashion when she was alone and in the direst misery.* She felt indebted to him for the *housing, the employment, the possibility of storing belongings, the chance to connect with the outside.* She also observed, perhaps a little wryly, that Otto was behaving ungratefully, as Engineer Langer had provided him *with protection from the moment he arrived.*

Eventually, thanks to files in the Jewish Museum and the archives in Brno, I was able to trace the youngest daughter of Ella's benefactor. Having grown up in Czechoslovakia, Beatrice is a retired pathologist, now living in Australia. We corresponded by email for a few months before finally meeting for an afternoon in London. Through Beatrice, my letters and the archives in the Czech Republic, I pieced together a picture of František Langer. Born in 1902 in Bohušovice, he had studied engineering at the University of Brno. He was a tall, lean, studious man, fond of reading, forest walks and open fires. He had married a Franco-Czech Protestant in 1932, and they had their first daughter, Beatrice's older sister, four years later. Ultimately, fearful of Nazi policies, František and his wife divorced to protect the family and their belongings. František had arrived at Terezín alone a month before Ella. He was soon put in charge of the *Bauhof*, the workshop in the camp. This was a position of considerable status, although, unlike the Elders, he held no decision-making power over administrative issues or lists for transports. Nonetheless, his position meant that his opinion carried weight in such matters. It also meant that he had access to rooms, storage and a measure of privacy that was unusual in Terezín. My grandmother acted as his cleaner and cook, and in the surreal conditions of their imprisonment they became friends.

By all accounts, my grandmother had always been charming and flirtatious. It is clear from the letters that she retained a sense of joy and fun even in Terezín. Regardless of the reason, Langer did whatever he could to help both Ella and Otto.

Ella may have flirted or done what she could to stay alive, to be reunited with her *golden boys*. All I know is that in that world of absurd choices, Ella chose to survive. Her letters were filled with hope but also pragmatism and a determination to maximise her and Otto's chances of survival. Ella consistently denied having anything more than a friendship with František Langer, who was, after all, not only younger than she was but also *loves his wife and daughter.* She accused Otto of being *irrationally jealous of everything, even his shadow.* I will never know if Otto's suspicions were well-founded or not. Either account could have been correct, or the truth could rest, as it often does, balanced somewhere between.

The fact remains that František Langer played an important role in my grandparents' lives in the camp. Despite my grandfather's reaction to it, he clearly afforded them both protection and was a source of comfort and kindness for Ella.

Beatrice and I had many conversations about Terezín, our families and the letters. I had been apprehensive about disclosing Otto's suspicions, but I should not have been. Joined by the invisible and improbable bond of being children of people who survived against the odds, we chatted openly and freely, on Skype, by email, in person. We agreed that we will never know the exact details of this relationship but that to us, so close but so far removed from the madness of the war, much can be beautiful and profound without being fully understood.

Engineer František Langer, having been liberated from Terezín in 1945, never mentioned either Otto or Ella Neumann to his daughter. Like so many survivors, he never spoke about the camps as he remade his life in Czechoslovakia and then Australia. His family keeps a portrait of him painted in Terezín by the renowned artist and painter Petr Kien. Kien died in Auschwitz in October 1944, but many of his drawings and paintings survive and are on display in Terezín. This oil, dedicated to František Langer, is simply inscribed *gratefully.*

Petr Kien's portrait of Engineer Langer.

By September 1943, most of Prague's Jews had been deported. Of the 118,000 who had been in the city in 1939, about 36,000 had fled and almost 70,000 had been deported. Only those of mixed heritage or those protected by intermarriages remained. This meant that the duties of the Council of Elders in Prague had diminished greatly. Yet the offices were filled with files of identification documents, declarations, paperwork concerning bans from public work, seizures, confiscations, deportations.

An average transport generated five hundred files of paper-work. Around a hundred transports departed Bubny between 1941 and September 1943.

At that time, the Prague Elders were in charge of all those Jews in the Protectorate who were not already interned in camps but to whom the Nuremberg Laws still applied. The Prague Elders operated under a complicated organisational structure with several hundred participants. Since most of the 'full' Protectorate Jews, including most of their own staff, had been deported by the summer of 1943, the organisation was in need of resources. Against this background, Lotar was recruited to work for the Council as a junior filing clerk in the transport office.

Among the other new recruits were two friends of Lotar's, a lawyer named Viktor Knapp, whom Zdenka knew from the law faculty at university, and Erik Kolár, Lotar's dear friend from the theatre and the clandestine school. They too were protected by mixed marriages and started to work there in September. And though many Elders themselves had been deported, Pišta, the family friend, had held on to his post as an assistant. Being among friends may have marginally eased the burden of working within an administrative machine devised by the Nazis. Any perceived protection was illusory, as being part of the Council did not afford anyone real security. All the original members of the Council in Prague and their families had been transported to Terezín in 1941. By September 1943 many had been tortured and killed.

To say that Lotar was asked to work in the Council implies there was a choice, that he could have refused. Two years before, Otto had tried to recuse himself from being a trustee, a request that had been denied. Lotar could have taken a similar stance and declined, but to do so would have had consequences not only for him but also for his parents in Terezín. All his family had been deported, and some had already been killed. The only one not to have been deported was Hans, but he was on the Gestapo list and in constant danger by hiding in plain sight.

Even though I knew him many years later, I can imagine Lotar's anguish. When faced with death, he had no real choice, merely the crushing sense of responsibility and torment that arises from the illusion of choice. Duress, as international law recognises, amounts to the removal of free will. Lotar acted under duress. Yet the conscience of a survivor is never so black and white. Many who were involved in the Councils across occupied Europe never admitted to it after the war. A number who became important in their communities and later assumed public roles erased this period from their biographies.

But my uncle Lotar did not erase it from his mind. Lotar's daughter Madla told me that he agonised about his involvement with the Council for the rest of his life. Unlike my father, who brutally severed himself from his past life, Lotar dealt with his traumas differently. In his fifties, he retired from the life that he had built and struggled in silence under the weight of a depression that never left him. He spent the last two decades of his life helping Holocaust survivors and refugees rebuild theirs.

Hans and Lotar had always supported each other. Yet Hans was not there to sustain Lotar during that terrible summer. Lotar could not discuss the Council or work through how best to send aid to their parents in the camp. Hans was not unaware of Lotar's plight, but he too was powerless to do anything more than heed their mother's entreaties to survive, day by day. Hans had vanished and become Jan, for whom nothing was more important than making sure that the name Hans Neumann remained unuttered:

I spoke to nobody about Hans. I had to become Jan completely. Even Míla wrote her coded letters to Jan. She would meet with Lotar and Zdenka and send me news about my parents in Terezín. She didn't write much about them, just enough to let me know that they were alive.

My brother Lotar had to work in the Council in Prague. Zdenka and he still managed to have parcels delivered to my parents at the camp. But I could no longer write to them. In Berlin, outside the moments I spent reading letters from home, Hans did not exist. He was never even mentioned by Zdeněk.

It saddened me at times. But it was the only way.

I 3

ONE QUESTION

Warnecke & Böhm's records show that in 1941 their workforce totalled 880; 369 of those were Jews from across occupied Europe who were coerced to work there. These Jewish forced labourers were given menial or dangerous tasks, cleaning, working with noxious gases or toxic chemicals. No protective equipment was provided. Their forced labour was brought to an abrupt conclusion when all were deported in February 1943, creating the shortage of manpower that Zdeněk and Hans had identified as a slim chance of escape.

Jan Šebesta was a gentile and, like Zdeněk, part of the human resources that the Reich drew from outside Germany itself. These people were compelled by circumstances. They were not obliged to wear a uniform and they received a nominal salary. Some were housed in specially constructed barracks around the city, but others could take lodgings and move around the city with relative freedom.

However, their status was drilled home relentlessly.

Czechs, as Slavs, were duly categorised within the obsessive racial classification of Nazi ideology. They were considered 'lapsed Aryans'. This meant that while they were discriminated against, they were treated marginally better than the Russians or Poles, who were deemed *Untermensch*, inferior people, subhuman.

A leaflet issued by Hitler's secretary Martin Bormann in April 1943, directing German behaviour towards all foreign workers, and offered as evidence at the Nuremberg Trials, paints the clearest picture:

> Everything must be subordinated to the winning of the war. Of course, treating foreign workers in a manner that is humane, but production-enhancing, and granting them concessions can easily lead to the blurring of the clear line between foreign workers and German compatriots. German compatriots are to be urged to consider it a national duty to maintain the necessary distance between themselves and the foreign peoples. German compatriots must be aware that disregarding the principles of National Socialist racial theory will result in the most severe punishment.

The Nazi approach to foreign labour was a pragmatic one, an attempt to balance the ideological objective of strengthening the purity of the Germanic race with the pressing practical need for labour, especially skilled labour. This created strained hierarchies where expertise did not denote status. The demand for non-German professionals to survive by propping up their less qualified German supervisors was often irresistible. So people like Jan were compelled to engage in the most dangerous and radical research but often without the protective measures provided for their German counterparts.

These pressured dynamics were set against the backdrop of a broader society that was febrile and fragmented, simultaneously embracing the propaganda and privately enduring solitude and grief, the realities of war. The safest course for

Berliners was to keep a low profile and meet or exceed allotted responsibilities. Any deviation from a slavish adherence to the rules was severely punished, and informants were everywhere.

Paradoxically, this provided a predictable environment for a person to get by, if they combined a devil-may-care daring with steely objectivity. The practical joker from Prague, it transpired, was just such a person.

He later wrote about his daily life:

As the months passed the job became routine. I woke early to arrive at the lab by 7 a.m. I had left Fr. Rudloff's room after a few months. I had become friendly with a young war widow called Traudl who worked in an office at the factory. Her husband had been one of the first casualties of the Polish invasion. Traudl had asked if I would move in with her. Her best friend, Ursula, also employed at the factory and whose army husband was presumed dead, had taken a liking to Zdeněk. They both lived in the same building and Zdeněk and I could not refuse the offer of cheap housing and better company. I left a suitcase of my belongings at the stern widow's home as Traudl's place was small. The move created a small scandal in the factory, but it was too convenient for the four of us. We ignored the whispered chit-chat behind our backs.

Traudl and I got on well as friends. She too was grateful for the company and between the four of us we figured out ways of sourcing food outside our meagre rations. We were less hungry than others. I worked out how to distil pure alcohol from the lab stores. This meant currency for bartering. My boss, Dr Victor Högn, turned a blind eye to our bootlegging as long as at the end of every week we handed him half of our proceeds.

Traudl let me use the bicycle that belonged to her husband.
As I pedalled the few blocks to and from my job, the simple hap-
piness of feeling the rush of the wind on my face — if just for a
second, made me forget who I was and reminded me of what it
was like to be free.

Jan was not free. He had to watch his every word, his every
step. Even in his living quarters, he had to keep up appearances
and be on his guard so as not to arouse any suspicion. Only his
thoughts could be free, and even those had to be controlled if he
was to focus on surviving. To fill his time and mind, he applied
himself to his tasks and even started to work late hours. He
conjured a discipline that he had lacked as a boy and crafted his
new persona with care. Obedient but not unconvincingly so.
There was a note of rebelliousness here and there to add authen-
ticity to the young Czech chemist working for his country's
oppressors. The illegal alcohol and the frowned-upon flirtation
with a war widow subtly made Jan Šebesta real.

Official paperwork continued to be a critical means of
operating within the brutal bureaucracy. Whenever the opportunity arose, my father continued to amass papers in the name
of Jan Šebesta. Documentary evidence shored up his credibil-
ity. It gave the impression that his presence had been validated
by diverse authorities, which made a challenge markedly less
likely, especially in a world where no one was inclined to call
into question anything that appeared to have an official stamp
of approval. In addition to his work permit and ration card,
another official paper was issued on 1 September detailing Jan's
move from his first home in Berlin to the apartment of Traudl
Schemainda, his friend and secretary at the factory. By October

1943, Jan Šebesta even possessed a genuine identity card issued by the German authorities, literally bearing the official stamp and complete with a confidently smiling portrait that was still recognisable to his young daughter in Caracas almost four decades later. A document from 1 November 1943 shows that Jan Šebesta had registered yet a new address with the police. The document states that he left his residence with Traudl and moved to Fr. Schaap's apartment at Tassostrasse 12a. He had moved three times in six months – this third time presumably to appease the chatter at the factory.

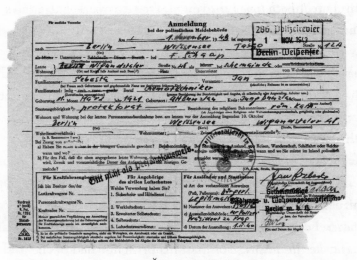

Police registration of Jan Šebesta in Berlin, November 1943.

For Jan, scrupulously maintaining the appearance of a mildly disrespectful yet compliant stranger to the city was a constant burden. Daily life was an extraordinary struggle, and as the war came to Berlin, it was indifferent to his personal loyalties. Since May 1940, the British Royal Air Force had attacked targets that were considered valuable to the German war effort, including many sites in Berlin. Warnecke & Böhm, which was developing products for the German military, certainly would have made a worthy target. While no air raid siren had sounded in Berlin during the first few months following Hans's arrival, 23 August marked the beginning of a concerted bombing campaign.

That day I oversaw distributing tasks to my colleagues in the lab. The blonde German chemist reminded me of an albino rodent, enthusiastic with twitchy hands. Her short and rotund assistant was another Czech. I knew she was miserable even if she did not say a word. Each time I tried to catch her eye, she looked down at the floor.

Dr Högn called me into his office. He looked like a goose with his wide-set blue eyes.

'Šebesta, you've impressed me. Your ideas have allowed us to improve our processes. Of course, I have had to present them as being from our investigations team.'

I looked straight back at him. 'Thank you, Herr Dr.'

What he didn't tell me was that he had presented my ideas as his own. He was an ardent Nazi, toiling to climb the political ladder. I detested him. He had even started to wear a little moustache, like the Führer, a blot of darkness on his idiotic round face.

He used to boast that he was so important for the Nazi Party that he was even allowed to skip the compulsory military service. He had told me with great pride that he was one of a handful of Austrians who were engaged with Hitler before the Anschluss. His role in this company was not that of a scientist but of a political emissary. He was useless as a researcher. That is why I was useful to him. He resented the fact that I had more imagination, simply because it contradicted his view that as a Czech, I was a lesser being than he was. If only he knew that I was even lower than that, at the bottom of his fabricated hierarchy, in fact, a stupid, lowly Jew.

'I wanted to tell you that I am going to get you involved in higher-level, important and confidential research,' he announced. 'You should be proud. I asked the Gestapo for clearance to promote you. Yesterday, I received the form authorising you. There is nothing in your past precluding you from access to confidential documents. Congratulations, Šebesta.'

I could not answer, appalled at the idea that he had requested the detailed Gestapo review of my file that a promotion likely entailed.

I dabbed, I hoped discreetly, at the perspiration on my brow. I tried to keep eye contact. I could not stop my knees from shaking. I shifted my weight from one leg to another, pretending it was excitement. I was shaking.

'I must go home, it's late, Šebesta,' he announced. 'You must go too.'

I think I must have smiled feebly at him as he waddled from the room.

It was not until a month later that after careful half-enquiries at the factory, I tentatively reconstructed what had happened. Dr Högn had referred the matter of my potential promotion to the Berlin Gestapo. The Berlin Gestapo had written to the Prague Gestapo, submitting a lengthy list of questions. Had Šebesta ever been involved in student protests? Had Šebesta ever been on any list of politically active students? Had Šebesta ever done anything in opposition to the interests of the Reich? Did Šebesta have a police record? Had Šebesta ever expressed any opinion that was critical of the Reich? Was Šebesta ever involved with anything arousing suspicion of any of the above? So the list must have continued.

*The list had omitted one question. Had a Jan Šebesta, born
in Alt Bunzlau on 11 March 1921, ever existed? This question had never been posed in Prague or in Berlin and was thus
never answered.*

*Dr Högn had been duly informed by the Berlin Gestapo in
Berlin that no criminal file existed for Jan Šebesta, against whom
nothing negative was known. He could proceed.*

Once again, the unfortunate boy from Prague was saved by
luck. The phrasing of a question and the rigidity with which it
had been answered had allowed him to remain undetected in
Berlin. My father had once told me that his life had been saved
during the war by others' lack of imagination. I had not known
what he meant precisely until I read this account.

Lotar was no longer permitted to assume any position of responsibility at Montana, so Zdenka had, as always, stepped in. After
the first Reich-appointed *treuhänder* had departed in 1942, the
factory continued operating under Alois Francek, another Reich-
appointed *treuhänder* who had written a letter in support of Otto's
work. Like all other Jews, the Neumanns never received any
payment for the 'sale' of their business to the Nazis, but Francek,
at least, always stayed sympathetic to the family. He was happy to
involve Zdenka, who was capable and knew the inner workings
of the factory. It was an unusual place for a female lawyer, but
the men had been deported or sent away to work or fight for the
Reich. Over the years, Zdenka had engaged in many a business
debate with the family, listened patiently to Otto's anxieties and

faithfully counselled Lotar. She knew what needed to be done. There was little for the dwindling factory staff to do, as materials were almost impossible to come by, and private orders were few and far between. Nevertheless, in an attempt to salvage whatever she could of the business, Zdenka worked in Montana every day. Yet the couple's focus continued to be on the growing challenge of keeping Otto and Ella supplied with letters and goods while the shortages and threats increased and the carriers became less and less reliable.

Otto marvelled at Zdenka's *indomitable optimism*, which lifted his own spirits. *Do not worry about us my darlings . . . we know you have all done all you could have for us and the rest we leave to fate . . . hopefully a favourable one.*

Zdenka worried, though, and determined that it was time to take the enormous risk of accessing Terezín again. Understandably, her memoirs dwell on her emotional response to the situation, and it is not clear from them precisely when she snuck in. It must have been during the early autumn months of 1943, when getting parcels through was becoming impossible, that Zdenka entered the camp a second time.

Once more, she dressed like an inmate and tagged along with the 'country unit' working in the nearby fields. She searched for Otto in the Hannover barracks, and there she found him, on his shared wooden bunk. She had stitched hidden pockets within her shirt and skirts, inside which she carried tins of shoe polish for his hair, money and other small items of value to him. Above all, she brought him hope.

One of the items in Lotar's box is an unusual-looking ring, made in metal that is coloured in bronzed pinks and dark greys. It seems to have been carved by hand from a piece of copper pipe.

It is not delicate or pretty. The ring is arranged around a curved, bordered rectangle with the letters 'ZN' intertwined. They are Zdenka's initials.

Madla explained to me that her father had told her once that Otto made the ring in Terezín. Grateful to Zdenka for the parcels, for the letters, for her help and what seemed like unconditional love, he had stolen some metal from one of the workshops and moulded it himself. Otto was an engineer, not an artist, and was unused to fashioning things using his hands. And yet somehow he managed to make this ring, which now sits on my desk as I write. Otto must have loved Zdenka very much. Perhaps it was during her brave incursion into the camp that a grateful Otto gave her the ring. Maybe he sent it out with one of their trusted couriers. Either way, this simple, essential symbol of love and gratitude made it out of Terezín. Zdenka kept it and wore it throughout the war.

I have some letters from the second half of 1943, but very few. Ella was convalescing, having been bedridden again in the hospital and unable to write much. The grapevine in Terezín worked efficiently, and Otto must have heard that Mussolini had been ousted and that the Russians were driving back the Nazis on the eastern front. Their optimism rekindled as the news spread through the camp. He wrote to Zdenka and his boys: *I think of you night and day. Slowly I am starting again to make plans for our future. My only aim is that your mother and I stay here until the end and there is hope of that given Ella's malady.* One of the many paradoxes of life in Terezín is that, for a while, at least, Ella's sojourn in the hospital protected her from being sent east.

In Berlin, Hans was also beginning to allow himself to think of the end of the war:

The noise of the dining room was overwhelming. The sound of cutlery, plates, people talking, laughing, shouting. It was so normal, so chaotic and so mundane. There must have been 500 people having lunch. The high-ceilinged room used to be a depository for raw materials. Nothing needed to be stored any longer, all materials that arrived were immediately transformed into products and the workforce had grown so quickly that a new dining place was needed. So here we were.

Conversations were being held in German, Russian, French, Polish, Dutch and other languages that I could not easily identify. At our table we spoke Czech. The majority of the workers were people from occupied countries. They were not the scientists, those were usually German. We, the others, were the ones made to perform the most dangerous tasks, handle the corrosives and the explosives. Many had the scars of scalds and burns on their hands and arms. They had been forced to leave their countries and work here for no real pay and no safety regulations.

Posters everywhere threatened us that this new Reich would span the globe and last a millennium. Images of Hitler were everywhere. He seemed perpetually to observe us all, unthinking and pitiless. A poster above us bore the words: 'One nation, one people, one Führer.'

We all devoured the food even though it was disgusting. As I cut the meal on my plate, I realised that there was a high likelihood that the brown concoction I was ingesting consisted of cows' lungs and rotten potatoes. As I cleared my tray, I noticed a man wearing the hallmark blue overall of a forced labourer standing slightly too close to me. He whispered with a Dutch accent: 'Šebesta, right? I have been watching you. I am a friend. I will wait for you by the main exit tonight.'

And before giving me time to get a proper look, he walked away. His broad shoulders, too big for his uniform, disappeared amid the blue and brown herds filling the corridor. That evening the broad man waited for me by the gate as he had promised. He looked straight at me and without hesitation said, 'Šebesta, let's walk.'

It was early autumn and the evening was filled with auburn light. I followed him, partly out of curiosity, partly because there was something familiar and compelling about him. As we turned the corner onto Gustav-Adolf Strasse and approached the cemetery, he spoke calmly.

'Let's go in here.'

We meandered among the ancient trees and tombs, taking our time and idly perusing the inscriptions.

'You are like me. You don't want this war to go on longer than is necessary.'

I did not say anything. Tombstones have always made me nervous.

He continued. 'The Nazis will lose sooner or later. You and I can do our best so that it is sooner.'

We stopped near a mossy cracked headstone, its engraving erased by time. I looked at him, unsure whether I should try to hide my surprise. This could easily have been a trap. Perhaps it was some sort of test, but something about him reassured me.

He smiled and said, 'It is okay. This seems unreal, I know, but then don't most days?'

He started to walk again. I caught up with him. I let him lead the way.

'I dislike the war. I mean, who doesn't?' I said carefully.

He paused and looked at me. For a moment neither of us spoke. He seemed assured for a mere labourer. He looked out of place in his overalls and thick grey jacket. I could tell by the way he spoke that there was a sophistication to him. He could not be much older than I was. He spoke German fluidly, with just the smallest hint of a Dutch accent. As I examined his face, I realised that I had seen him before at the factory and that I had heard him chatting in French as well.

I no longer hid my surprise. 'Are you some sort of academic?' I pulled a crumpled pack from my pocket and offered him a cigarette. We headed to the exit as the light faded.

'University student,' he replied. 'But that was another life.'

Looking around him, he spoke quietly and deliberately now. 'You have the opportunity to obtain information that could be interesting to the Allies. If you get the papers to me I will ensure they fall into the right hands. Just make eye contact in the lunch hall and I'll *wait for you by the gates. I'll be in touch, Šebesta. I trust you.' He stared straight at me.*

That was it. He didn't ask for an answer or a promise. Nothing. He was measured and determined. He didn't waste words. He seemed to know what he was doing. Or did he? He left me on the side of the street, didn't turn around, didn't say goodbye.

I was not sure what to do. I couldn't ask anyone's advice. Not Zdeněk. Obviously not Traudl. There was no one I could trust with this. The decision had to be mine. I could not get anyone else involved. It would have been a risk for me and could also be their death sentence. I was utterly alone. Alone in a ridiculous situation. I had a false name. Hunted by the Gestapo, I had come to the centre of their world. Pretending to be a technical specialist, I was working in a factory for the very people who were starving my parents, torturing and killing my family. I was living with a German war widow. I was in a city that was constantly being bombed by the people whose side I was on. As my new Dutch friend had remarked, it was all entirely unreal.

And it wasn't really a choice. There was only one thing to do. The longer the war went on, the less tenable my situation. My odds of surviving were minimal anyway. The sooner this war ended, the more chance I had of coming out alive and seeing my family and my friends again. The Dutch student was right. I wanted to help end this war. I made up my mind as I walked the few blocks back to Traudl at 48 Wigandstaler Strasse. The next day I would find the Dutch student and tell him that I would do it. I would find him at the lunch hall and just say yes.

That night I had to drink three cupfuls of my revolting alcoholic mixture to fall asleep. I had made it to barter for supplies, but that evening I was thankful to have not traded it all.

I will probably never find out who the Dutch student was. My father's writings are filled with names, most of which I have been able to verify either from Warnecke & Böhm's employee records or from the old Berlin phone books. But the name of the Dutch student is never given. I wonder if my father even knew it. Perhaps he had never been told for reasons of security. Maybe he thought that omitting the name was the correct thing to do.

Instead of the Dutch student's name, my father left me a document in the box, stolen from the factory, which details the kind of work that he carried out. This document, dated 14 December 1943, was signed by Dr Högn and marked 'Sebesta/3'. It detailed research that had been undertaken to assess the effectiveness of sealing lacquer that was being developed for Messerschmitt, the aircraft manufacturer.

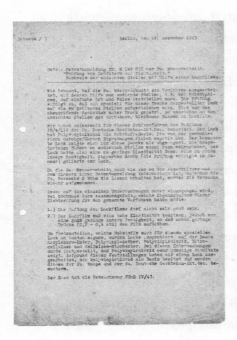
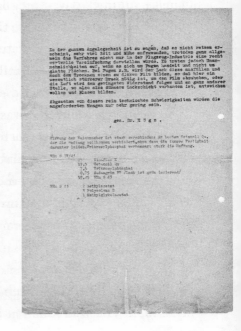

The boy from Prague was defying the Nazi system by living in the middle of it all. Sharing details about his work in the defence industry made the defiance even more acute. He could not share this further fact with his best friend, as doing so would endanger him as well. It was risky enough for them both that Zdeněk knew Jan Šebesta's real identity.

There was one photograph in the box that took me years to place. My father is in it, a mischievous grin on his face, one of two young men in shorts, at some park in front of a statue. My father looked so young and happy that I assumed it must have been taken before the war and left at the bottom of the box for sentimental reasons.

I realised that the other man in the photograph was Zdeněk when I finally found his passport photograph in a Czech archive. The photograph was of the two of them, taken on some outing during a summer day. Much later, it occurred to me that it would be interesting to locate the exact site of the photograph, so I used Google to look up statues in Central Europe. I scanned hundreds of online images until I found it. Any Berliner would have recognised it at once.

The Bismarck Memorial was moved by Hitler in 1938 to its present location in the Tiergarten, the principal park of Berlin. The imposing bronze of the first chancellor symbolises German might as mythical heroes pose beneath him. Atlas signifies force. Siegfried forges a sword as a metaphor for industrial strength. Sibyl personifies learning as she peruses a book of history. Germania bears down on a panther to symbolise the suppression of rebellion.

When I finally traced Zdeněk's son, he sent me the same photograph. His was stamped by the photographer and years later inscribed on the back with the words, *Handa and Zdeněk, taken during an 'educational' walk in Berlin*. In the image taken by Otto Kohler in 1943, the two friends are standing in front of the Bismarck Memorial. Two Czech boys with their secrets. Two pranksters grinning, in their shorts, in front of a symbol of German power.

Hans and Zdeněk in the Tiergarten in Berlin,
summer of 1943.

I 4

FRIGHTENED EYES

On 10 December 1943 Otto wrote a letter to say that his *only worry is that your life may not be as peaceful as ours*. A few days earlier, Ella had been admitted once more to the hospital in Terezín for emergency repair of her gall bladder. She wrote her children a brief note saying that before going into surgery she had placed the photographs of the three of them, Lotar with Zdenka and Handa, by her bedside so they would be the first thing she saw as she came around from the anaesthetic. She reassured them that she retained her *iron will to live*, and asked them to focus on *nothing else other than of the time that they will meet again.*

She also entreated them to tell her something about her *everything, her Handa*. It seems she was in good spirits; after warning them not to laugh, she requested mascara and face powder. As always, she conveyed her gratitude and love. Even Otto sounded hopeful that this surgery would put an end to the ailments that Ella had suffered over the last eight months. He mentioned that with winter encroaching, his thoughts had turned to Zdenka, who hated the cold, and that he imagined her traipsing through a freezing Prague to Montana to handle the bureaucracy.

At the end of his letter, he added:

*We thought we would be able to spend these holidays together.
Last year I cried all through them but this year I am not going
to cry any more. I hope with all my heart that you enjoy the
holidays in peace and that we do too. I am certain that we will
not remain separated for long. Only then, when we are again
together, will we truly start living.*

I will never know if Otto and Ella knew what Hans went
through that December 1943. It certainly was not the peace
that Otto had wished for him. There is no coded reference to
Hans that I can find in the very few letters and postcards that
remain from the period.

In November 1943, the British Royal Air Force led a series
of air raids in a bombing campaign that became known as
the Battle of Berlin. Newly developed fast-bombing planes
equipped with radar technology enabled them to unleash
increasingly damaging attacks on the city. Initially, the raids
were conducted at night to minimise the inevitable losses
from anti-aircraft fire. Though Berlin seemed to withstand
the attacks, the damage was devastating and widespread.
Residential buildings, factories, churches, barracks and ware-
houses were obliterated. The Charlottenburg Palace, the zoo
and the Tiergarten, where Hans had stood with Zdeněk the
previous summer, were all bombed. Many structures and
entire neighbourhoods were destroyed. Between November
1943 and January 1944 alone, there were thirty-eight major
bombing raids on Berlin. Thousands of civilians in Berlin were
killed in those two months, and hundreds of thousands were
rendered homeless. The war was far from over, but the city
had begun the final terrible descent through fire into rubble.

Warnecke & Böhm and the surrounding area were bombed on 22 and 23 November 1943. My father was in the middle of it all, a period that he described in depth in the writings that he left for me.

When I narrate my father's account of late 1943 and early 1944, I struggle to do it justice. It is better read in full as it was written, by an older man living in Caracas reviving memories that were then indistinguishable from the nightmares which woke him screaming in the night.

A visitor is welcomed at the gates of Warnecke & Böhm
in Berlin in the late 1930s.

Nietszche wrote that what separates humans from animals is the ability to find one's condition risible. Nazis tended to solemnity and humourlessness. They always showed what Nietszche called 'Tierischer Ernst', a certain 'animal earnestness', a complete inability to laugh at themselves.

With every passing day I spent in Berlin, this became more evident. They could not recognise their own ridiculousness or indeed appreciate the absurdity of anything. Without imagination they were predictable. This realisation enabled me to take calculated risks. I figured that by acting in an unexpected manner or in any way that ran contrary to their expectations, I could increase my chances of survival.

I must be clear. I behaved as I did out of an instinct to survive and not bravery. As was my intention, my colleagues found me eccentric. If they argued that the Germans were winning the war, I casually put forth a doubt, but without feigning much interest in the subject. At Warnecke & Böhm, as in all German factories, we were obliged to greet one another with a salute and a 'Heil Hitler'. I refused to do this and instead would offer a simple but cheerful 'guten tag'.

There were five of us Czechoslovaks in the company. I had convinced all in our group to adopt a similar approach. The others were tentative at first, but there is nothing like the comfort of numbers, united in nationality and hatred, to embolden one. These acts of mild insubordination confused the Germans, who expected absolute compliance, but at the same time represented a problem that they could tolerate. This meant that the focus on Jan Šebesta's very identity was less intense, and any slips might more easily be explained as being merely a consequence of the cussedness of a lowly Czech. Paradoxically, drawing a little hostile attention might help me, as long as it was always consistent with Jan Šebesta's character — a naive young Czech who was useful in a lab.

We had been doing this for months, so when the political commissary finally called me in, it took me by surprise.

'Šebesta, I have received a complaint from your superiors. It seems you are not saluting in the appropriate manner.'

I made up my answer as I went along. 'In my family, we always greeted one another with "guten tag" and it's very hard for me to break the habit. My father used to say that it was important for one's greeting to have meaning. The first thing to do when you encounter someone is to wish them a good day. It would be inconsiderate to do otherwise.'

He appeared unconvinced.

'Also, to proclaim "Heil Hitler" when the Führer clearly does not need a simple worker's support when he is doing so well just doesn't seem right. So I prefer to greet people with words that have significance.'

He seemed baffled. 'Very well, Šebesta, I will include it all in my report.'

Just when I thought we were done, he looked at me again and his upper lip twitched slightly. His tone changed. 'There is something else. You are scandalising the company with your relationship. She is the widow of a hero.'

This made me uncomfortable and I hesitated. He stared up at me from behind his desk as I locked my fingers behind my back. I was no longer registered as living in Traudl's apartment although we often spent evenings together. I knew of the prohibition on relationships between German women and 'fremdarbeiter', foreign labour. I reminded him that Dr Högn was very happy with my work and pointed out that I had a contract approved by the Ministry of Work.

I added cautiously, 'The widow needs protection during the bombardments, sir.'

He looked at me with repulsion. I could tell that he despised *me, abhorred the fact that I was different. He wanted me to be scared, and this was enough to make me defy the fear that took hold of me when he first mentioned Traudl. He snapped the pen down onto the desk. 'Go, Šebesta, out!'*

That night in the apartment, Traudl burst into tears and said that she too had been called in for questioning about her living arrangements.

In March 1944, to compound the assault on Berlin, the US Air Force started to execute raids during the day. At night, the British attacked. The Allied assault on German cities was unprecedented. Hundreds of thousands of civilians were killed between 1943 and 1945. Each raid by the Royal and US Air Forces consisted usually of a thousand bombers, each dropping tons of explosives and incendiaries. It would have been impossible for my father to know what to wish for, more bombardments that heralded death but also the defeat of Germany, or a hiatus from the bombardments. My father was forced to join Berlin's effort to soldier on.

The day after the first daylight raid, the political commissary of Warnecke & Böhm called Zdeněk and me to his office. He never bothered with niceties and went straight to the point.

'Tůma, Šebesta, you should be honoured. The Allies, in their desperation at losing the war, have taken to bombing defenceless cities. We do not have enough firefighters in Berlin, so I have chosen you both. I have volunteered you to represent the company. You are young and strong and should continue your tasks as you have been doing them, with the same working hours. But whenever you are needed you will make yourself available to work as firefighters as well.'

Just as we were wondering if we would get paid for this honour, he said wryly that we would each be rewarded with a weekly pack of cigarettes.

It was not clear why we had been chosen. We were indeed young, and I am tall, but neither of us was particularly strong. Zdeněk and I debated the reasons for the 'honour'. Perhaps it was because as Slavs we had cohabited with German women, even if, officially, it had only been for a couple of months. Or perhaps it was revenge for refusing to say 'Heil Hitler' despite the rules. I wanted to be thought of as a slightly mad scientist, uninterested in anything political, focused simply on his formulas and experiments.

Now I was going to have to be a mad scientist who fought fires.

The father I knew was softly spoken, but it masked a relentless tenacity. His underlying boldness and strength of purpose were inviolable. Despite this, I never saw him as someone who was physically brave or daring. The strength he embodied was in every way connected to his mind and had very little to with his body. It was not that he particularly lacked physical strength. He was tall and rangy. He jogged, played tennis, skied. As he approached sixty, he would carry me on his shoulders and twirl me in circles in the garden. He loved to play. When he was closer to seventy our massive Rottweiler would pick up a long fallen branch from one of the dozens of tall palms that bordered the garden, and my father would join in a tug-of-war with him, leaning back with me against the weight of the determined dog.

Still, I cannot imagine him as a firefighter, as for that he would need a physical strength that was devoid of caution and fear. My father was always dynamic and brave, but also careful and considered. Any risk was taken after a prudent weighing of the potential benefits and costs. Perhaps he knew that his stint as a firefighter would be surprising to me; perhaps he felt the same need I do to prove his story, to me, to others, to himself. And so, once again, he left me a document that did just that.

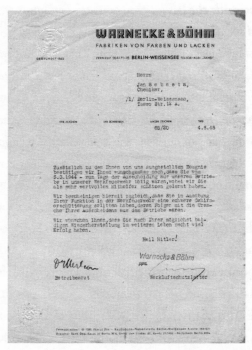

A letter from Warnecke & Böhm stating that my
father was part of the volunteer fire brigade.

This letter, dated May 1945, confirms that my father was a *valued member of the fire brigade* for fourteen months, starting in March 1944. It was signed by the manager of defence and the medical officer of the company, who noted that Jan Šebesta had to stop after suffering a severe concussion while on duty.

*The explosions threw us off our feet. The air pressure hurt our
ears. The thumping was so deafening that I failed to realise
the chaos around me. I shouted for Zdeněk because I wanted to
know that he was alive, that I was alive. People were screaming,
pushing and running away from the plant.*

I ran towards the destruction.

*I could see a small fire being put out through a smashed
window. There were wounded to take to the hospital. My eyes
found Zdeněk's in the crowded and smoke-filled corridor.*

We were among the lucky ones.

*A colleague from the lab, the head of another section, a tall
man, gloomy but sympathetic, had died in the bombardment.
His lungs exploded with the pressure, his face and torso were
so disfigured that he was unrecognisable. Two German workers
placed his body in a sack to be collected in the morning. I
watched as they closed the bag with a double knot of thick
string and attached a tag. They also attached a note saying
'Do not open', ensuring the parcel would pass the security guard
stationed by the warehouse door without interference. Once they
were done with their grisly wrapping, the men made a careful
record in the lab book, accounting for the materials that had
been used.*

The tag attached with string around the sack read:

'From: Warnecke & Böhm. Berlin.

Contents: Dr Ing, Carl Kemph.

Weight: 78 Kgs.'

*It struck me that these were the tags we used when we sent
out packages of lacquers. But I don't think the Germans found
this strange. They simply called the relevant office for the collection of corpses. Somehow the phone lines were working still.*

Everything that could be fixed after each bombardment was efficiently put right. The Germans were remarkable that way. Water, electricity, transport, phone lines. Everything that could be mended would immediately be repaired. It was a clear order from the Reich and the Germans were good at following orders. It was one thing at which the Nazis, especially, excelled. So a few hours after every bombardment, life carried on as if nothing had happened. Everything that could be repaired, would function again.

Except for Dr Kemph.

Sadly, poor Dr Kemph could not be put right.

Each time, the bombardments seemed to grow in intensity and duration. The cars in the city had all been adapted so that their lights cast light no more than two metres ahead. In homes, lights were seldom used unnecessarily, and curtains or blackout sheets were secured with tape around the windows to control the escape of light. As soon as the sirens howled below, and the engines roared above, everyone turned everything off. Each squadron's pathfinders marked the areas to be targeted with coloured flares. We called them 'Christmas trees'. The planes then carpet-bombed the marked area in waves.

As firefighters, Zdeněk and I had to go towards the Christmas trees and guess whether we were inside or outside the targeted square. He was as terrified as I was. More often than not we found ourselves inside the square.

The destruction in some parts of town was unimaginable.

Now that we were 'volunteered', we had to leave our shelter

even when bombs still rained down all around us. But our
dismay at the 'honour' bestowed upon us did not last long. On
the first night we realised that by directing the water hoses
we could control the fire. We could try to stop it or allow it to
propagate. We could effectively direct it. If there were no people
in danger and no one was watching, Zdeněk and I would allow
the flames to dance from building to building. As there were
fires everywhere and 'volunteers' were scarce, we were often quite
alone. Sometimes, even in the stench and roar and heat it felt
that we were Hans and Zdeněk, sixteen and in Prague again,
dressed up in our outsized uniforms and heavy hats playing a
game of make-believe. Our initial fear at being unsheltered was
temporarily overwhelmed by the simple joy of playing at fanning
the fire, but the harrowing reality would soon pierce the smoke
and ash and end the game. People were dying all around us and
we had to rescue them if we could.

A huge bomb had completely demolished a building a few
metres away from where we lived. Clouds of dust and fire rose up
from the pile of shattered cement that remained. We could hear
wailing and shouts from beneath. Chunks of concrete and metal
barred the exits from the air raid shelter there, and the living
were trapped with the dead inside. Peering through the cracks,
we realised that a wedding party had reached the shelter before
the raid began. The bride and groom were still recognisable,
their elegant clothes covered in blood, soot and dust. Through a
small hole I thought I could see them holding one another, sob-
bing. Bodies, people writhing, bricks and beams lay strewn all
around them.

We started moving the rubble by hand and scraped around
the cracks, but soon realised that we were making no progress

at all. The building had been rendered into immovable chunks of stone, millions of pebbles and dust. We ran for help through smashed streets. The bombing continued, but we managed to keep on moving, shielding ourselves when we heard the deafening clamour and whistling too close. Everyone hid underground in the shelters and the streets were deserted. We ran towards the centre of the city in the hope of finding other firefighters.

Then a shadow making deep, horrible noises advanced towards us, blocking our way forward. A small man, pushing a crooked wheelbarrow, emerged through the thick smoke. In the basin was a tiny body wearing a dress. Like a forgotten marionette, it lay with its limbs broken, deformed and immobile. It was obvious to Zdeněk and me that the child was dead. The noises we had heard were the man's guttural animal howls of grief.

The only light on the street came from the crackling flames. Everything else seemed to disappear and we were left alone with his cries and the explosions. Zdeněk was still next to me, but neither of us could speak. We stood paralysed, watching as he slowly made his way towards us on the pavement. Then, as if out of nowhere, a wall crumpled and collapsed, burying him and the girl. We ran towards the mound. There was nothing but a pile of brick and debris. Still dazed, we shifted the bricks to one side and hauled at the rubble. The man's face emerged, his eyes closed, his hands still holding the handles of the cart which carried his child.

Then there was silence. There were no more planes, no more screams. Even the crackling of the fire seemed to have stopped. Only quiet dust, settling everywhere like snow, covering the

devastation. I don't remember any more details or how Zdeněk
and I made it home that night.

It took two days and a dozen of us to get to the wedding
party. When, exhausted, we manage to dig a hole large and
safe enough to crawl through, the corpses of the bride and groom
were on opposite sides of the shelter. Somehow, among all the
horror, that is what surprised me.

I don't know if they had moved or if I had just imagined
seeing them together.

The weeks passed, but no day was like another. The raids
seemed to happen more often. Buildings crumbled all around us.

One evening we were summoned to Langhansstrasse. Fr.
Rudloff's apartment building, where I had spent my first night
in Berlin, had also been destroyed by the direct impact of a
bomb. No one managed to escape the inferno that ensued.
The fire brigade couldn't even attempt a rescue. Zdeněk and
I got there soon after the bombs hit but were kept back by
others. We couldn't do anything but watch it burn. I prayed
Helene Rudloff died instantly. Despite her severity, she always
was so courteous and proud. I could not bear to think of her
distressed.

She had not managed to rent the room after I moved.
People were going away from Berlin. No one wanted to be
in the city. No one was moving in. Despite my departure,
Fr. Rudloff had allowed me to store a suitcase in the cupboard
of my old room in her apartment. She had promised to keep
my things for me as long as I brought her some of my alcoholic

brew every week. I had lost only some clothes and shoes. Now my brown fireman's suit had become my second change of clothes. I was grateful to have it. It was thick and warm and easy to clean after a night's work. If I used it without the helmet, it looked quite smart.

It had been two consecutive nights of sirens. We had worked in the factory all day. The fire brigade operated in a rotation and that night we had been allowed to rest. As the sirens blared, Traudl and I hurried out of the apartment and ran into Ursula in the hallway. When the three of us entered the shelter, Zdeněk was not there. The whistling and explosions surrounded us. The shelter filled with people, and Ursula huddled up to Traudl and began to cry. Zdeněk was supposed to be in the apartment that night, waiting for her. He should have been with us by now.

'I'll get him,' I said as I scrambled my way out.

I ran to the building, bounded up the stairs and pushed open the door to their apartment as I screamed his name. There was no answer.

'Zdeněk!'

The sirens still moaned, and I could hear explosions to my left.

'Zdeněk!' I shouted, trying to make my voice heard as I paced the apartment. I was about to give up when I noticed something through the cracked bathroom door. It was the dark silhouette of Zdeněk in the shadows, sitting on the toilet. I ran in. He was completely naked and shivering.

'What are you doing? Did you not hear the sirens?'
I shouted.

'Handa. I am so tired. I didn't hear anything. I was sleeping.
I didn't have a chance to put clothes on. I just came to sit here.
I can't do it any more.'

He was looking at me steadily, but he was not himself. His
usual dark, darting eyes were slow and wide and vacant. I
took up a knitted blanket from the bed to wrap around him
and stop the shivering. 'Zdeněk, it's fine. But why are you
sitting there?'

His usual stutter was much more pronounced when he
was nervous. He stammered: 'Have you not noticed, Handa,
that when the buildings crumble under the bombs, the toilets
all remain attached to the walls? Even when everything else
falls down?'

I held his gaze and held his face in my hands as he sat
hunched, wrapped in the blanket.

'You are right, Zdeněk. But I need you to come with me
now,' I said urgently.

Zdeněk was correct. I had noticed it too. As the buildings
were obliterated, the toilets withstood the bombs, almost always
unharmed and exposed. We had noticed and had laughed
together at the randomness of it.

'Come, Zdeněk, come with me to the shelter.' I grabbed his
freezing hand and tried to lead him out. 'It's still safer than
the toilets.'

He continued to be frozen and looked at me without understanding. I put my hands under his legs and shoulders to
carry him down. He was short and very skinny, but I was still
surprised at how slight he felt. As we made it to the bottom of

*the stairs by the entrance to the shelter, he wrapped his arms
around my neck and shook and sobbed.*

'Remember, it's Jan, not Handa, here,' I whispered.

*As Traudl and Ursula made space for us I realised that I was
shaking too.*

Luck was still on Hans' side. The world in which he lived
continued to forge the haphazard boy poet into the robust
and controlled man he had become by the time I came along.
Others had always taken care of Hans – his parents, Zdenka,
Lotar and Míla. Lotar was the responsible older brother; with
their parents gone, it fell upon him and Zdenka to keep Hans
safe. Now, at twenty-three years of age, Hans was alone with a
solitary friend, living among enemies in an unfathomably dangerous city. He had scarcely fed and clothed himself unaided
before arriving in Berlin.

At times he had to take care of others, too. He had to help
rescue victims of the bombs. He also be had to be strong for
Zdeněk. For the first time in his life he could count only on
himself. The sickening fear created by his life in Berlin must
have been relentless. I had always thought my father's nightmares had to do with Czechoslovakia, but as I read his writings
about the war, it seemed to be his nights in Berlin that were
the stuff of terrors.

The days brought a different kind of fear as Hans continued
diligently to seek information that might usefully be passed on.

*The Dutch student and I met again, and as we walked to the
cemetery I explained what we were working on with Högn. He
said it would be best to get actual documents that he could get to*

the right people. The information was technical and most easily communicated in written form. It was tricky to get actual papers. I figured that I could take notes of conversations or transcribe documents. I started walking around the office with a note-book, a detail which I thought would be in keeping with Jan, the quirky Czech work-obsessed scientist. I constructed a plan to access material.

All the important documents were in a locked file in the office of the head of laboratories, a Prussian aristocrat named Von Straelborn. He had a secretary, Frau Bose, who sat in an anteroom to his office. I had heard colleagues say that she was unmarried. They had also mentioned that she was a racist and a ferocious Nazi. She had, however, flashed me a shy smile a couple of times when we passed in the hallway, so I retained hope that she might be open to a bit of flattery. She seemed to me to be my only way of accessing the information. The real problem was that all in the company knew I was spending time with Traudl, and starting a conversation would be tricky. But then everything fell into place. There had been a rumour that the company would be moving some operations to the plant in the south in Bavaria, away from the bombs. A few evenings later, Traudl cried as she told me that she was part of the team being moved. She had to pack and would leave with the others in the next days. She said that she was worried about me and made me promise I would visit her apartment. She wanted me to take care of it and also wanted to ensure I had a place to live. Sweet Traudl. We drank a bit of brew. It burned our throats but helped assuage our fears.

As soon as Traudl left for the south, I stopped by the desk of Frau Bose and asked her for help locating a file with the name of a compound for one of my experiments. At first she seemed *suspicious and didn't talk much. I started stopping by her cubicle every other day with one excuse or another. Eventually, the strategy began to work, and she told me to call her Inge. A few visits later she agreed to come with me for a Sunday stroll. It took only a few Sundays and a couple of beers to get the friendship established. She no longer found it odd that I lingered around her desk, which was always filled with interesting papers. I sensed that she finally trusted me when one afternoon she asked me to help her fix some loose floorboards in her apartment.*

From then on, she even sat next to me when we were in the same shelter during the raids. She also lived alone. The apartment was stark, the walls mostly devoid of decorations except for a shelf by the table which held a few ornaments, postcards from the Black Forest, and a framed photo of the Führer. As I worked to endear myself to her, he observed us with his dark eyes and expression of strained formality. It struck me then that I had rarely seen the Führer smile. He was always shown shouting or fierce and unforgiving.

I mentioned this to Zdeněk, in part to allay his concern that I was spending time with a true Nazi and to change the subject from his anxiety for my welfare. We agreed that the only people smiling in German propaganda seemed to be little blonde girls, their faces illuminated by laughter, their hair in two perfect plaits and their hands clutching wild flowers. It seemed to Zdeněk and me then that it was only German girls who were genetically capable of smiling. My assurances made little difference; Zdeněk continued to fear for my safety.

I had learned the useful skill of appearing to listen without letting the words get past my ears. I had to be able to hear without letting it affect me or betray my feelings. Inge was adamant that I understood her views on the war. She believed all killing could be justified as a means of establishing an empire governed by the superior Aryan race. She believed that this would ultimately be for the benefit of all people, as they would be led by the wise Nazis. Of course, it was true that those dominated would be serfs and subservient, but then they would all have the advantage of living in a world of order and general well-being. She claimed that the British and the Americans, who were not as pure of thought as the Germans but made of similar stuff, would soon see the error of their ways and align themselves with Nazi interests. She explained gravely that the Anglo-Saxons were currently fighting the Germans only because they had been conned into doing so by the wily Jews. She seemed entirely serious when she explained that Roosevelt's name was originally 'Rosenwelt', and she suspected that Churchill too might have a few drops of Jewish blood circling in his veins. I tried to focus on the fact that she apologised before saying that the Slavs were so inferior as to not belong fully to the rest of the human race.

'Of course, there are exceptions, Jan. In some rare cases, Slavs can have a similar mental capacity to Germans. You, for example. I heard Dr Högn say that you are quite bright. But in that case, it must be because your Czech ancestors had the foresight of mixing with Germans to improve their stock. Do you understand what I'm saying, Jan? Lots of Czechs have mixed in the past with Germans for this simple reason.'

I endured this imbecilic drivel in the hope of picking up a morsel about developments in Nazi technical capabilities. I tried to get her to move on from her racial pontification and talk more about her boss.

'Von Straelborn seems worried lately. You are always working late. I hope he is not making your life too difficult. Is he all right?'

'He is just busy and under a lot of pressure. They are in the middle of developing some finishes for new planes that will fly faster than anything before.'

Having got my morsel, I immediately started rambling on about office gossip. I did not want her to think I was too interested in her boss. And then, as usual, I escaped as quickly as I could.

I asked Dr Högn what innovations the Germans were accomplishing in aviation. He got so excited he decided to draw me a diagram of a jet plane. I kept this paper and put it together with some notes of the new camouflage system that the company was developing and passed it on to the Dutch contact after work the next day. He seemed very pleased. He never spoke to me much, to avoid arousing suspicions; but I could see gratitude in his eyes.

With Traudl in Bavaria, it was easy for me to stay late at the factory and try to get more details for the Dutch student. Dr Högn was so pleased with me he almost treated me like one of them. One evening, as we were finishing, he announced proudly: 'Now it is true that we are going to win this war. The Führer is finally going to have vengeance weapons that will make us unstoppable, and we are working on their development. You will work with me on this project. We must develop a finish for the weapons that will only allow high-pressure gases to escape from the exhaust.'

A few days later some men that I had never seen before brought a cylinder containing a dark solid mass. We covered it with our experimental concoction, leaving the bottom part uncovered. We left it to dry. The next day when I arrived, the men were already there, chatting with Högn. The youngest held a note-pad and looked at me studiously. The other brusquely asked me to light up the uncovered base of the cylinder. They took a step back as I held out the flame. As I focused on the cylinder, they disappeared from my sight. The cylinder seemed to need a lot of heat and initially would not ignite. As I looked around, I real-ised that I was standing alone. The two men and Dr Högn, the brave Germans, were in the corners of the room, on their knees, crouched under tables. I was aware of the danger of an explosion and the fact that I was being used. Being a Slav made me dispos-able. For a second, I hesitated. Could I refuse the role of guinea pig? But of course, I didn't have that choice. I pretended to be calm and lit the flame. The cylinder finally ignited with a flame so intense the whole thing propelled forward and fell with a crash to the floor. It hadn't lit properly and yet the force was extreme. I turned off the gas ignitor that was still in my hand. I spoke loudly with an attempt at authority.

'It is clear that this is an effective coating for a propellant rocket with liquid fuel.'

The other men rose to their feet and walked grandly towards me, somehow inflated by my assertion, as if they had never been cowering on the ground. 'This is excellent,' the one with glasses boasted. And then to Högn he said triumphantly with a chuckle: 'Werhner von Braun was correct. We will carry out proper, bigger tests in Peenemünde. Perhaps your team will be sent to help with the application of the lacquer there.'

That same day at lunch I signalled to my Dutch friend to meet me. As we walked aimlessly on the Berlin pavements, I told him about my morning. I had no papers for him, but it was the first time that his face betrayed intense surprise and interest. We agreed that next time I would obtain whatever documents I could and pass them to him folded inside a book.

A portrait of my father, composed and elegant, was among the papers in the box. A historian in Berlin in 2018 pointed out the pin on his lapel. It was the official corporate insignia of Warnecke & Böhm that was positioned to the left above his heart. The photograph was taken in 1944, when Hans was twenty-three years old. It would have been the photograph for his employee file with the firm. His head is held upright and proud, and he wears that perfected half-smile of Jan's.

It seems to me, though, that if you look closely, you can see fear in his eyes.

15

CHARADES

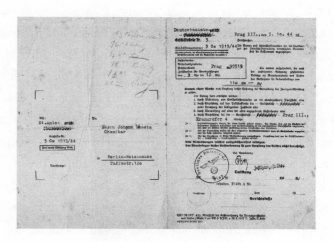

One document from my father's box seemed problematic as I worked on a timeline of his life during the war. The yellowing form, issued by the German District Court in Prague, stamped with the swastika on 5 October 1944, made no sense. It was addressed to Johann (the Germanised version of Jan) Šebesta, chemist at Tassostrasse, his registered address in Berlin. The form stipulated that a fine was to be paid as a result of the court case against him. Jan lived in Berlin from 1943 onwards. Why would a case have been brought in Prague in 1944 against a man who did not officially exist?

His writings explained.

Dr Högn called me into his office. As I entered, I was struck by the bumptious grin. His chubby fingers clasped in self-importance, he seemed very proud as he muttered, 'Ahh . . . I have a task for you that will bring you great pleasure. We have some issues with suppliers in Prague. This is not really your field and I'm sure they could be sorted out by someone else here, but I thought you'd like to take the opportunity to visit your home.'

I tried to absorb the news with the open joy that he expected. In reality, I was terrified. I could not go to Prague and pretend to be Jan. There were lots of people there who would recognise me. Under what name would I stay and where? I could not possibly spend time near the factory. I could not risk being seen. People there knew I had absconded from a transport. They knew I was wanted by the Gestapo. There would probably even be a reward for information on my whereabouts. Someone, anyone really, could turn me in. But I couldn't betray my terror, so I smiled broadly and countered, 'Dr Högn, thank you, it is truly so kind of you. But I don't think it's my area of expertise. I am no good with people.'

'I know,' he said, coming towards me. 'But you've been doing a good job, and I think you'll enjoy going to see your old Bohemian friends.'

He patted my back. I felt like I was going to collapse.

'You will travel as the company's official envoy next week and you can stay for a whole week.'

'Thank you, Herr Dr. Thank you for the great news.'

I could see no way out. I had to go. I shared my fears with Zdeněk. He was scared for me too but agreed that there seemed to be no avoiding it. Jan Šebesta would have to return to Prague.

As before, I decided to travel on the night train. This time, though, I could not travel first class. The carriages were more than half empty. People didn't really want to move unnecessarily in the middle of a war. It was safer to stay close to home. When I had taken my seat, I put my head down and then strained to peer up to scour the other faces for familiarity. I grew calmer as I realised that I had not seen any of the people in my compartment before.

I had an official travel permit and a German identity card. I kept on telling myself there should be no problems this time. There was no need for the cyanide capsule to be taken out of my briefcase. Everything went smoothly, and I managed to sleep a little after we had passed through border control. As we had agreed in our brief telephone call, Míla was waiting for me at the station. She tried to embrace me. I pushed past and grabbed her hand to leave the terror of a public space as quickly as possible. She drove me directly to the small apartment where I had hidden with my brother and Zdenka after my parents had been sent away. There, Zdenka met us and greeted me with an enormous embrace. She handed me a bundle of letters and assured me that my parents, Lotar and she were all fine. She whispered over and over that I must be careful. We determined it would be best if she and Lotar stayed away. We were desperate to see each other, but simply could not take the risk of someone following them or spotting me. I phoned them every morning and evening, to reassure myself that they were well and close. The first day I called the two suppliers and explained that I had just arrived from Berlin and fallen ill. I asked them whether we could deal with our business over the phone and offered to send my assistant to their offices to collect any paperwork or materials that needed to go back to Berlin. They both agreed. Míla, always helpful, played the part of my assistant and went to their offices to collect the papers and chemicals.

*I stayed a week in the apartment without taking a step outside.
I barely dared to look out of the window. I longed to walk along
my old streets, visit my parents' house, see Lotar and Zdenka,
but even thinking about it made me nervous. Míla came only at
night, to minimise the chances of running into acquaintances
along the way who might ask too many questions. She brought me
food that she'd prepared at her parents' apartment. She left some
pâté, bread and her rohlíčky sugar cookies in the shape of crescent
moons. I could barely touch them, and they had always been a
favourite. The constant knot in my stomach left no space for food.
I was careful that there were no smells or noises to create any
unnecessary reminder of my presence. We moved around barefoot,
spoke in hushed words as we played cards and shared stories. We
wanted to spend time together, but I was an anxious wreck. I tried
to remain positive to get through it. Things in Prague did not
seem to be worse than in Berlin. At least there were no bombs and
one could sleep, albeit fitfully, at night.*

*I read and reread the dozens of letters from Terezín that
Zdenka had given me. I imagined my parents' tones and voices
and was happy to feel them with me despite the conditions
they described. They knew I had left Prague and had only been
addressing the letters to Lotar and Zdenka. But I knew they
were for us all. My mother's letters were usually addressed to 'My
golden ones'. She had always called us that. One of my earli-
est memories was of falling down the stone steps at Libčice. My
mother had cleaned my cuts and, as I flinched at the sting of
the powdered antiseptic, she comforted me with murmurs that
I was her golden one. My father, as I expected, filled his letters
with lists and detailed descriptions. Stern as always, he had
decided that my mother was having an affair. He had always been*

enraged by the fact that men adored my mother. It seemed to me that men couldn't help but be happy in her presence; all men, that is, except my father.

I spent the noiseless, lonely days writing letters that I hoped would reach my parents. I played solitaire with the old deck of cards and peered out of the window. I tried to write poems, but nothing came out. Jan was not a poet. I felt like a prisoner caged in the apartment. At least I was able to see Míla and hold her. She was so gentle and thoughtful, it almost made me forget what was happening around us.

The night before I was due to return to Berlin, Míla and I went over my documents as we ate dinner. I thought my eyes were failing me as I stared in horror at my permit. Dr Högn had said that I could take a week. In my alarm, I had failed to check my papers. My permit was not valid for a week but for four days. I should have returned to Berlin three days earlier. How could I have been so foolish and not checked it before? Travel was restricted, and Jan's permit to be in Prague had expired. I was there illegally.

Legally, I was required to seek an extension of the permit from the Gestapo, but that would have been suicide. Míla agreed. She tried to calm me and said we'd come up with a plan, but she too was frantic at the discovery. She left me with a plate of half-eaten food and said she would find Lotar and Zdenka to get their advice. She didn't feel the phone was safe. She promised to be back as soon as she could. She left and I grew more desperate. In a complete panic, I decided to alter the ink on the permit and change the date from a 24 into a 29. Once done, there was no reason to wait around in further agony, there was nothing to do, no point in putting it off or saying goodbyes. I pencilled a short note for Míla, telling her not to worry and that I would write from Berlin.

I pulled the brim of my hat down low and walked quickly to the station without glancing up at the streets I knew so well. Once again, I took my seat on the night train and braced myself. This time I put the cyanide capsule in my breast pocket and eventually transferred it to my mouth. Then I waited.

After a while, the inspector came. He asked to see my permit and began to study it with care, turning it in both hands. He looked at me without a hint of humanity in his eyes. Then he walked away. I pressed the tiny vial in my mouth nervously with my tongue until he came back.

'Your return date is irregular. The authorities need to check your document. Come with me.'

Numb, I climbed down from my carriage and followed him into the border station. The train sat entirely silent on the tracks, as if asleep. The world around me seemed frozen. Another guard on duty pointed me to a room. I went in and stood against a wall, frail with fear. Too weak to bite into the vial.

The second guard asked where I worked and why I had been in Prague. Before I could answer, he looked steadily at me and asked why I had altered my permit. I pushed the capsule to the side of my mouth. I started to tell him the truth.

'I was sent by Warnecke & Böhm, where I am employed, for a week to fix some matters with suppliers back home.'

Much to my surprise, he seemed to believe it. I nudged the cyanide with my tongue and spoke slowly and more nasally. 'The company organised it all. I had not read the date until tonight and I just panicked.'

It was always hard to speak while holding the vial, but I'd had a lot of practice by then.

'And you've taken this opportunity to see your girlfriend, right?'

He winked at me. I tried to smile weakly, unsure of him, careful not to commit to a response. He continued. 'I know how you feel. A few extra days with your girl, and she makes you brave enough to change the date. You rascal!'

Still in shock, I realised that he almost approved, as if he would have done the same. And then I saw that he was my age and had no wish to be stationed there. He probably missed his home too. He laughed as he filled out a form. Reassured, I coughed the vial out into my hand and pretended to laugh too. I pocketed the poison. When he looked up at me, he seemed to have cheery tears in his eyes. I smiled back at my fellow conspirator.

'Unfortunately, this is a matter for the tribunals, not for us. Get back on the train and go to your job. I am sure they'll need you there. The authorities will get in touch with you in due course to sort this out.'

The incident must have taken less than five minutes, though it felt like hours. I ran back and was taking the seat in my carriage as the train started to pull out. The journey was sleepless, there was only adrenaline running through my arteries. I was so relieved to arrive in Berlin that the incident seemed a faraway dream.

I told no one about this other than Zdeněk. We convinced ourselves that the whole thing would be forgotten in the chaos of the war, but a few weeks later a letter arrived from the Czech police. The usual bureaucracy: forms to fill out, a description of my offence. When I read the last part, my heart stopped. I was summoned to appear in front of a tribunal in Prague in three weeks.

After another sleepless night, I figured that approaching Högn was my only hope. Hoping that he'd remember that he had told me I'd have a week, I walked into his office and confessed the whole thing.

'I got carried away by seeing my girlfriend and didn't check the documents until the last night. You remember, Herr Dr, you told me I had a week?'

Luckily, yes, he remembered.

'Please, Herr Dr,' I begged. 'You are such an important man, you have important friends. You have so much influence, could you not help me out? What good would it do us all if I went to the trial and they decided to throw me in jail? Please.'

And then, I don't know if out of vanity or kindness or pity or because I was useful to him, he spoke and told me not to worry. He would do what was needed.

'Your Czech girlfriend must be quite something.'

A few weeks later, Högn again called me into his office. From a neat file on his desk, he handed me a piece of paper saying I had to pay a fine of 110 marks. 100 for the fine, 10 marks for the administration fee.

'It's all fixed, you just pay the fine. I have even arranged it so it won't appear in your penal records.'

Then he winked at me, as the guard had done, and his round eyes gleamed with pride. Högn had, once more, unintentionally saved my life. Not that I cared if the incident appeared in any records. I prayed that Jan Šebesta could soon disappear for ever. I asked for permission to leave the building and walked the few streets to the bank in Weissensee to pay the fine immediately.

I was beside myself with fury. How could Jan Šebesta have been so careless? If Högn had not intervened, there would have been no other option but to run away again and cross over to Holland or France in the hope of finding a group of Maquis [members of the underground French resistance during the German occupation]. And that would have been next to impossible.

The official papers detailing the fine and the cancellation of the court appearance found their way eventually from the German District Court in Prague to the Czech who did not exist but who was working in Berlin. Jan Šebesta was saved once more by extraordinary luck. He was also becoming more resourceful and resilient. The transformation of the young man who had left Prague was almost complete. Yet Hans the unfortunate one, still a little careless, had let matters slip. He would never again permit any lack of attention that could cost him his life.

Another odd scrap of paper was preserved in my father's box. It was a torn bank receipt, the teller's proof that on 4 November 1944, Jan paid his fine of 100 Reichsmarks to the Czech police, with an extra 10 to cover the administration fee.

Jan continued to work at Warnecke & Böhm during the day and perform his duties as a firefighter with Zdeněk at night. By April 1944, the Allies had temporarily paused their campaign of bombing Berlin as all efforts were redirected to prepare for the advance of the troops who landed in Normandy on 6 June 1944. Berlin was not left undisturbed, though. Nuisance and diversion raids, as well as false alarms, continued to terrorise the city's inhabitants. News of raids on other cities reached them daily. Peenemünde, the military research centre that was supplied by Warnecke & Böhm, was itself targeted. Shortages of food, clothing and materials compounded the misery.

The Germans were now fighting on two major fronts, in the East and in the West. In spite of the Nazi propaganda machine and their attempts at absolute control of information, news from abroad seeped into Berlin, and for Jan and Zdeněk, there was hope that the defeat of Germany was near. Jan did what he could to hasten it.

Aside from three or four things, the papers that I had obtained from Dr Högn's office seemed to hold very little of interest for the Allies, and I was thoroughly disheartened. The Dutchman encouraged me to remain positive and said that all information about the company's developments for the Luftwaffe was useful. The more information I gathered and passed on, the greater the chance that the war would end soon. These words were what I repeated to myself as I sifted through each tedious note of an experiment, one slow word at a time, looking for something that might be important.

For a while in 1944, the bombings seemed to have stopped. I pretended to be interested in creating a highly combustible substance similar to nitrocellulose that would accelerate the man-ufacturing of our lacquers. I asked Dr Högn if I could have his permission to perform experiments alone. Dr Högn agreed, as long as I worked during my free time.

This meant that I could stay late in the labs. I was given a special permit allowing me to access the factory after hours. I had all night to search the desks for documents or notes that might carelessly not have been locked away and try to find something useful to pass on. I opened every drawer of every desk in my department but, despite my enthusiasm, found only details to add to what I had already passed on to my Dutch friend.

I considered this a defeat and it troubled me enormously. In some way, my failure to lay my hands on something more substantial felt like another victory for them.

The few letters that I have from 1944 tell me very little about Otto and Ella's state of mind. They are more staccato, and the lyrical tone has faded. While Otto made brief mentions of his protégées Olina and Stella, the letters focused largely on practicalities, parcels and Ella's state of health. By April 1944, Ella was unable to write and was once more bedridden in the hospital in Terezín.

In June 1944, envoys from the Red Cross visited Terezín. The visit had been negotiated by the Danish Red Cross, who requested an inspection following the deportation by the Germans of 476 Danish Jews to the camp. The Nazis, obviously aware of the importance of this visit and its propaganda potential, prepared for it. A sham 'beautification' programme was implemented, which included planting gardens, renovating barracks, painting buildings, constructing a sports field in the middle of the square and, to ease overcrowding, deporting thousands to Auschwitz. In the three days from 16 to 18 May, more than 7,500 people were transported.

My grandparents managed to avoid selection. Discreetly supervised by SS officers, on 23 June the Terezín inmates acted out the charade of being content with their lot for the benefit of the three Red Cross visitors. People who were ill or mal-nourished were confined to their rooms. An orchestra played on a newly constructed bandstand, children were made to sing, the streets were filled with people chatting, and a football match was played on a newly laid pitch. The gendarmes were given the day off to support the illusion that the prisoners were happy. Despite the rumours that they must have heard, none of the Red Cross visitors asked a question sufficiently probing to establish the truth. The inmates themselves by then would have known of the Normandy invasion and would have been hopeful that the end of the war was near. This, in addition to the ever-present fear of reprisal, must have been a further incentive to maintain the artifice. There is no record of any of this sham in my possession; I have no postcards or letters from June 1944. Ella was in the hospital, and I cannot imagine that my grand-father, so stern and righteous, would have played much of a role in the pantomime. The Red Cross visit was deemed so success-ful by the Nazis that they decided to re-create the charade for a propaganda film to be shown to the Allies to counter reports of genocide. The filming lasted three weeks. The cast and crew were among the tens of thousands subsequently deported to Auschwitz in September and October 1944.

The last pieces of correspondence that I have from my

grandparents are two brief postcards to Lotar and Zdenka dated 15 September 1944, one from each of them. Ella and Otto both thanked their *golden ones* for all their letters and kindnesses, enclosed short messages for their friends, talked about restrictions and asked for news. They explained that they would be allowed to write only once every eight weeks. Ella ended her card by saying that she thought of her loved ones constantly and prayed for their well-being.

Ella and Otto bade their children farewell with kisses.

There was one more communication from Ella, the original of which was not among the others, probably because it must have been almost unbearable for Lotar and Zdenka to read. Its contents were recalled much later by Lotar. Ella, weakened and desolate, had a note smuggled out from the hospital to report that on 29 September 1944, my grandfather had been deported alone to Auschwitz in a transport she referred to as 'labour'.

Otto had remained strong and healthy, and the family continued to be hopeful, given the classification of the transport, that he would survive.

There is one more piece of paper, undated, among the letters from the camp. Initially, it baffled both the translator and me. It was a note, written by someone with little formal schooling and signed *Mrs Rosa*. The writer, who was clearly panicked, scribbled that she could not *find Mrs Mother at her usual place.* She promised that she had *looked everywhere and asked at the camp, but no one knew where she had gone.* Mrs Rosa explained that she had been unable to deliver the package, as she had promised to do. She asked Mrs Jedličková, which was Zdenka's maiden name, to *confirm a day and time to meet at Bohušovice station so she could return the parcel of goods in a wheelbarrow.*

Note from Mrs Rosa.

Mrs Rosa, anxious to return the undelivered parcel, was the unwilling bearer of the news that Lotar and Zdenka had dreaded.

Ella was deported to Auschwitz on 19 October 1944, with her niece Zita in a special transport that included those who were unwell.

The letters and cards were the last link between the parents and their children. When the letters stopped, the lives of Otto and Ella were plunged into darkness. It was almost impossible to have any communication with the inmates of Auschwitz and camps in Eastern Europe.

In Prague, the offices of the Judenrat were instructed that all the remaining Jews, including those who had intermarried or worked on the Council, were to be deported. It was only a matter of time until Lotar found his name on a list. It would be impossible to hide from the Gestapo. Denunciation for reward was highly likely, given the miserable conditions that people were enduring as the Reich crumbled. Lotar and

Zdenka were living in one of her apartments and did not trust their neighbours. Zdenka later recalled that decisive action was required. The increasingly obvious disintegration of the German military machine had created opportunities. Soldiers were becoming nihilistic, reflective or desperate. Others were just running wild in a frenzy of violence, a terrifying prospect for anyone who caught their attention. Zdenka, as astute in her judgement as ever, identified an SS guard who, for some reason, was susceptible to her approach. She did not record how she prevailed upon him, whether it was bribery, a desire to protect himself in the future or perhaps even kindness. He agreed to help.

Early one February morning in 1945, this man, in SS uniform, barged noisily into their apartment building on Podskalská Street. He shouted, slammed doors, knocked down pictures and threw furniture around as loudly as he could. The commotion woke all the neighbours. He acted the scene so perfectly that Lotar and Zdenka became scared and wondered whether they had been duped and the man actually intended to arrest or shoot them. He chased Lotar and Zdenka down the stairs at gunpoint and then out, around the corner. When they reached an alleyway, to Lotar and Zdenka's great relief, the SS man declared: 'Well, that does it, I guess. Goodbye now. Good luck.'

Satisfied that there were now multiple witnesses to his arrest, many of whom might have been potential informers, Lotar returned as quickly and discreetly as he could to Zdenka's apartment on Trojanova Street. Just as before, when they had sat out the aftermath of Heydrich's assassination, only the building's caretaker was entrusted to keep their secret. To complete her pretence, Zdenka burst into the offices of the Judenrat and, later that day, the SS headquarters and hysterically protested that her beloved and innocent husband had been taken at dawn. All those who heard her recounting the arrest concluded that it was unlikely that Lotar Neumann would be heard of again.

Their ploy succeeded. The charade served to throw the Gestapo off Lotar's scent. No one would be looking for him now. As an added precaution, Lotar started to use Ivan Rubeš's identity once more. The Federation of Jewish Communities in the Czech Republic holds a record card for Lotar, bearing a red stamp dated 10 February 1945: *HAFT*.

Imprisoned.

16

WHAT REMAINS OF US

On 14 February 1945, four days after Lotar was officially declared imprisoned, the Allies set out to bomb Dresden, the German city some 115 kilometres northwest of Prague. Allied planes had been seen over Prague before, but they had never attacked. That day, those involved later explained, a combination of faulty radar, high winds and heavy clouds led to a navigational error. Disorientated, between twelve-twenty-eight p.m. and twelve-thirty-three p.m., sixty-two American bombers descended on Prague in three waves and carpet-bombed it. It was so unexpected that the city's air raid sirens wailed only after the first bombs hit. Most people were unable to seek shelter. In those five minutes, the planes dropped 152 tons of explosives.

More than seven hundred civilians were killed and close to a thousand injured. The crisis was exacerbated by the fact that most Prague firefighters had been despatched to help in Dresden. Hundreds of historical monuments and buildings were damaged. One of Zdenka's buildings, where her mother and sister lived, was hit. In the panic that followed the extraordinarily brief but savage onslaught, Lotar and Zdenka abandoned caution and ran to find them. Zdenka's mother was hurt but was able to walk. Marie, her nineteen-year-old sister, was badly injured, with a severe concussion and serious wounds to her legs. It was Lotar, supposedly in prison, who took her in his arms and, in plain daylight, carried her down the streets to the University Hospital. There, in a bombed-out infirmary, her life was saved.

Much of Europe succumbed to chaos in the early months of 1945 as war raged and the Reich crumbled. Berlin and Prague were no exceptions. The Russian army was advancing, and the Germans were staging an increasingly desperate defensive war. The bombing of Berlin by the Allies had started up again on 3 February with the largest daylight attack on the city to date. Thousands lost their lives, tens of thousands were injured and hundreds of thousands were displaced as a result of that raid alone. Through the smoke and dust of the bombs and fires of the Allied raids, Berliners could see and hear that the Soviet army was drawing ever closer.

In January 1945, my father found himself dealing with a wholly unexpected challenge. He was temporarily blinded in a laboratory explosion at the factory. This was followed by a brief enforced respite from the fire brigade as a result of having suffered a concussion while on duty. One of my documents from the box is a medical note from 31 January 1945, signed by Dr Hermann Gysi, stating that Jan was being treated three times a week for Vegetative Dystonia, a disorder of the nerves that does not seem to be caused by a physical illness. Among its common symptoms are heart palpitations, chills, fear, insomnia, feelings of suffocation and panic attacks. It is clear that Jan Šebesta's life was taking a toll on his health.

By then, four months had passed without news of his parents or any of the family members who had been sent east. Amid the work, the firefighting, the bombings, the impending arrival of the Soviets and the fear of being uncovered, my father's only links with his former self were Zdeněk and an occasional surreptitious telephone call to Lotar or Míla. Berlin grew more dangerous with each passing day. It was time to go home to Prague.

In what was by now a characteristically careful way, Jan Šebesta approached the question of a transfer to Prague with complete professionalism. He made an official application for permission to return home so that he could apply his talents there and even obtained a letter of reference from Warnecke & Böhm.

Dated 5 April 1945, the document from my box was printed on official company letterhead and read:

Mr Jan Šebesta, born on 11 March 1921 in Alt Bunzlau, was employed as a chemist in our laboratory between 3 May 1943–5 April 1945.

Mr Šebesta successfully performed all tasks assigned to him which spanned the fields of synthetic lacquer chemistry, analytical chemistry, the development of special lacquers and sealing materials. Endeavouring to keep up-to-date with the latest scientific advances and continuously inspecting industry publications relating to synthetics and the specialised lacquer sector, Mr Šebesta acquired sound professional expertise. He distinguished himself by his exemplary diligence and a deep enthusiasm for the work entrusted to him. Mr Šebesta was highly regarded by his co-workers due to his helpful and friendly nature.

Mr Šebesta is leaving our company at his own request in agreement with the employment office in Berlin in order to return to his home country. We wish him all the success for the future.

Warnecke & Böhm

I was struck by the phrase *exemplary diligence*. It was exactly the language that anyone would have used of the father I knew, but not of Hans the happy-go-lucky boy from Prague. If Otto had read this reference, he would have been surprised. He also would have been proud.

The boy who had come to Berlin in the spring of 1943 was not the man who, two years later, fought his way through the crowds to leave it.

The journey began in Berlin. I had managed to get on board outside the main station as the carriages were being prepared. I boarded an hour before the scheduled departure and I wasn't alone. There were many who, like me, had thought to do this. I was prepared to bribe the conductor and the cleaners, but I didn't have to. We fought our way up the step to the door of the wagons. No one really seemed to care too much about the rules any more.

Nothing mattered. Everyone wanted to escape.

Everyone expected the Russian army and the Americans and their allies to meet and defeat the Nazis in a matter of days or even hours. The Germans had lost the war. Everyone knew it by then. Rumours of extreme cruelty by the Russians were every-where. We were all scared that they'd speed up their advance and stop our train. I prayed it would not be the Russians.

The train was packed. It was the second week of April and outside you could feel that spring was approaching. The carriages were not heated, but it was swelteringly hot inside the train.

It was evening and there was no light inside the carriages. Lights attracted attention, made trains and stations easier targets from the air. Our periodic stops were pointless, as no one could get on the train. There was simply no room. In the dimness, you could see the desperate faces on the platforms, the shoving, the fights for a small space. Everyone wanted to get out of Germany.

Only a handful made it into the carriages and, then, only when another handful had disembarked. The movement of the train didn't affect the passengers at all, as we were all closely wedged together. We were a dense human mass with no air in the gaps, composed of hot, malodorous bodies that seemed to melt into one.

In front of me in the throng, a man stepped on my shoe. He turned to apologise, his breath full of onion, garlic and weeks without toothpaste. I could not escape the smell. I could not kneel to tie my shoelace.

I was wearing an old striped shirt, an even older pair of trousers and tennis shoes. No socks and no suitcases. Just a small valise with my papers, the case of cyanide, some Reichsmarks and Míla's good-luck doll. Everything else had stayed behind in Berlin. Not that there was much.

One of the later bombs in the recent raid, one that caused destruction using air pressure, had razed the building next door. It half-destroyed ours too. I took it as a warning and had been lucky to escape before a second bomb fell and caused our building to collapse into a pile of dust. No one from our building had died. For one more day, we were the lucky ones.

This was still Germany, of course; there were formalities even to escape. I still couldn't believe that I had managed to get the paperwork from the bureaucrats in the Ministry of Labour. I had walked into the hall and picked the person who looked the most terrified, a fidgety middle-aged man. I watched him as I awaited my turn and then told him, 'I have been in Berlin for two years. I have my papers. If you give me a permit to return to Bohemia, I will not forget you and will report that you have helped me.'

He had a nervous tic that made his eyes blink repeatedly. He carefully explained that they were only issuing travel permits for exceptional cases, cases of importance to the Reich. I looked at him and focused my eyes intently on his. I said in a hushed tone,

'This is not a matter of importance for the Reich. This is a matter of importance to you. If you deny me the permit, I will remember you and you will regret it.'

I continued slowly to ensure he heard my every word.

'I will remember your name and your face. If you give me the permit to go back home to Bohemia, I will give you my address and you can find me. If there is a case against you, I will be a witness to your kindness when the Reich falls apart.'

This was a risky approach, but it was the only leverage I had, my only hope. If I didn't leave now, I might not be able to do so later. I looked at his face as he blinked furiously back at me. He looked around, sweating copiously, and stammered out something unintelligible. He cast his eyes downward and nodded. He had filled out the permit.

No one bothered to check the tickets or the permits in the chaos. Twice during the journey to the border, the engines of approaching planes terrified us. The noise made by the aircraft outside and above us was overwhelming and seemed to seep into all in the carriage. We froze. We held our breath. During the second approach, we heard explosions and gunfire. From a corner, there was a sob. For a moment, we all thought the train was under attack. And then, as we neared the Czech border, the noise receded and disappeared. All fell silent and, once more, all I could hear was the sound of the incessant rumbling and churning of the wheels of our train.

We crossed the frontier and the first colours of morning started to light up the train. I tried to imagine the smells outside, the flowery breeze of the Bohemian countryside in spring. The man next to me started retching. I could not move away, and he stained the shoulder of my only shirt. I had never stopped to think before about how sour the smell of vomit is.

The metallic screech of the brakes heralded our arrival into Prague. The hordes started to sputter from the wagons, each person eager to get off, to flee.

Míla had been waiting for me at the station. I locked my eyes on hers as I pushed through the crowds. Even from afar, I was grateful for their blue beauty and their peace. I could barely speak as she held me.

'You are home, Handa, we are together, it is safer here.'

We walked through Prague to Lotar and Zdenka's apartment, where I would hide again, hopefully not for long and for the last time.

It was a beautiful morning. I felt the familiar uneven cobblestones through the thin soles of my shoes. Míla and I walked side by side, one small hand around my waist, the other clasping my hand. I was so tired, so hungry. I just wanted to feel the sun on my face and eat and sleep. There was so much to tell her, but I had no words.

There were still some German soldiers on the streets, but very few. The city seemed surprisingly calm and whole. We walked

along the river. The cool breeze erased the acrid smell from the
train. To one side of us were the remnants of shattered build-
ings, mistakenly bombed by the Allies in February. Next to us,
the Vltava flowed, indifferent and calm.

  My only identity card bore the name Jan Šebesta. I would
have to wait until the city was liberated to become Hans
Neumann again.

Hans was reunited with Lotar and Zdenka in their apartment at
Trojanova 16. From Zdenka's writings, I know that the city now
concealed many others alongside him, and so did the apartment.
Conditions in Prague were typical of the chaos that reigned across
Europe. Though Terezín itself was not liberated until 8 May,
some of the concentration camps had been liberated as early as
the autumn of 1944. This continued through to the spring of
1945, as the Allied armies advanced deeper into Europe.

  Several survivors of the camps, whom Lotar and Zdenka had
helped during the war, showed up on their doorstep, homeless
and destitute. A German cousin of Zdenka's, who had deserted
from the army, also appeared, asking for shelter. The apartment was filled with people of all creeds and political factions,
united by hunger, exhaustion and desperation, all scared of
every doorbell ring and of every noise. They passed the days
just trying to stay alive and to get along in this makeshift
refuge. Zdenka and Lotar distributed their clothes and shared
the contents of their pantry. Through friends, they sought extra
blankets and a little more food. Zdenka wrote that for weeks,
they were 'like sardines sleeping on the floor or the sofa or
wherever they could', and that, for her new guests, 'anything
was better than the camps or the fronts'.

The resistance in Bohemia and Moravia had regrouped after the Heydrichiáda in 1942 and grown to a few thousand after years of war. In early May its members organised an uprising against the remaining German forces in Prague. Emboldened Czechs took to the streets, vandalised German property, tore down Nazi flags, painted over German signs. Fighting ensued between the residual SS forces and the Czechs who had been joined by the so-called Russian Liberation Army, a faction of Russians who had been fighting with the Nazis but had switched sides. Prague was bombed by the Luftwaffe while the German troops on the ground massacred, tortured and injured thousands. The Czechs in turn, after years of oppression, exacted retribution from the Germans and their collaborators. The brutal fighting in the streets, train stations and within key buildings in the city lasted for four days. Eventually, on 9 May 1945, a day after the liberation of Terezín and a day after the official Victory in Europe Day, Prague was liberated by the Red Army. After more than six years, the occupation was finally over. On 23 May 1945, Zdenka wrote to Otto's brother, Uncle Richard, in America. I have the letter:

Dear Uncle Richard,

We are using the first opportunity that we have had to report to you what remains of us. We are devastated to tell you that only three of us are left from the entire Neumann family, Lotar, Handa and I. From the Haas side, only our cousins Zdeněk Pollak and Hana Polláková survived. We do not know about the others. There is very little chance that any will come back. The three of us only survived because we lived underground, Lotar and me in Prague and Handa in Berlin. All three of

us are completely healthy and we are trying to earn our keep
somehow. We need you and your advice, as we will have to take
care of various family matters and issues relating to Montana,
which withstood the war reasonably well. We are living in an
unimaginable chaos and we really could use your opinion on all
matters. As you can see, the family suffered terribly.
  What a price we paid for not listening to your advice in 1939.
Please, please send us your reply by return.

Gradually, weakened survivors began to trickle into Prague
with news of the concentration camps in the east. That
summer, Zita Polláková and Erich Neumann returned home.
I do not know precisely when Lotar and Hans discovered
that their mother had travelled from Terezín on transport
ES with her niece Zita, but it was in those days of appalling
reckoning immediately after the war that they learned their
mother's story.

On arrival at Auschwitz, there had been a selection process:
250 men were selected for work in the coal mines and a few
dozen women, among them Zita, were chosen to be transported further east to work in the camps. Zita was one of 51
people on a transport of 1,500 who survived the war. Ella,
along with the rest of the sick, had been sent directly to the
gas chambers. I cannot imagine the grief that Hans, Lotar and
Zdenka must have felt on hearing the news.

Lotar wrote the American family a five-page letter dated
29 June 1945, informing them that Ella had been gassed upon
arrival at Auschwitz. This was the document my father had
shown me on the dawn that followed my brother Miguel's
funeral. After sending the letter, none of the three, Hans,

Lotar or Zdenka, wrote or spoke about Ella's death for the rest
of their lives.

Stella Kronberger, Otto's protégée from the camp,
returned to Prague and told the family about his last months
in Terezín. He had kept up his good spirits and stayed healthy
and strong. Stella told Otto's anxious sons that he had been
sent away on a labour transport, so they also clung to the
hope that he could have worked his way out of the camps and
might make it home.

Records show that Otto had been sent on labour transport
EI on 29 September 1944, with the number 164. On arrival
at Auschwitz, he too faced the selection process. SS doctors
and guards designated some for labour in various camps.
Those deemed old or weak were put aside and sent to the
gas chambers.

My father recorded in his memoir the account that he had
pieced together:

*Like everyone there, my father knew that the trick to maximis-
ing your chances of surviving was to appear young. You had to
look healthy, strong. Able to work. The Germans needed evidence of your potential as a labourer.*

*In our family, our hair turns grey early, salt and pepper by
thirty, alabaster by middle age. I had always been told that this
made us look distinguished. I suppose in more normal times that
might have been true. Yet our hair, to Nazi eyes, would make us
look older than our years. At a crucial moment, that could make
us seem useless, expendable.*

We were acutely aware of this. We had been warned.

For my father, with his distinguished hair, it was just a

matter of time until they deemed him too old. Too old and worthless, simply because he had white hair at the age of fifty-three. Between Zdenka, Lotar and friendly contacts, we'd arranged for some gendarmes to allow into Terezín parcels of 20 kg containing currency, goods and letters for our parents. The brave couriers would bring their letters and news back to us. At first, we had sent hair dye. And when it became impossible to source hair dye even on the black market, we had to find something else. Zdenka, Lotar and I had tried everything and eventually decided that black shoe polish would have to do. We had tried it and it worked. It had a foul smell and it washed off, but it coloured the hair well enough. Zdenka even sneaked it into Terezín herself when we could not get the gendarme to help us. And when she could not get in to the ghetto, she bribed a guard there who agreed to take it to my father.

My father, who always appeared so distant, with a sternness that seemed rooted in the worries of all humanity. He was constantly trying to solve problems, always weighed down by the existence of evil and injustice. And yet he repeated that the war would soon be over and reminded us to hold on to hope, as peace, he said, was just around the corner. He always wrote in his letters that the family would survive and maintained that soon we would all be together again.

But then, as summer ended, we found all our efforts and letters to the Elders had failed. My father had been included in one of the dreaded journeys to the east. Always cautious, he had brushed his hair with the polish and placed the tin in the inner pocket that my mother had sewn near the seam of his shirt. In a world where little made sense, his shoe polish had become the most precious commodity. As important as food to guarantee life.

The transports were always 1,000 people. It was a perfect round number that allowed for 20 wagons of 50 people, each with their permitted 40 kg of belongings, though whatever they had left after all the confiscations and the desperate barter of the ghetto never amounted to that. The healthy stood, the others, treated like numbed animals, lay one on top of the other. As soon as the train was ready, the doors were sealed. There was no ventilation, no fresh air inside. It took twenty-four hours to reach the destination. Then the doors opened again.

Exhausted and dizzy from the long journey and the stale air, the people struggled to form queues. The shouts of the officers and the black of their guns would have been enough to jolt them. Links! Rechts! Left for older people. Right for the young. The wait for the selection seemed interminable despite the elite SS soldiers' renowned efficiency. As they all stood there, ghosts of the people that they had once been, waiting to be examined and classified, the icy November fog slowly turned to rain. Heavier and more frequent drops came down until the rain became unrelenting.

The shoe polish started to wash down my father's back and face, travelling in streamlets of black that stained his face and clothes. A guard saw this and hauled him out of the queue. He called another guard. They knocked him across his face with a gun and made him go to the left, with the old and weak ones, first in line to the gas.

I could picture it all.

My father, with his patrician profile and dignified bearing, bent in two, hit by a German brute. I imagined him walking into the concrete room, naked, the black staining his face, contrasting with the limpid blue of his eyes. His lips contorted into a grimace of death as he tried to not breathe the poison.

I remembered his words to me as a young boy.

'You have to fight. Not with violence but with your mind, not for people but for ideas. Fight and work for what you believe in, Handa. That struggle is all that matters.'

I could see his face in front of me, aquiline nose, high cheekbones, slicked-back hair that always made me think of freshly fallen snow. His thoughtful pauses that punctuated each conversation laden with advice. His struggle had not mattered to them. Neither had his sense of justice.

'If you want to be truly just in this life, when you see people who are weak, you must stand with them. Because you are strong, and it is the weak who need you more, not the strong.'

My strong father had stood with the weak. I wasn't strong. I imagined or remembered, I am not sure which now, that as a boy I was sitting on his knees. He caressed my face affectionately but was still distant, inaccessible. His hand was very soft and enormous, and it made me feel entirely secure. He wiped my tears with his thumb and said, 'Now, now, Handa. Strong men never let anyone see them cry. Never.'

And now my father was gone. They had murdered him.

I wanted to scream but my jaw was locked. I had no air left inside, my lungs were made of stone. I sat on the step of the building hallway, leaned my head against the yellowing wall and cried.

My father made a mistake in his retrospective diary. Otto's transport did not consist of a thousand people but of fifteen hundred. Of those, 750 were grouped to the right and selected for labour, of whom 157 survived. One of them found the Neumann brothers in Prague and told them how their father had been killed in the camp. He recounted the story of how the rain had revealed Otto's distinguished silver hair and washed away his luck.

I have visited every place where my grandparents lived and worked. Their apartment in Prague, the Montana factory, their beloved house in Libčice, the many buildings that housed them as they were moved around in Terezín. And now I realise that without having meant to search for them in particular, I finally have found my family. In attempting to piece together the puzzle, in my search for my father's past, I found his life in Europe. Amid the details of that life, I have discovered the family that was never spoken about, the one that was not so much forgotten as veiled in the silence. And I finally have the grandparents I secretly longed to meet. I now know Otto and Ella Neumann. I have found them in the photographs, through the words of their letters and anecdotes that have emerged from the boxes and the research. I have retrieved an intimate sense of who they were, and I carry them in my heart. They are no longer distant figures in a picture of faded greys.

Maybe one day I will decide to go, but for the time being I cannot muster the courage to visit Auschwitz. I simply cannot go to the place where they died.

Now that, after all these years, they are finally with me, I refuse to say goodbye.

There are two photographs of my grandparents in Lotar's album that I particularly love. In one, taken in the mid-1930s, Ella is skiing. She is happy, carefree and perhaps a little

coquettish. In the other, Otto is relaxed, smiling with his dar-
ling Zdenka in the garden at Libčice.

In my memory, this is how they remain.

17

WHERE TIME DOES NOT MATTER SO MUCH

My father did not wait for the official end of the war in September to become Hans Neumann once more. Eager to restart his life and deeply grateful to her, he married Míla as soon as he could. The wedding took place on 2 June 1945. Records show that they had announced their intended marriage to the Prague Registry Office only a couple of days earlier, just a few weeks after his return from Berlin. At the time, it was obligatory to wait a minimum of six weeks, but the registrar dispensed with the rules, and they were allowed to skip all three rounds of the reading of the banns of marriage.

A wedding photograph shows that Míla beamed as she held on to Hans, who wore a suit that was too big for his gaunt frame. The witnesses were his brother Lotar and his best friend Zdeněk. There were few other guests, just Míla's parents, Zdenka and her mother, and a few friends. Otto and Ella and almost everyone else in the family were still unaccounted for. A small celebratory lunch was held in Prague, although the city was still reeling and food was scarce.

Hans and Míla's wedding, 2 June 1945. In the photo taken by Zdeněk
are Lotar, Zdenka, and Zdenka's sister Marie, among others.

Shortly afterwards, Hans and Zdeněk went back to work at
Montana, but it was not until March 1946 that Hans and Lotar
managed to restore the family's factory to a semblance of its
previous productivity. Lotar had also taken on another job.
From May 1945 he was part of the National Committee for the
Liquidation of the Jewish Council of Elders in Prague. In this
capacity, he took care of distributing to survivors any assets
that could be recovered from the Germans. The committee
was also in charge of using funds collected during the war
by the Jewish Council of Elders to help repatriated survivors
start again. In June 1945, together with his friends Erik Kolár
and Viktor Knapp, Lotar also joined the National Fund for
Recovery, a government organisation set up to help reconstruct Czech institutions and provide aid to the repatriated. In

January 1946 he decided to go back to university to finish his engineering degree, while Zdenka continued to work for the fund. Lotar decided to leave the fund permanently on 1 April 1946 in order to conclude his studies and focus on business at Montana.

A grateful letter from his colleagues praising him for his *hard work and sense of justice* remains in the files today. By all accounts, Lotar, who had always tended to melancholy, was deeply debilitated by his experiences during the war. His sorrow and a misplaced sense of guilt at having survived were obvious to those who knew him then and later in his life.

Zdenka too had been acutely marked by the war. Five years of hiding and subterfuge, the sustained efforts to help her friends and the Neumanns to survive the war and the loss of her beloved in-laws had all taken their toll. She was exhausted by the burden of being the constant source of strength and support. Lotar in 1945 was a very different man from the one she had fallen in love with in 1936. Perhaps a love as pure as theirs was incompatible with the people they had become.

As Zdenka recalled in her writings, everything came to a head in 1947. Lotar had travelled to Switzerland on business for a week and, upon returning to Prague, collected Zdenka from the fund's office with an enormous bouquet of *gorgeous green flowers*. There, Lotar encountered and chatted with his old colleagues. With his characteristic eye for detail, he noticed that his friend the lawyer Viktor Knapp's wristwatch was missing its protective glass. Later that day, when he and Zdenka arrived home and turned on the lights in their apartment on Trojanova Street, Lotar spotted two tiny shards glinting up at him from the living room floor. As he knelt to pick them up he realised they were unmistakably fragments of glass from a broken watch face.

Incapable of lying to him, an agonised Zdenka collapsed on the floor next to him and explained that Viktor's watch had accidentally smashed when they had been together. She confessed that, while working alongside each other, she had fallen in love with him and he with her. She explained to a dumb-struck Lotar that she wanted to be with Viktor, who in turn had promised to leave his wife. Lotar was crushed.

Viktor was true to his word. Zdenka promptly asked for a divorce.

The anxieties and grief of previous years had almost over-whelmed Lotar. This further blow of an unexpected betrayal by his wife and his friend plunged him into the most profound gloom. He moved out of their apartment immediately. Scant information remains about the period that followed, as no one in my family spoke about Lotar and Zdenka's relationship again. All I know is that the official records show that Lotar enlisted in the army as a reserve, went away for months for military train-ing and, in a state of physical and emotional dislocation, moved residence five times between September 1947 and June 1948.

The family and friends who had all relied on and embraced Zdenka were equally distraught at the news. Hans, Míla and the few remaining cousins gathered around Lotar. Despite wrestling with traumas of their own, they tried their best to support him and help him regain strength.

Zita had just opened a small boutique designing women's clothing. Trying to cheer up Lotar when he returned from army training, she introduced him to a pretty and sparkly-eyed nineteen-year-old named Věra, who worked as a model and also helped at the shop. Much to everyone's astonishment, the new relationship flourished. Věra admired Lotar and affectionately hung on his every word. With her soft-spoken manner, she managed to coax the broken young man back to happiness. He was besotted by her youth, beauty and charm. More than anything, he desperately needed her nurturing and positive presence in his life.

On 19 June 1948 Zdenka and Lotar signed divorce papers once more, only this time the separation was real. A mere three weeks later, Lotar and Věra quietly married. It was a modest gathering, but the family was both thrilled and relieved that Lotar had managed to find a supportive and beautiful woman with whom to rebuild his life.

The photograph from Věra's identification card
after her marriage to Lotar in 1948.

I do not know precisely when the Neumann brothers decided to leave Czechoslovakia, but little remained to hold them there. Their family had been torn apart by the war. Lotar's marriage to Zdenka had disintegrated. Perhaps carrying on in the country where all those they had lost had lived just proved too difficult. Every step at Montana, in Libčice, on the cobbled streets of Prague would have elicited memories. There must have been ghosts everywhere.

It was not a swift decision. Everyone who knew them in Prague could see that they were bent on rebuilding their lives there after the war. Lotar was part of the official reconstruction programmes. Together with Hans, they hired employees, restarted production and completed the process of restitution for the Montana factory. They reclaimed the ownership of the apartment and the country house. Throughout the immediate post-war years, they remained in constant touch with their uncles Richard and Victor in California. They continued, as they had during the war, to research possible countries where the Czech family could start a new life as refugees.

Perhaps it seemed that there was more hopefulness and opportunity elsewhere. The Communist putsch must also have had an impact on their decision. The Communists seized power in Czechoslovakia in February 1948, buoyed by anti-fascist sentiment and the fact that the Soviets had liberated Prague. Perhaps politics proved to be the Neumann brothers' accelerator. The decision clearly had been made by the autumn of 1948, when Hans and Lotar sold the house in Libčice, complete with the contents of the safe, to the Peřina family.

So, in late 1948, Hans and Míla, with their one-year old son,

Michal, and Lotar, accompanied by a very pregnant Věra, left Czechoslovakia behind. They departed separately to reconvene in Zurich, Switzerland, by January 1949. Of all the destinations considered, Venezuela seemed to be the best choice. While many Europeans migrated to the US, Venezuela lacked a developed paint industry and thus presented a real opportunity to the Neumanns for a new start. It also welcomed immigrants from war-torn Europe. A letter to Hans and Lotar from Uncle Richard in January 1949 reads:

My dear ones,

Welcome to free Switzerland. As I am writing this, you are probably already there and have completed the first, most difficult, step on your way to a new life.

I have not yet received a single piece of news from Benes, who is organising things for you in Caracas; he must have acclimatised himself so much that he has started to act like the locals who put everything off till 'mañana'. Time there does not seem to matter so much. Nonetheless, a letter from him must be on the way and I will confirm once everything is set.

In any case it does seem that Venezuela is the best option among the countries that come into consideration. However, you must be prepared for a country without culture or the weight of history and with little by the way of civilisation. But one can live there; it is relatively easy to make enough for daily needs. A satisfactory living can be quickly established, and it is a good environment to set up a new Montana. The only things you'll need are to maintain your good health, learn a bit of Spanish and a dose of optimism . . .

At the end of February 1949, Věra gave birth to their first daughter Susana in Zurich. Hans, Míla and Michal crossed the Atlantic by boat and were the first to arrive in Caracas. Lotar and Věra waited a few weeks, until their newborn was strong enough to travel, and then flew. To help them settle, their uncle Richard moved to Venezuela as well. Many Europeans like them arrived as refugees in Venezuela after the war.

The brothers threw themselves into their new adventure. They took Spanish lessons. With the help of a loan from Richard, they bought a house in the Chapellín neighbourhood, where both families lived together initially, near other newly arrived European immigrants. They made ends meet with odd jobs and set about getting back into business. To begin with, they used the garage to mix paints and lacquers to sell. Then, when their finances allowed, they managed to hire the premises for their first company, which they named Pinturas Montana, in honour of the Prague factory that their father and Richard had started in 1923. It was a team effort. The brothers operated the business and hired a handful of fellow Czechs and Europeans who had also settled in Caracas. Věra took care of everyone, and Míla designed and hand-painted the labels.

My father had spent twenty-eight years of his life in Czechoslovakia, but he always maintained that he was Venezuelan because that country welcomed him as a refugee. Nonetheless, his fifty years in Caracas did little to disguise his heavy Czech accent or his passion for Bohemian artists or his love of rohlíčky sugar cookies.

He adopted many Venezuelan traditions but never their attitude towards keeping time.

In all the Czech letters that have emerged during my research, aside from a few notes written when he was a boy at camp, only one was written by my father.

It was sent to Uncle Richard when Hans was twenty-four years old, on 28 June 1945, after Germany had surrendered.

Today I attempt to write you a few lines that I hope will reach you.

We are so happy to know that you are well and that you were spared all this. It was not as terrible for me as it was for others. I spent the worst time under a false name in Berlin, where I was employed as a varnish chemist. It was really an adventure and maybe someday I will be able to tell you all about it. Lotík will probably talk to you about Montana, but I am only writing to tell you that we really need you. It might be a bit pointless to ask you to come, as I am sure you are doing your best to visit us as soon as possible. You have been in all our minds, throughout the war, the whole time.

We have not gone back to Libčice yet, it is too difficult. Much has changed. Only Gin, the fox terrier who was a puppy when you left, is still the same.

News? I have a thousand stories. But most of them are so terribly sad that there is no point in repeating them.

As you must know by now, I am married to a girl named Míla whom I have known for years and who helped us through it all.

I now work in the paint industry. I just work and work and work. So much. All the time. It's the only way I have of trying to forget how many did not come back, how few of us are left behind.

Give our love to Uncle Victor and to cousins Harry and Milton.

Handa

Or you might remember me best by my nickname, 'the unfortunate boy'.

This letter was not in the box that my father left me. It was kept by Uncle Richard in America and eventually given by his widow to my cousin Madla. She had mislaid it among other papers and brought it to me later, when I had finished my research and was writing this book. I sent it to the Czech expert, as I had done with every other document.

She emailed me a translation of the letter. When I read it, my hands started to tremble uncontrollably, just as my father's had all those years ago at Bubny and then again at his son's funeral. I had encountered much sadder things during my investigations, and yet only these words provoked such a response.

I recognised the voice in that document. The father I knew had worked indefatigably, obsessively. He repeated often that this was because he loved the challenge of building things, because he had to stretch time. But this was only a fragment of the whole truth. He was doing whatever he could to bury an unwavering pain under layer upon layer of work. He was simply attempting to escape his past. Reading his words, I was sad for the person who my father had been, the shambolic poet, the prankster, the unfortunate boy whose heart had been shattered. I cried on reading the gentle voice of that grieving young man, little more than a child. I now recognised that twenty-four-year-old in my father, still just discernible among the resolute pronouncements of the hardened man I had thought I knew.

I could not write for weeks afterwards. My sleep was broken with nightmares. I woke in the small hours, sometimes shouting or in silent fear that my heart had stopped. Each time my husband ushered me back to the present. The dream was always the same. I was surrounded by crumbling walls and ceilings, in a space filled with unidentifiable crowds. The precise setting changed. Sometimes it was a subway station, or some type of hall, or a vast building. Invariably, there was a man whom I had to find among the people, the debris and the clouds of dust. I had to explain something to him, to keep a promise of obscure but overwhelming importance, that would, somehow, save his life. Every time, I raced towards him, yelling desperately. But each time, as I fought my way to him, he vanished into a fog of ash and anonymous faces.

Eventually the dreams waned and I started again to write. And then I realised that an essence of that boy from Prague, whom I had at first thought lost, had actually endured.

When I had travelled to the Pinkas Synagogue in Prague in 1997 and spotted his name inscribed next to the question mark on the memorial wall, my father was living in Caracas in the house he loved, surrounded by sunlit gardens, his art collection and his frenziedly furious dogs. He had already suffered his first stroke and it had left him mostly paralysed. Undaunted by this, and ignoring a bleak prognosis, he had continued to work, write and be active in his philanthropic pursuits. I phoned him that night from the hotel and told him that I had visited the memorial and found the name of his parents on the wall. He was silent as I spoke and, afraid to upset him, I did not wait for his response. I moved swiftly on to explain my surprise at finding his name and the question mark on the wall.

'What does it mean, Papi?' I asked. 'If your name is on the wall, they must think you are dead.'

He paused for the briefest moment.

'What does it mean?' he said, chuckling quietly. 'It means that I tricked them. That is exactly what it means.

'I tricked them. I lived.'

EPILOGUE

In 1939 there were thirty-four members of the Neumann Haas family living in Czechoslovakia. Three were either gentile or 'mixed' and too young to be deported. Only two, Lotar and Hans, escaped the transports altogether.

Everyone else, twenty-nine of them in all, ranging in age from eight to sixty, was deported to concentration camps in Czechoslovakia, Germany, Latvia and Poland.

Four came back.

Erich Neumann, my father's first cousin, whose brother Ota was tortured and killed in Auschwitz in 1941 for swimming in the river, was liberated in Magdeburg. He was one of the few survivors of the camps of Riga. After the war, he married again and in 1946 had a daughter named Jana. Their family initially lived in the small Czech town of Třebíč but were forced to move to Prague in the late 1950s, when the local senior school refused to educate Jana because she was Jewish.

Erich was then imprisoned by the Communists both for being Jewish and for maintaining ties with his cousins and uncles in the West. Jana now lives in Paris with her husband and daughter. I met her for the first time a few years ago, and despite having never cast eyes on each other before, we recognised each other immediately among the hordes of people on the arrivals platform of the Parisian Gare du Nord. Her father never spoke about the war, but when Jana shares what she knows of his experiences, still today, her large blue eyes fill with tears.

Three of the four Pollak children, my father's first cousins, Zdeněk, Hana and Zita, complete the quartet of survivors. They saw internment in a number of camps, including Terezín, Kurzbach, Dachau and Auschwitz. I have met many of their children and grandchildren. The three Pollak siblings have twenty-nine great-grandchildren between them.

Zdeněk Pollak was liberated from Dachau. In June 1945 he returned to his family home in Teplice, Czechoslovakia, before moving to Israel in 1949, where he remarried and had a son. In 1956 he went to Yad Vashem, the Holocaust memorial in Israel, and filled out testimony pages on behalf of every victim in his family. Two months later, he took his own life.

Hana Pollaková, who had lost her husband in the camps, married a survivor of Buchenwald in 1945. They had two children. She lived the rest of her years in Teplice and died in 1973.

Zita Pollaková was one of the fifty-one survivors from her and my grandmother's transport of fifteen hundred to Auschwitz. She escaped from a death march and, after hiding in a barn in Poland, was rescued by Russian soldiers who eventually took her to Prague. Zita married a Czechoslovak army veteran and moved back to Teplice. There, they raised their daughter Daniela. In 1968 Zita moved to Switzerland where she lived until 2002. She committed some of her memories to paper later in life, but otherwise the Pollak survivors seldom spoke of the war.

Stella Kronberger, my grandfather's protégée in the camp, was liberated from Terezín in 1945. After finding Hans and Lotar in Prague, sharing her stories of Otto and waiting in vain for his return, she moved to the US in 1946 to be with her daughter. A few months afterwards, she travelled to California to meet Otto's brothers, Victor Neuman and Richard, who had changed his last name to Barton. Stella shared with them how their brother had lived the last few years of his life. Eventually, Stella married Victor and became Stella Neuman. The two lived quietly in San Diego, where Stella wrote a weekly cooking column for the *Times of San Diego*. She never spoke of the war to Victor's children or grandchildren. When I connected with two of the grandchildren, my cousins Greg and Victor, they had no idea that they had any Jewish heritage or that their step-grandmother had ever been in a camp. But Stella did confide some of her experiences to her own daughter and her granddaughters, who have generously shared their memories.

Richard Neumann (later Barton) stayed in Caracas for a few years to ensure that his nephews had settled well. He then moved back to the US where he married a Czech woman named Edith. They had no children. They lived in La Jolla and kept in touch with Lotar and Hans until Richard's death in 1980. Edith lived until 2003. I met her a few times but she never mentioned the war or the existence of any other family members.

Having built up a conglomerate of companies with his brother, Lotar left Venezuela for Switzerland in 1964, fifteen years after he had arrived. There, with Věra, he lived a quiet life in the small village of Gingins, raising their two daughters Susana and Madeleine (Madla), collecting paintings by socially committed artists like Daumier and Kollwitz, as well as pieces of art nouveau. Throughout his life, Lotar privately supported Czech refugees and Holocaust survivors.

Zdenka had her only child, a daughter, Lucia, with Viktor Knapp in 1949. Zdenka's relationship with Viktor ended in 1955 when he left her for another woman. Lucia told me that no one who came after ever matched Lotar's love for Zdenka. She explained that Zdenka had confessed, towards the end of her life, that she bitterly regretted having left Lotar but that by the time she realised this, it was too late.

Zdenka never lost her independence of mind. She worked at the literary publication *Literární noviny*, where she wrote many articles. She also acted as a lay judge. In 1968 Zdenka and her daughter Lucia escaped from Czechoslovakia, fearing the aftermath of the Prague Spring. They showed up unannounced at the door of Lotar's home in Switzerland. Lotar and Věra took them in for some days and then helped them resettle in Switzerland.

Lotar and Zdenka tried to remain friends. However, in the early 1970s they decided it would be best if they continued their lives separately and consigned their shared experiences to silence. During the last days of his life, when his mind and body were weakened by Parkinson's disease, Lotar cried out for Zdenka. A few months before, she had suffered an accident that meant she could not walk or travel to visit him. They never saw each other again. Lotar died in 1992. Zdenka herself died eleven years later. Unlike all the other women I traced and despite two subsequent marriages Zdenka never changed her name. She kept the name Neumannová, the Czech feminine adjective of Neumann, throughout her life.

Lotar and Věra donated pieces from their art collection, as well as photographs taken by Lotar, to museums in Prague. Věra sent me Lotar's boxes of letters, documents and his photograph album, through their daughter Madla, in 2012. Věra died in 2013.

Zdeněk Tůma worked at Montana in Prague after the war and in 1947 moved to the town of Staré Město with his wife; there, they raised two boys. He worked with paints all his life. Unlike Hans, he shared some stories of his time in Berlin with his family. He continued to read and write poetry for pleasure and translated Rilke's lyrical poem 'A Song of Love and Death' from German to Czech. Despite the very different worlds that they inhabited, Zdeněk and Hans stayed in touch. Their secret partnership and lifelong friendship brought them both great joy until Zdeněk died, surrounded by family, in 1991.

Míla and Hans's marriage was fraught with difficulties from the start, but they built a life in Caracas and raised their son, Michal, who became Miguel, my half-brother. They separated much earlier but divorced in 1969. Despite having risked her life many times to bring Hans food and solace, Míla also never spoke about the past. As a child, I visited her a few times with my father. Each time she made his favourite, rohlíčky sugar cookies. Míla and Hans were friends until her death in New York in 1990. After she died, my father began keeping the good-luck doll that she had made him in a drawer by his bedside, beneath the photograph of his parents. I do not know exactly when he placed it in my box.

Hans went on to accomplish so much after the war that I would probably need another book to tell you about it all. He was a businessman and philanthropist whose seemingly boundless energy and drive spanned countries and industries — manufacturing, newspapers, agriculture, tourism. His passion for the arts and education drove him to establish programmes that benefited thousands. Still today there are two streets in Venezuela named after him, one in Caracas and one in Valencia. The fire never left him, and as he wrote to his uncle Richard in 1945, during the whole of his life he continued to *work, work, work*. He had recently founded the principal opposition newspaper to the Chávez regime, whose catastrophic legacy he had foreseen, when he died after a series of strokes on 9 September 2001.

In my early memories of my father, he was always sitting, fixing the mechanism of a watch in the long room at the back of the house that nestled in its vibrant garden. But now I can picture him, young and chaotic, in Prague. I cherish the mental images that the photographs, letters, writings and anecdotes have helped me create. I see my father lying in the middle of a cobblestone pavement in Prague, with Zdeněk giggling around a corner, waiting to scare an unsuspecting passer-by. I picture him on a bench by the banks of the river writing poetry, wildly pedalling and falling off his bicycle, arriving late, always dishevelled, for meals. I imagine him with Otto, Ella and Lotar, joyously playing with the dogs in the honeyed light of their garden in Libčice. The sounds of laughter, the rush of the Vltava and the wind in the trees are so loud that one can no longer hear the ticking of time.

I spent my childhood willing a mystery to come my way.

When it finally did, it took decades to solve. As an adult with children of my own, I found the reason for the question mark on the wall of the memorial at the Pinkas Synagogue in Prague. I learned why my father awoke screaming in the night. I solved the puzzle of the identification card and everything else that had baffled me about my father when I was young.

I have kept my promise to him that I would help him write his story. I have searched through time and found him and, in the process, his family and mine. I can make connections between my children and those who came before. I can see traits of a generation that disappeared in a generation that will never forget. My children share Hans's relationship with time.

'It is nine o'clock,' I once said to my youngest daughter, then five. 'Time to go to bed.'

'It is nine-oh-four,' she frowned predictably, though it was not my sending her to sleep that irked her, it was my lack of precision. Still today she corrects me.

My middle daughter keeps a brass clock pendulum, as a memento, by her bedside. She steadfastly spins it eight times before falling asleep every night. I have repeatedly asked her why she does this. Once when she was much younger, she proffered, 'It's to ward off the nightmares.' Now, if I insist, she replies: 'Because I have to do it, maybe it's for luck. I just have to, I don't know why.'

My eldest must have a clock by his bedside or he simply will not sleep. He has always maintained that he needs to know the time. Even without an alarm and regardless of where he is, he wakes up every morning at six-thirty. Everyone assured me that this would change, that all teenagers sleep in. He never has, though he is almost an adult.

My children never met their grandfather, the watch repairer. They have heard me speak of him often. Yet, until recently, I had never told them of his watches or the obsessive timekeeping. Some say that trauma is, to some extent, inherited, no matter how distanced or sheltered the environment into which you are born. My children and I have heated debates on the issue. They firmly believe that we each decide and shape who we are, that we learn from our own experiences and from observing others, that unspoken traumas and lessons are not somehow imprinted in our cells. How we behave and who we become is up to us. I do not entirely agree with them. Of course we have control over our identity, but it is not absolute.

I like to believe that life lessons are etched into us and passed on. We choose who we are, but our choices are always moulded by where we come from, even when we do not know where that is. The past is intrinsic to the present, despite any attempts to dismiss it. It is a part of the mechanism that pivots who we choose to be. I look at my three children as they chatter and laugh, and I pray that, in addition to the timekeeping and tenacity, they also have my father's boldness, his poetry and his strength. And hopefully too a little of his luck.

My father's collection of clocks and watches includes one of which I have no childhood memory. I checked with my mother, who confirmed that it held a special place for him. I still love all the others, with their complexities, ornamental engravings and colours, and yet this timepiece has become my favourite. It resembles a book. It tells the time, but it makes no sound. It is actually not a watch at all.

It is an astronomical device called an ivory diptych that was manufactured in the German city of Nuremberg. Most similar pieces were produced by members of six families between the sixteenth and early eighteenth centuries. This particular one was probably crafted by Paul Reinmann, in the early 1600s.

It is minute, just a few centimetres across, and fits neatly in my palm. It is composed of two panels of ivory. On one side, it has a carved spine that is hinged and decorated with gilt brass. On the other, it has two tiny, elaborate brass latches that hold these panels closed.

The book opens to reveal two perfectly symmetrical circles, one on either leaf. Each is marked with numbers which are framed within patterns of finely engraved garlands and flowers, pigmented in burgundy and black. A tiny brass lever near the hinges can be adjusted to keep it open.

335

On the left panel is a sundial, to tell the time. On the other is a compass for direction. The sundial has a face on it that, depending on the angle at which you look at it, seems angry or content.

When I press it between my hands, when I open it, I feel a connection to my father. It is simple. There is no complex mechanism to wind, maintain or repair. There is no case to prise, no moving wheels to ascertain if time is indeed going by. For direction, you just need to hold it steady. To tell the time, you have to tilt it carefully. Time will be marked by the position of the shadow. All you need is patience to capture the fallen light.

Sometimes I lose my bearings. I forget that time has passed. And for that briefest moment, I want to rush again to my father. I want to tear along the chequered floor of the hall to the long windowless room and, as he raises his visor and looks up from his watches, explain that I finally solved the puzzle. I have to let him know that I found the boy he was, the unfortunate boy, and that I love him. I love that boy just as much as I respect the man he became. I long to tell my father that I strolled around the garden of his house in Libčice and wrote our book on a desk crafted by the person who now lives there. I need to reassure him that there are no more questions. I want to wrap my arms around him, place my head on his heart and, as the sounds of the mechanisms fade, in the stillness, whisper that I understand.

ACKNOWLEDGEMENTS

I am hugely grateful to so many people who have helped in manifold ways with my research and the realisation of this book.

To begin with, I thank those closest to me. My beloved, Andrew Rodger, for being my first editor, my biggest fan, my gentlest critic, for fuelling my dreams, for keeping me grounded and for using me as the main butt of his jokes. Mostly I thank him for being my best friend and the most fabulous husband, father and shrink and always, unhesitatingly, being a source of love. I could have never done this if it were not for him and our three marvellous children, Sebastian, Eloise and Maria-Teresa. I thank each of them for their endless patience, the constant love, for their laughter, for engaging with it all and putting up with so many years of this quest and my many monothematic days. They have constantly made my present such a joyful and cossetting refuge from the past. The darkness would have been too daunting if it were not for their light.

I owe a special debt of gratitude to my mother Maria Cristina Anzola, for falling in love with my father, for teaching me so many things, for the hundreds of hours of conversation, her love, wisdom, guidance and friendship. I thank John Heimann for being her beloved companion for over thirty years, for his wise counsel and kindness to my family and to me.

An enormous thank you is due to my aunt Mayalen Anzola, who plunged into the darkness with me. Her advice and love, her help with the letters, the Terezín history and the writing have been invaluable. I am lucky to have her as both my real and my fairy godmother. To her husband Enzo Viscusi for always being my supporter, for the wonderful stories he tells, for the hundreds of poems that he has pulled out of his jacket pocket through the years.

To my brother Ignacio for throwing me into the pool, for our chats, his memories and for his patience and love. To Kai and Grace for keeping him whole.

To my cousin Madla for her trust, affection and companionship on this wonderful adventure. To her husband Stephan Strobel for all his support of us both during it. To my cousins Susana and Philippe also for allowing me to tell Lotar's story and for their encouragement.

To all my uncles, aunts and cousins on the Anzola side of the family for their support and for their recollections of my father. To Alfredo José for watching over me. To Florinda Pena for sharing her memories and those of my brother Miguel and for always being a sister to me.

I am grateful as well to all my new family, my wonderful Czech, British, French and American cousins who have put up with my endless questions, shared their memories and searched their attics and boxes of mementos to help me, thank you for all the positivity and support. My only regret is that I could not include every single marvellous story that you shared with me. I am especially thankful to Greg Neuman for sending his father's stamp collection, Victor Neuman for all the information and chats, Jana Neumannová and her husband Serge Wietratchny for their stories, affection and rohlíčky, to my cousin Daniela Schmidova for the photos and her translating and sharing her mother's words. All have been exceedingly warm and kind and so generous with their time and their recollections. Also, a special thank you to the two Zuzana Panuskovas for the lovely day in Leeds, for the family tree, the photos and the stories. Thank you to their families and also to Jan Sik and Karolina Mrkvičková.

To Carolina Herrera for always being there and for remaining still a fully committed and loyal member of the Mysterious Boot Club since those Saturday mornings in the Caracas garden. May we have another thousand adventures and mysteries to solve together. To Lisa Train for being my reader, my sounding board, for listening to me prattling on for endless hours about my quest and for checking the insanity levels. To Aurelie Berry for reading, listening, commenting, for her constant supply of books and articles and a particularly enormous thank you for her talent as a photographer of watches, diptychs, postcards and dolls. Many of the images of objects in this book are hers. To Caroline Schmidt Barnett for the friendship, German cuddliness and religion lessons. To Emma Bleasdale for the numerous walks and the endless talks.

To Tad Friend, for all his advice, mordant insight, patient guidance, Brooklyn teas and his unusual ability to read and write while travelling by bus. To Magda Veselská for her tenacity in scouring every archive, for her detective skills and her patience with my hundreds of emails filled with questions. To Anna Hájková for her knowledge, guidance, tolerance, sense of humour and friendship.

To Lukáš Přibyl for deciphering so many letters and

documents and helping me solve so many mysteries, for always thinking out of the box, for never being more than a call away, for his constant rallying and, above all, for his friendship. I hereby appoint you, Señor Přibyl, honorary chairman of the Mysterious Boot Club (even if you owe me some of your mother's rohlíčky). To Gabriela Přibylová also for her help with the original translations of the Terezín letters.

To Ivan Nedvídek, Eva Nedvídeková and Jana Straková, thank you for your time, continuous smiles and your immense kindness towards me and my family. I could never thank you enough for the enormous risks your mother and stepfather took in hiding and helping my father. My father survived, and I am here to tell the story of my family and yours, thanks to their courage.

To Zdeněk Tůma Jr and his niece Barbora Tůmova for their time and sharing the wonderful stories, memories and photos of my father's supremely brave and loyal friend.

To Michal Peřina, for the documents in the safe, for my beautiful desk, for the wonderful afternoon in Libčice and his kindness in welcoming me to his family home.

To Jiří Havrda for being a fabulous source of knowledge, for his documentary on Kolár, for being so forthcoming and so full of joy, and of course for helping me find Lucia. To Lucia Aeberhard, my new friend, for allowing me to write about her fabulous and valiant mother Zdenka. For trusting me, for her generosity with her mother's past, for her kindness and all her lovely letters and photos. To Bozena Macková for her time and recollections of the family and of her cousin Zdenka.

To Alena Borská for the recollections of her best friend, and my cousin, Věra. For sharing the story of the clandestine school and allowing the use of her wonderful photographs.

To Beatrice Susil, another new friend, for her immense empathy, for trusting me with her father František Langer's memories, photographs, stories and for sharing her family's painting by Kien. Her father and my grandparents were friends at a terrible time; we continue that friendship along the generations in what, hopefully, is a gentler world. A special thank you to Stan Mares, grandson of Engineer Langer, for all his efforts in providing a good photograph of the Kien portrait.

To Evelyn Epstein and her sister Margaret Polikoff for their candour and warmth and for sharing the story of their grandmother Stella Kronberger.

To Mafe Machado, Kevin Travis and Elliott Bross for always being there and believing in me. There are many others whom I must acknowledge, who helped me directly with my research and the writing process and sometimes also helped unknowingly, recently or a long time ago, often by answering or asking questions, devoting their time or saying the right thing, among them Cesare Sacerdoti, Natalie Harris, Charlotte Cunningham, Mark Cunningham, Olina Pekna, Stanley Buchthal, Roger Moorhouse, Jessica and Adam Sweidan, Guy Walters, Barbara Schieb, Martina Voigt, Karolin Steinke, Ulrik Werner Grimm, Florian Luddecke, Martin Navratil, Milada Cogginsová, Claudia Zea and Johannes Schmidt, Sophie Fauchier, Eloy Anzola E, Rodrigo Anzola, Patricia Anzola, Diego Anzola, Robert Jamieson, Peter Rosenberg, Joanna Ebner, Nick Clabburn, Meredith Caplan, Camilla Partridge, Roberto Chumaceiro, Eliza Arcaya, Jordana Friedman, Lisa Rosen, Alba de Aponte, Cecilia de Luis, Romulo Zerpa, Eric Shaw, Bryan Adams, Alicia Grimaldi, Ben Passikoff, Howard Fahlkson, Aaron Izes, Leonie Mellinger, Tom Gross, Keith

Craig, Florian Luddecke, Paul Bird, Robin Johnson, Martin Navratil, Luis E. Alcalá, Cosima Carter, Ricardo Neumann, my cousin Eloy Anzola for his eye for detail and his tech expertise, Vanessa Neumann for caring for the doll, Sam Endacott for his help with the initial organisation and research, Daniel Recordon for his love of watches, Jessica Henley-Price for her beautiful map, Michael Haslau for his fabulous expertise on Weissensee and his photos, Alba Arikha for her comments and her encouragement, Menena Cottin for her art, Giles Nelson for taking care of Fluff, and to Pedro Meneses Imber (I pray that where you are there is no time) for, among many things, giving me my first book on Judaism. To Juan Alonso, a brilliant writer and my fabulous college literature professor, for the inspiration and encouragement. I promised him in 1993 that I would write a book and I apologise it's taken me so long. To everyone else, who may have temporarily slipped my mind before this goes to press, but remain always in my heart, thank you.

Lastly I am hugely grateful to those that were directly involved in the creation of this book.

To my two superb editors, Suzanne Baboneau and Rick Horgan, a heartfelt thank you for understanding the idea from the get-go, for making the book so much better, for helping me to achieve what I set out to do. I am grateful to Suzanne for the careful polishing of the manuscript, the myriad lovely chats, the ducklings, the hugs. Thank you to Rick for the fab creative advice, our lunches, the enthusiasm and the laughter. A huge thank you also to the brilliant teams at Simon & Schuster and Scribner, especially to Ian Chapman for his constant encouragement and his beautiful emails, and to Nan Graham for my dahlias, and to her and Roz Lippel for all their wonderful advice and support.

To Kaiya Shang, for her thoroughness, the wheels and the metaphorical hand-holding. To Emily Greenwald for having all the answers. To Beckett Rueda for his help and for hitting the ground running. To Brian Belfiglio for his enthusiasm and kindness. To Beth Thomas for her careful copy-editing and, particularly, for reaching out. To Francesca Sironi in production and M Rules for typesetting the book. To the immensely talented Sian Wilson for designing our beautiful jacket. To everyone at Aitken Alexander, especially Geffen for her generous support and her awesome ability to answer emails in record time. I could not have been better guided or cared for – it has been an absolute joy to work with you all.

I am grateful to Wendy and Bill Luers who, with their usual brilliance and generosity of spirit and ideas, led me to the right people so that I could turn the research into a memoir.

To Maria Campbell for being kind to a stranger and for her incredible foresight in introducing me to Clare Alexander with whom I have much in common and who happens to be the best agent in the world.

Clare is the most brilliant woman I have encountered and without her belief in me, in the story and her unwavering endorsement, this would have never been a book at all. In so many ways, this is her story too. I thank her for helping me capture the light, for her guidance in shaping it into a coherent whole, for her constant sage counsel, for being my champion and, above all, my friend. She also has sensational taste in earrings.

Thank you also to all those that helped me with their time and expertise at the following institutions and archives:

Archiv bezpečnostních složek, Praha (Archives of Security
    Services in Prague)
Archiv hlavního města Prahy (Municipal Archives
    of Prague)
Archiv města Brna (Municipal Archives of Brno)
Archiv mesta Košice (Municipal Archives of Košice)
Archiv Městské části Praha 8 (Archives of the Prague 8
    Municipality)
Federace židovských obcí v ČR (The Archives of
    the Federation of Jewish Communities in the
    Czech Republic)
Národní archiv, Praha (National Archives in Prague)
Moravský zemský archiv, Brno (Moravian Land Archives
    in Brno)
Památník Terezín (Terezín Memorial)
Pinkasova synagoga, Židovské muzeum v Praze
    (The Pinkas Synagogue and the Jewish Museum
    of Prague)
Státní oblastní archiv v Praze (State Regional Archives
    in Prague)
Státní okresní archiv v Hradci Králové (State District
    Archives in Hradec Králové)
Státní okresní archiv v Teplicích (State District Archives
    in Teplice)
Státní okresní archiv v Třebíči (State District Archives
    in Třebíč)
Vojenský ústredný archív, Bratislava (Central Military
    Archives in Bratislava)
Landesarchiv (The Berlin Archive)
Centrum Judaicum, Berlin

ARIANA NEUMANN

Gedenkstätte Stille Helden (The Silent Heroes Memorial
  in Berlin)
The Auschwitz-Birkenau Archives
Yad Vashem, Jerusalem
The Wiener Library, London

SOURCES

This is not a history book, but it narrates as accurately as possible the lives of my family and many of the people that they encountered. The personal stories described within it are drawn from the letters, official and personal documents, memoirs and anecdotes, written and oral, of those who lived through them. The recollections and anecdotes have inevitably been tinged by time and memory, but as much as such things can ever be, they are true.

Most of the objects, documents and photographs belong to my own family. A handful have been loaned to me by archivists or the families of those involved.

Other specific and general background information, data and inspiration for this memoir was gathered through many years of research and reading history and fiction relating to remembrance, identity, trauma, the Second World War and genocide. It has been drawn from a wide range of materials, including the following invaluable sources.

Articles and books

H.G. Adler, *Theresienstadt 1941–1945* (New York: Cambridge University Press, 2017).

Madeleine Albright, *Prague Winter. A Personal Story of Remembrance and War 1937–1948* (New York: Harper Collins, 2012).

Hannah Arendt, *Eichmann in Jerusalem. A Report on the Banality of Evil* (New York: Penguin Books, 1994).

Alba Arikha, *Major/Minor. A Memoir* (London: Quartet Books, 2011).

British Intelligence Objectives Sub-Committee, G. Palmer, A., Mc Master, H. Hughes, *German Aircraft Paints*, 18 October–10 November 1945, Final report 365, Item 22. London 1946.

Donald de Carle, *Watch & Clock Encyclopedia* (London: Robert Hale, 1999).

Hans Fallada, *Alone in Berlin* (London: Penguin, 2010).

Viktor E. Frankl, *Man's Search for Meaning. The Classic Tribute to Hope from the Holocaust* (London: Random House, 2004).

Saul Friedländer, *The Years of Extermination* (London: Weidenfeld & Nicolson, 2007).

Jeremy Gavron, *A Woman on the Edge of Time. A Son's Search for his Mother* (London: Scribe, 2015).

Nancy R. Goodman, Marilyn B. Meyers, *The Power of Witnessing: Reflections, Reverberations, and Traces of the Holocaust: Trauma, Psychoanalysis, and the Living Mind* (London, Routledge, 2012). The quote by Norbert Fryd is from p.191.

Ulrich Werner Grimm, *Zwangsarbeit und 'Arisierung'. Warnecke & Böhm-Ein Beispiel* (Berlin: Metropol, 2004).

Anna Hájková, *The Last Ghetto: An Everyday History of Theresienstadt, 1941–1945* (New York: Oxford University Press, forthcoming).

Anna Hájková 'Sexual Barter in Times of Genocide: Negotiating the Sexual Economy of the Theresienstadt Ghetto', *University of Chicago Signs*, Vol. 38, No. 3 (Spring 2013), pp. 503–33

Trudy Kanter, *Some Girls, Some Hats and Hitler. A True Story.* (London:Virago, 2012).

Sven Felix Kellerhof, *Berlin Under the Swastika* (Berlin: Bebraverlag, 2006).

Gerda Weissmann Klein, *All But My Life. A Memoir* (London: Indigo 1995).

Ivan Klíma, *My Crazy Century. A Memoir* (New York: Grove Press, 2013).

Heda Margolius Kovaly, *Under a Cruel Star: A Life in Prague 1941–1968* (London: Granta, 2012).

Zdenek Lederer, *Ghetto Theresienstadt* (New York: Howard Fertig, 1983).

Primo Levi, *If This Is a Man, The Truce* (London: Abacus, 2014).

Primo Levi with Leonardo de Benedetti, *Auschwitz Report* (London: Verso, 2006).

Steven A. Lloyd, *Ivory Diptych Sundials 1570–1750* (Cambridge: Harvard University Press, 1992).

Daniel Mendelsohn, *The Lost. A Search for Six of Six Million* (London: William Collins 2013).

Anne Michaels, *Fugitive Pieces* (London: Bloomsbury, 1997).

Patrick Modiano, *La Place de L'Etoile* (Paris: Gallimard, 1968).

Patrick Modiano, *Livret de Famille* (Paris: Gallimard, 1977).

Melissa Müller and Reinhard Piechoki, *A Garden of Eden in Hell: The Life of Alice Herz-Sommer* (London: Pan Macmillan, 2008).

Gonda Redlich and Saul S. Friedman, *The Terezin Diary of Gonda Redlich* (University Press of Kentucky, 1992).

Livia Rothkirchen, *The Jews of Bohemia and Moravia – Facing the Holocaust* (Lincoln: University of Nebraska Press and Jerusalem: Yad Vashem, 2005).

Philippe Sands, *East West Street. On the Origins of Genocide and Crimes Against Humanity* (London: Weidenfeld & Nicolson, 2016).

Simon Schama, *Belonging. The History of the Jews* (London: Random House, 2017).

Vera Schiff, *Therensienstadt: The town the Nazis gave to the Jews* (Michael Schiff Enterprises, 1996).

W.G. Sebald, *The Emigrants* (London: Harvill Press, 1997).

Gita Sereny, *Into That Darkness. From Mercy Killing to Mass Murder* (London: Pimlico, 1995).

Mary Jalowicz Simon, *Gone to Ground* (London: Profile Books, 2014).

Ervin Staub, *The Roots of Evil. The Origins of Genocide and Other Group Violence* (New York: Cambridge University Press, 1989).

Bernard Taper, 'Letter from Caracas', *New Yorker*, 6 March 1965, pp. 101–43.

Richard Tedeschi and Lawrence Calhoun, *Trauma & Transformation. Growing in the Aftermath of Suffering.* (Thousand Oaks: Sage Publications, 1995).

Marie Vassiltchikov, *The Berlin Diaries 1940–1945* (London: Pimlico, 1999).

Edmund de Waal, *The Hare with Amber Eyes: A Hidden Inheritance* (New York: Picador, 2011).

Jirí Weil, *Mendelssohn is on the Roof* (London: Daunt Books, 2011).

Jirí Weil, *Life with a Star* (London: Daunt Books, 2012).

Sarah Wildman, *Paper Love: Searching for the Girl my Grandfather Left Behind* (New York: Riverhead Books, 2014).

These institutions and sites have provided articles, data and information:

Websites

Auschwitz.org

cdvandt.org

www.holocaust.cz

The Holocaust Encyclopedia United States Memorial Holocaust Museum, www.ushmm.org

www.forgottentransports.com

The Visual History Archive of USC/Shoah Foundation, sfi.usc.edu

Yad Vashem, The World Holocaust Remembrance Center, www.yadvashem.org

Archives

Archives of the Prague 8 Municipality

Archives of Security Services in Prague

Auschwitz-Birkenau Archives

Berlin Archive

Federation of Jewish Communities in the Czech
    Republic, Prague

Central Military Archives in Bratislava

Central Technical Library of Transport, Prague

Centrum Judaicum, Berlin

Moravian Land Archives in Brno

Municipal Archives of Brno

Municipal Archives of Košice

Municipal Archives of Prague

Museum Pankow, Berlin

National Archives, Prague

State Regional Archives in Prague

State District Archives in Hradec Králové

State District Archives in Teplice

State District Archives in Třebíč

Terezín Memorial Archives

PICTURE CREDITS

BRUNNEROVÁ ARNOŠTKA 12.III 1883 ~ 20.II 1943 *FIŠER
MILIE 8.III 1877 ~ 20.II 1943 *GÜNSBURG JOSEF 23.VIII
1894 JIŘÍ 2.IV 1921 ALENA 30.XI 1922 OLGA 26.III 1879 ~ 2
5 JAN 18.III 1926 ~ 20.II 1943 *LUSTIG MAX 16.X 1865 ~ 1.
~ 20.II 1943 *NEUMANN ZDENĚK 18.III 1900 ~ 28.IX 19
II 1943 *VLADIMÍR 25.V 1882 OLGA 28.IX 1891 ~ 6.X 1944
OŠT 16.VIII 1913 MARIE 3.III 1885 ~ 20.II 1943 *WEISS
II 1943 EMILIE 2.II 1883 ~ 23.II 1943 *LIBČICE NAD VLTA
HANUŠ STANISLAV 9.II 1921 ~ ? *WEISS JIŘÍ 8.III 19
1939 ~ 10.VI 1942 *LIBĚJOVICE: *BAŠTÝŘOVÁ BAR
GA 26.X 1899 ~ 25.IV 1942 *KOHN LUDVÍK 26.VII 1866 ~
SEF 31.XII 1896 ~ 28.IX 1944 *LIBĚŠICE: *FRIED BOH
MILA 6.II 1891 ~ 17.V 1942 *KLEINOVÁ ARNOŠTKA 18.V
II 1914 ~ 1.X 1944 *KRAUS LADISLAV 30.VIII 1904 ZD
VII 1900 ~ 15.V 1944 ARNOŠTKA 22.II 1928 ~ 25.II 1943 *
IL 11.VII 1908 ~ 22.X 1942 GUSTAV 11.VII 1908 ~ 25.VIII 1
ERTA 14.VII 1875 ~ 22.X 1942 *REICHEROVÁ MARIE
1899 JIŘÍ 13.VIII 1926 ~ 6.IX 1943 *ROUBÍČEK RU
5 ~ 1.II 1943 *LIBICE: *PICKOVÁ KAROLÍNA 29.I 185
3 IDA 14.VII 1912 LUDMILA 12.III 1938 ~ 12.VI 1942 *K
NOŠT 2.II 1878 MATYLDA 27.IV 1880 ~ 12.VI 1942 *POLI
VI 1942 *LIBÍŇ: *SCHWARZ JAN 18.V 1904 ~ 26.VIII
A 17.IX 1917 ~ 20.II 1943 *SAUER ALFRÉD 1.II 1885 FRA
ROSLAVA 24.VIII 1934 ~ 25.IV 1942 *LIBLICE: *HR
II 1912 ~ 1.IV 1942 *FISCHER ZIKMUND 22.VII 1919 ~
IBNÍKOVICE: *ROSENBACH JAROSLAV 17.I 188
2 *LIBOCHOVICE: *BRILL KAREL 26.XI 1883 BE
III 1942 *DUB EMIL 29.XI 1892 FRANTIŠKA 7.II
ANTLOVÁ ANNA 19.XI 1879 ~ 23.IV 1942 *FLO
OGES RICHARD 2.II 1865 LEOPOLDA 22.II 1879 ~
II 1929 ~ 17.III 1942 *GRÜNHUT OSKAR 8.IX 1884 VI
AMLISCHOVÁ TEREZIE 3.VII 1900 ~ 17.III 1942 *JA
2.VII 1942 *PAVLA 28.V 1879 BEDŘIŠKA 5.I 1892 MA
1866 ~ 19.X 1942 *KRÁTKÁ JEANETA 11.IX 1893 ~ 12.
RA 2.VII 1921 ~ 19.X 1944 *NEUMANNOVÁ ELSA 24.II
IL 24.VI 1870 ~ 19.X 1942 KAMILA 11.I 1885 ~ 7.IV 1942 *PIO
4 ~ 26.X 1942 *PROPPEROVÁ EMILIE 11.IV 1905 IVAN
RNOŠTKA 5.I 1860 ~ 20.III 1942 IRMA 14.VI 1886 ~ 19.X
1896 ~ 23.IV 1942 *SPIELMANNOVÁ JANA 6.XI 18